MERRY
CHRISTMAS!
LOVE,
PAUL + LEANNE

Prayers
and Devotions
from POPE JOHN PAUL II

Prayers and Devotions
from POPE JOHN PAUL II

Edited and with an Introduction by
BISHOP PETER CANISIUS JOHANNES VAN LIERDE, O.S.A.
Translated by FIRMAN O'SULLIVAN

VIKING
A GINIGER BOOK

VIKING

Published by the Penguin Group
Penguin Books USA Inc., 375 Hudson Street,
New York, New York 10014, U.S.A.
Penguin Books Ltd, 27 Wrights Lane,
London W8 5TZ, England
Penguin Books Australia Ltd, Ringwood,
Victoria, Australia
Penguin Books Canada Ltd, 10 Alcorn Avenue,
Toronto, Ontario, Canada M4V 3B2
Penguin Books (N.Z.) Ltd, 182–190 Wairau Road,
Auckland 10, New Zealand

Penguin Books Ltd, Registered Offices:
Harmondsworth, Middlesex, England

First published in 1994 by Viking Penguin,
a division of Penguin Books USA Inc.

1 3 5 7 9 10 8 6 4 2

LIBRARY OF CONGRESS CATALOGING-IN-PUBLICATION DATA
John Paul II, Pope 1920–
Prayers and devotions from Pope John Paul II.
1. Devotional calendars—Catholic Church. 2. Catholic
Church—Prayer-books and devotions—English. I. Lierde,
Peter Canisius Johannes van. II. Title.
ISBN 0-670-86179-0
BX2170.C56J626 1984 242'.3
84-42799

Printed in the United States of America
Set in New Baskerville

Contents

Prayers and Devotions
from POPE JOHN PAUL II

Introduction

The Aim

This book is arranged to offer the modern reader, at grips with various daily tasks, a chance of getting to know and entering into the broad and ample thought of the Supreme Pontiff, John Paul II, day by day, without too much trouble, in calm reflection — in a word, a moment of repose from the occupations of life.

The compiler has gathered a harvest from the mind and heart of Karol Wojtyla, over the days of the liturgical year — an authentic breviary of Pope John Paul II's thought, but never a burdensome one.

There is but one entry for each day. Its text is intended, in the first place, for Catholics and all Christians believing in Jesus Christ, but also for any and every human being of good will who aspires to that liberty which does not disappoint.

The Contents

The liturgical year is a period of twelve months. It extends from the beginning of December through November and is entirely concentrated on the most lovable person of Jesus Christ. It studies, meditates, and enters into His life, from His birth in time down to His glorious return at the end of time. Over that period the liturgical year reveals His person, His work, the deep reasons for His coming among mankind, and His present vitality for every human being.

It forms an authentic cycle of events which are simple but extremely precious. It is a far-reaching, richly adorned arch; a film, projected rapidly but with stirring effect, sometimes with moments of suspense, down to the final solemn and universal scene. It is a singular, unique voyage of the heart. The cycle of the liturgical year marvelously depicts the divine and human mysteries of Jesus, true God and true man.

A point of great weight and value: the mysteries of Jesus Christ have a twofold aspect. The historical aspect consists of the concrete, precise, punctual succession of acts, happenings, and determining events. The spiritual aspect consists of the interior and psychological attitude, equally concrete, precise, and punctual, lived by Jesus in every circumstance of His life, in each of His mysteries.

The historical aspect is called "mystery" — *mysterium*. The spiritual aspect is called the "interior power" of the mystery — *vis mysterii*. It means the very high charge accumulated by Christ and put into every historical event of His existence and mission. It is His mind, His heart, the most beautiful sum of all His virtues in all His daily activities. It means the hidden core of the various states which He accepted or underwent.

So, as we begin the spiritual journey at the end of November or beginning of December, we are all invited to contemplate Him hidden in the immaculate womb of Mary of Nazareth, to follow Him in His silent birth, and to observe His threefold manifestation or epiphany — of the visit of the Wise Men of the East, the baptism on the banks of the Jordan, the miracle of the water changed into fine wine at Cana. Then we find Him again at Nazareth, as He grows "in wisdom and age and grace before God and men"[1] and as, in the liturgical readings, He is presented as the worker of Creation.[2] We are led by the hand through His public life: made up of temptations, healings, miracles, teaching, and guidance. The austere period of Lent is one of rich and extensive preaching on penitence, conversion, reconciliation, but also the time of the secret plot woven by pharisaical formalism and the envy of the powerful, culminating in the drama of the Cross, Death, and Burial, which is then transformed into splendid Resurrection. Then follows His marvellous Ascension, with the consequential promise of the Holy Spirit to be sent down upon the Apostles and Mary Most Holy.

Then we have the beginning of the second part of the liturgical year. It is marked by the tangible, proclaimed operation of the Holy Spirit. Through this operation, the inward power of all Christ's mysteries, after having been at work in the first part of the liturgical year, is now even more accentuated, and continued in the life of the Church. The Church was born from the sacred side of Jesus on the cross and was publicly proclaimed by the Holy Spirit on the day of Pentecost: "Go, therefore, and make disciples of all the nations. Baptize them in the name of the Father and of the Son and of the Holy Spirit. *Teach them* to carry out everything I have commanded you. And know that I am with you always until the end of the world."[3] "The Paraclete, the Holy Spirit whom the Father will send in my name, will instruct you in everything, and remind you of all that I told you."[4]

So it is in any case undeniable that Christ founded His Church *in* the world; it is also supremely true that He raised the Church up *for* the world, not so as to annul and obstruct the world's life but to orientate all who are born in the world toward "possession" of God, who is loved and served on earth and seen and enjoyed in an inexpressible way to eternity: "God did not send the Son into the world to condemn the world, but that the world might be saved through him."[5] "I solemnly assure you, the man who hears my word and has faith in him who sent me possesses eternal life. He does not come under condemnation, but has passed from death to life."[6]

So it becomes fitting and useful to be able to condense the value and preciousness of the liturgical year in three key words: *Christ* living and true, who revitalizes and continues his mysteries the members of his *Church,* for the good of the *world.* "Through Christ our Lord, you, O God, ever create and hallow, ever give life, bless and present every good thing to the world."[7]

Christ, Church, World

In the first six months of the liturgical year everything is concentrated on Christ of course. How is the vital current traced out in the second six months of this book?

Christ's vitality and His mysteries derive from Him, head of the Church, in the Church's members, through the Holy Spirit, who is the soul and heart of the same Church.

Pentecost is the annual renewal of the descent of the Holy Spirit. It is therefore the starting point. In accordance, then, with the path taken by the liturgy and pastoral usage, the reader is presented with the action of the Holy Spirit. This is manifested also in the Sacrament of Holy Chrism or Confirmation; there has already been meditation on the Sacrament of Baptism at Epiphany and during Lent, while the Sacrament of Penance finds its pastoral place in the time of Lent, too.

After the Solemnity of the Most Holy Trinity, there follows intense reflection on the august Sacrament of the Holy Eucharist, through the solemnities and feasts of the Body and Blood of Christ, and His Most Sacred Heart, and of the Immaculate Heart of the Blessed Virgin Mary.

We thus arrive at the point where we begin to go deeply into the reality of the Church. We thus consider, in order, the Church's evangelical spirit and spiritual life, with her virtues; essential tasks, such as evangelization, catechesis, and missionary action; and the elements composing the Mystical Body of Christ: the Supreme

Pontiff, cardinals, bishops, priests and seminarians, men and women religious, laity, the married, secular institutes, confraternities, and ecclesial movements.

A fundamental reflection on the contemporary world forms a useful introduction to the Church's presence and activities — *pro mundi vita,* "for the life of the world" — not for the purpose of exercising hegemony or supremacy but for the sake of service. The Pope's words deal with harmony between modern technology and moral conscience; faith and culture; schools and universities; the family, meditation on which is particularly marked; work, and the Gospel of labor; peace; mass media; sport; tourism; Europe; and the United Nations.

The liturgical year conceals yet another luminous and transparent gem: the faithful and, as it were, silent presence of Mary, Virgin, Mother of Jesus Christ and of the Church, the New Eve of the human race. In drafts for the Constitution on the Sacred Liturgy, distributed to the Fathers of the Second Vatican Council, there was explicit mention of the idea of a "Cycle of Mary Most Holy," to be inserted in the yearly liturgical cycle. The word "cycle" was not used in the final version, but there is nothing to forbid us from assigning an eminent role to Mary of Nazareth, in the successive series of the Mysteries of Christ and in the mystery of the Church, as was solemnly affirmed in Chapter 8 of the Dogmatic Consituation on the Church, *Lumen Gentium.*

Without any exaggeration, we may therefore affirm that the humble and immaculate Mary accompanies Christ Jesus, her Son according to human nature, in all His mysteries which are contemplated one after the other in the liturgical year, and that she is associated in an intimate manner — though subordinated to Jesus — in the work of redemption, which is carried on in the Church's life and is inserted by merciful love in the dynamism of the world.

The reader of this book may therefore discover

Mary's lovable presence beside her Son, Jesus, and follow that presence, which is gentle in its apparition and strong in the inspiration it gives for the harsh path of human living. In Mother Church's mind, the entire month of May is dedicated to Mary.

Also present will be the saints: men and women, eloquent witnesses of great wisdom and most concrete goodness. Mary is their Queen, and Christ their imperishable Crown.

This book also contains a section where the reader may reflect to full advantage on the movable feasts, those events in the life of Christ and His Church which are commemorated on dates which vary from year to year. Examples are the precious Holy Week and the Octave of the Solemnity of Easter.

Choice of Material

The purpose of the present publication and the wide and varied panorama provided by its contents clearly show how material was chosen and in what way the numerous excerpts composing it were sought out.

While following with dutiful attention the pastoral activities and overall teaching of the Holy Father, John Paul II, I sought to grasp with strict objectivity the Pontiff's thought on a vast series of mysteries, events, celebrations, and commemorations, which the liturgical cycle postulates, represents, and propounds in its course of three hundred and sixty-five days.

A further effort was made. Within the variety of the Holy Father's doctrinal, spiritual, and pastoral declarations, research also brought to light a line of continuity in his thought on not a few matters. Without doing any harm to the liturgical bias of the work, it was possible to indicate the chain of reasoning, together with its development and enrichment, and the fitness and value of single statements or expositions. By way of example, we may mention December 1–7, the nature of the time of Advent; December 15–25, the spiritual riches in Christmas; Holy Week; the Octave of the Resurrection, and so on.

In presenting the Mysteries of Christ and inserting them together with their vitality in the Church's life, with positive and beneficent effects on the world and human society, there was rightful need to respect feast days and commemorations of saints, men and women, each on the day assigned in the liturgical calendar. This presence is necessary. While it gives prominence to devotion to the saints, it does not break into or even concretely diminish happy linkages of themes which are very important and cover a whole series of days. Here are some examples: April 16–29 goes into the Mystery of the Resurrection; in the same period of time, we find the Holy Father's thoughts on Our Lady of Jasna Gora (22 April), St. Adalbert (23 April), St. Mark (25 April, and on 26 April) Mary, Mother of Good Counsel. The same may be said of the period 19–29 June, dedicated to meditation on the Most Blessed Eucharist. Again, the period 18 January– 7 February is devoted to reflection on true and authentic ecumenicism, etc.

It will be readily understood that Pope John Paul II has dealt with one specific theme on more than one occasion during the liturgical year. So it is that, at well-defined moments, he speaks of Jesus Christ, he explains the theme of the Church, he discourses on man, on the family, on labor. It is easy to see that this manner of proceeding leads to a happy development of thought and more marked impact upon the minds and hearts of all.

How the Work was Done

Mention has already been made of the respectful, constant research into the Pontifical texts. While remaining faithful to his purpose, the compiler also had to pay proper attention to the requirement that no single excerpt should exceed a page.

Because of the need to be guided by this, it sometimes seemed very proper, I would say even necessary, to abbreviate the Pontifical text without, however, at any time harming the integrity of the thought and diminishing the authenticity of any particular text. I can honestly declare that even in such cases the text loses nothing of its eloquence and incisiveness.

I would conclude the introduction to this book with the words uttered by the Holy Father, John Paul II, when inaugurating the Jubilee Year of the Redemption on March 25, 1983:

Jesus Christ, Son of the Living God,
Grant that . . . all of us may love You more,
As in ourselves we live the mysteries of Your life again,
From the conception and birth
Up to the cross and the resurrection.
Be with us through these mysteries,
Be with us in the Holy Spirit.
Help us to change the direction of the increasing threats
*   and misfortunes of the world of today!*
Lift man up again!
Protect the nations and peoples!
O Lord Jesus Christ,
Show how more powerful
— In man and in the world —
Is the work of Your Redemption!

The Vatican, 22 February 1984
Feast of the Chair of St. Peter

✝ PETER CANISIUS JOHANNES VAN LIERDE
Vicar General of His Holiness

[1]*Lk* 2:52; [2]*Jn* 1:3; [3]*Mt* 28:19–20; [4]*Jn* 14:26; [5]*Jn* 3:17; [6]*Jn* 5:24; [7]*Eucharistic Prayer I.*

December

December 1

The Liturgical New Year

Angelus Domini nuntiavit Mariae, et concepit de Spiritu Sancto — "The angel of the Lord declared unto Mary, and she conceived of the Holy Spirit."

Let us concentrate on the content of these words at the beginning of the new liturgical year.

Once again there opens up before us the prospect of the time that the Church fills up every year with meditation on the divine Mystery, which operates in the history of man and the world. The liturgical year is an abridgement and summing up of the story of salvation, from its beginning down to its final completion. *Jesus Christ is the culmination and center of this history.* He gives their full significance to the single parts of the liturgical season and endows them with due order.

He is that Jesus whose coming was announced by the Angel of the Lord to the Virgin Mary — and she conceived Him in her womb through the power of the Holy Spirit.

It is through the power and operation of the Holy Spirit that man's time and the world's time are consecrated to the Father in Jesus Christ.

It is through the operation of the Holy Spirit that the Church's time is consecrated to the Father in Jesus. That time, today, in accordance with the cyclic nature of human time, makes a new beginning.

Let us enter this liturgical New Year with faith and hope! Let us enter upon it with that love which has been poured out into our hearts through the Holy Spirit who has been given to us" (*Rom* 5:5).

The Virgin of Nazareth received this gift most fully and through the operation of the Holy Spirit became Mother of God.

December 2

Advent: The Coming of the Lord

Adventus means "coming." *God comes to man.* This is a fundamental dimention of our faith.

We live our faith when we are open to God's coming, when we persevere in His advent. The Angelus which we are going to recite reminds us how much the Virgin Mary was open to God's coming: she introduces us to Advent. I am thinking most of all of the Advent which is accomplished in the Sacrament of Holy Baptism. You see, a human comes into the world. He or she is born as the child of the parents and comes into the world with the inheritance of original sin.

The parents are aware of that inheritance. Inspired by faith in Christ's words, they take their child for Baptism. They wish to open up the child's soul to the coming of the Savior, to His 'Advent.'

So Advent shows *the beginning of new life.* In certain sense, the seal of original sin is removed from the child, and the beginning of the new life, the divine life, is engrafted in him. For Christ does not come "with empty hands." He brings us the divine life; He wishes us to have life and to have it to the full *(cf. Jn* 10:10).

Every parish is a place where Baptism is performed. So it is the place of the "Coming"; it continually perseveres in the Advent and awaits "the Coming of the Lord" in every new parishioner.

December 3

The Grace of the Coming

Christian expectation: Perseverance in faith and in struggle.

Advent makes us see that salvation has been given to us through *the grace of the coming* of our Lord, Jesus Christ. Let us open our hearts afresh so that the grace of this year's Advent may work in us with the fullness of its riches and depth.

Advent is the period of waiting: of Christian waiting and perseverance in faith and in struggle, by virtue of Christ's grace in us. Advent opens a new chapter every year in that book of salvation which God writes in the Church through the story of man.

It is necessary to be humble to receive the divine teachings; there is need to be humble so that divine grace may operate in us, transform our lives and bring out fruits of goodness.

Elevation of the soul is accomplished through *knowledge of the Lord and His ways:* Your ways, O Lord, make known to me; teach me your paths, guide me in your truth and teach me . . ." *(Ps* 25:4–5).

As you see, it is not a matter of abstract knowledge but of knowledge *having influence upon life.* "Teach me your paths" means teach me to live in conformity with God's will.

In this internal effort it is given to us to discover once again and convince ourselves that *"the Lord is good."*

There are "Advent wishes," "Advent requests." I express them to you in prospect of the feast of Christmas.

December 4

Prepare the Ways of the Lord

"Prepare the ways of the Lord, make straight in paths. Every man shall see the salvation of God." *Alleluia. Alleluia. Alleluia.*

Is it possible to see salvation? What does salvation mean? What does it mean to be saved?

It means being freed from evil, liberated. It means being embraced by the good. It means irreversible *participation in the unalterable and definitive good.*

"Every man shall *see* the salvation of God." Advent actually speaks of the salvation which comes to man from God, from God alone.

What *credibility* have these words *today*? Man, today as then, knows from experience that his existence in the visible world *does not let him share* in the unalterable and definitive good. The whole of the goods existing in the world, taken all together, are not capable of "saving" man, that is, of liberating him from all evil.

On the contrary, man of today, with the cosmic dimension of his existence, feels *a threat from a manifold evil.*

This, however, is an exclusively negative argument. Not even the prophet Isaiah made use of such an argument. He said outright: "God will save you.... Every man shall see the salvation of God."

God has said that He wills to save man. He said it through Isaiah and all the Prophets.

He said it through Jesus Christ.

He says it constantly through the Church.

He says it in a special way in Advent.

December 5

Make Straight the Paths of the Lord

"Prepare the way of the Lord."

I ask you to accept this call with all the simplicity of your faith.

Man prepares the way of the Lord and straightens His paths — when he examines his own conscience; when he searches his works, his words, his thoughts; when he calls good and evil by their names; when he does not hesitate to confess his sins in the Sacrament of Penance, repenting and resolving not to sin again.

This is what is meant by "straightening his paths." It also means receiving the good news of salvation. Each of us may *"see God's salvation"* in his own heart and conscience when he participates in the mystery of remission of sins, as at the very Advent of God.

He thus professes that Christ is "the Lamb of God," He who takes away the sins of the world.

December 6

Everyone Shall See the Salvation of God

"All mankind shall see the salvation of God" (*Lk* 3:6).

God's salvation is the work of a love greater than man's sin. Love alone can wipe out sin and liberate from sin. Love alone can consolidate man in the good; in the unalterable and eternal good.

It is exactly this God of our Advent: the Creator and Redeemer, who makes this profession of such love for man, for man the sinner: "Though the mountains leave their place, and the hills be shaken, *my love will never leave you*" (*Is* 54:10).

Let us make straight the paths of the Lord. And let us get ready for the meeting with this love which will reveal itself, during the night of the birth of the Lord, in the shape of a shelterless Child. Let us remember once again that this saving love, coming to man during the night of Bethlehem, and revealing itself in the Cross and the Resurrection, remains incessantly written in the Church's life as *the Sacrament of the Body and the Blood* as nourishment of souls.

Each time we receive this Sacrament, whenever we accept this food, we prepare the way of the Lord, we make straight his paths. May we always have hunger and thirst for this nourishment, above all in the period of Advent!

May we, through the Sacrament of the Body and the Blood, build the way along which God will come to us in the mystery of his majesty.

December 7

ADVENT: A Call to Be at Peace with God

What does Advent mean?

Advent is discovery of a great aspiration of men and women and peoples toward the house of the Lord.

The Lord is *the God of peace,* He is the God of the Alliance with mankind. When, during the night at Bethlehem, poor shepherds will set off to walk to the stable where shall be accomplished the first coming of the Son of Man, the song of the angels will lead them, "Peace on earth to those on whom His favor rests" (*Lk* 2:14).

This vision of the divine peace belongs to all the Messianic expectation in the old Alliance. " One nation shall not raise the sword against another, nor shall they train for war again" *(Is* 2:4–5). Advent brings the *invitation to the peace of God* for all mankind.

It is necessary for us to construct this peace and continually reconstruct it in ourselves and with others; in families, in relations with neighbors, in workplaces, in the life of the whole of society.

To serve such peace with manifold dimensions, there is need to listen to these words of the prophet as well: "Come, let us climb the Lord's mountain. . .that He may instruct us in His ways, for from Zion shall go forth instruction, and the word of the Lord from Jerusalem" *(Is* 2:3).

Advent is the time when the law and the Word of the Lord must again penetrate hearts, must find once more confirmation in social living. They serve the good of man. They build peace!

December 8

The Most Redeemed of All

Blessed be God the Father of Our Lord Jesus Christ, who filled You, Virgin of Nazareth, *with every spiritual blessing* in Christ. In Him, You were conceived Immaculate! Preselected to be His Mother, you were redeemed in Him and through Him more than any other human being! Preserved from the inheritance of original sin, You were conceived and came into the world in a state of sanctifying grace. *Full of Grace!*

We venerate this mystery of the faith in today's solemnity. Today, together with all the Church, we venerate the Redemption which was actuated in You. That most singular participation in the Redemption of the world and of man, was reserved only for You, solely for You. Hail O Mary, *Alma Redemptoris Mater,* dear Mother of the Redeemer.

You who are *the first among the redeemed,* help us, men and women of the twentieth century moving toward its end and, at the same time, are people of the second millennium after Christ. Help us to find once more our part in the mystery of the Redemption. Help us to understand more profoundly the divine dimension and, at the same time, the human dimension of that mystery. Help us to draw more fully on its inexhaustible resources. Help us — redeemed by the most precious blood of Christ. All this we ask of You in the solemnity of today, O clement, O pious, sweet Virgin Mary. Amen.

December 9

Prayer to Mary Immaculate

To Mary Immaculate, Mother of Our Advent
Hail!
Blessed are you, O full of grace.

Today with the greatest veneration, the Church recalls the fullness of this Grace, with which God filled You from the first moment of Your conception.

The Apostle's words fill us with joy, "Despite the increase of sin, grace has far surpassed it" *(Rom 5:20).* We are glad at this particular abundance of divine grace in You, who bear the name of "Immaculate Conception," Mother.

Accept us, just as we are, here by You.
Accept us! Look into our hearts!

Accept our cares and our hopes!

Help us, You, full of grace, to live in grace, to persevere in grace and, if it should be necessary, to return to the grace of the living God, which is the greatest and supernatural good of man.

Prepare us for the advent of Your Son!

Accept us with our daily problems, our weaknesses and deficiencies, our crises, and our personal, family and social failings.

Do not let us lose good will! Do not let us lose sincerity of conscience and honesty of conduct!

Obtain justice for us through Your prayer.

Save the peace of the whole world!

Be with us, You the Immaculate.

Be with us. Be with Rome. Be with the Church, and with the world. Amen.

December 10

Mary Believed

Mary says to us today: "I am the servant of the Lord. Let it be done to me as you say" (*Lk* 1:38).

And with those words, she expresses what was *the fundamental attitude of her life: her faith!* Mary believed! She trusted in God's promises and was faithful to his will.

When the angel Gabriel announced that she was chosen to be the Mother of the Most High, she gave her *"Fiat"* humbly and with full freedom, "Let it be done to me as you say."

Perhaps the best description of Mary and, at the same time, the greatest tribute to her, was the greeting of her cousin Elizabeth, "Blest is she who trusted that the Lord's words to her would be fulfilled" (*Lk* 1:45). For it was that continual trust in the providence of God which most characterized her faith.

All her earthly life was a "pilgrimage of faith." For, like us, she walked in shadows and hoped for things unseen. She knew the contradictions of our earthly life. She was promised that her son would be given David's throne but, at his birth, there was no room even at the inn. Mary still believed. The angel said her child would be called the Son of God; but she would see him slandered, betrayed, condemned and left to die as a thief on the cross.

Even yet, Mary "trusted that the Lord's words to her would be fulfilled" (*Lk* 1:45) and that "nothing is impossible with God" (*Lk* 1:37).

This woman of faith, Mary of Nazareth, the Mother of God, has been given to us as *a model in our pilgrimage of faith.* From Mary, we learn to surrender to God's will in all things.

December 11

Joseph Believed

Saint Joseph of Nazareth was a "just man." It was said to his credit, "as justice," that he believed in "the God who gives life to the dead and calls into existence things which do not yet exist."

That happened at the *decisive moment for the history of salvation,* when God, the eternal Father, "sent His Son into the world" to accomplish the promise made to Abraham.

It was exactly then that the faith of Joseph of Nazareth was manifested. It showed itself to be up to the measure of the faith of Abraham.

It was manifested even more when *"the Word of the living God became flesh in Mary,"* the Spouse of Joseph; by the announcement of the angel, "she was with child through the power of the Holy Spirit." The faith of Saint Joseph was bound to be manifested *"before the mystery of the Incarnation of the Son of God."*

Then it was indeed that Joseph of Nazareth underwent the great proof of his faith, just as Abraham had seen his faith tried. And now Joseph, "the just man," believed in Him who "calls into existence things which did not exist."

In fact, *God Himself,* through the power of the Holy Spirit, called into existence the humanity which was that proper to the only begotten Son of God, the Father's Eternal Word, in the womb of the Virgin of Nazareth, Mary, the bride promised to Joseph.

And Joseph of Nazareth believed in God: "Joseph, son of David, have no fear about taking Mary as your wife. It is by the Holy Spirit that she has conceived this child." Joseph took Mary to himself — and That which had been engendered in her.

December 12

To the Virgin of Guadalupe

O Immaculate Virgin, Mother of the true God and Mother of the Church! You who from this place show forth your clemency and your compassion for all those who have recourse to your protection, hear the prayer which we address to you with filial confidence and present it to Your Son Jesus, our sole Redeemer.

Mother of Mercy, teacher of hidden and silent sacrifice, to You, who come to meet us, we sinners consecrate all our being and all our love on this day. We also consecrate our lives, our work, our joys, our infirmities and our sorrows to you.

Grant peace, justice and prosperity to our peoples, for we confide all we have and all we are to your care, Our Lady and Our Mother. We will to be completely yours and to follow with You the road of full fidelity to Jesus Christ in His Church. Hold us always lovingly by the hand.

Virgin of Guadalupe, Mother of the Americas, we pray to You for all the bishops, that they may guide the faithful along the paths of an intense Christian life, of love and of humble service to God and souls. See how great the harvest is and intercede with the Lord so that He will infuse hunger for holiness into the whole People of God and grant abundant priestly and religious vocations, strong in faith, zealous dispensers of the mysteries of God.

Grant our homes the grace to love and respect life as it begins, with the same love whereby You conceived the life of the Son of God in Your womb. Virgin Saint Mary, Mother of Beautiful Love, protect our families so that they may always remain united and bless the education of our children.

So, Mother Most Holy, with the Peace of God in our consciences, with our hearts free of malice and hate, we shall be able to bring true joy and true peace to all, which come from Your Son, our Lord Jesus Christ, who lives and reigns with the Father and the Holy Spirit for ever and ever. Amen.

December 13

St. John the Baptist, Forerunner of Jesus Christ

Christ *gives testimony* of His Precursor. He bears witness to John in the Jordan region. He does so in metaphorical and powerful terms. He asks his hearers: "What did you go out to see in the desert — a reed swayed by the wind? What, really, did you go out to see — someone dressed luxuriously?" (*Lk* 7:24–25).

Christ put this question in a rhetorical form so that, through the negation, the evident truth of who John was could be seen even better. He was not *swayed* like a reed in the wind but professed the truth in a simple and fundamental way and proclaimed it. He was not dressed in fine raiment but "in a garment of camel's hair" (*Mt* 3:4). This is only one of the details regarding his harsh and mortified life.

Yes, John was a prophet. He was "something more" (*Lk* 7:26). Christ says of him, "There is no man born of woman greater than John" (*Lk* 7:28). Why do we dwell on *this testimony* which Christ gives to John? To make us aware as well of the significance of the word of truth, we profess that Christ is "the Lamb of God," He who takes away the sin of the world (*cf. Jn* 1:29), exactly what John professed.

You see, each of us *pronounces such words* when he or she confesses sin in the Sacrament of Penance so that the Lamb of God will take away that sin. To whoever among us confesses that word of truth with humility and contrition Christ gives similar testimony, like that which He gave to John. He says, in fact, "Yet the least born into the kingdom of God is greater than he" (*Lk* 7:28).

So. I ask you, brothers and sisters, to meditate on Christ in the period of Advent . . . and hunger and thirst to receive such a testimony on you by examining your consciences and receiving the Sacrament of Penance.

Prepare the way of the Lord! Make straight His paths! Everyone shall see the salvation of God.

December 14

St. John of the Cross, Spiritual Master

St. John of the Cross is the great master of the paths which lead to union with God.

He shows the ways of knowledge through faith, for only such knowledge of the faith disposes the understanding to *union with the living God:* "For, as God is infinite, so such understanding propounds Him to us as infinite: as He is Threefold and One, so it manifests Him to us as Threefold and One . . . and so, through this sole means, God manifests Himself to the soul in divine light surpassing all understanding" (*Ascent of Mount Carmel*).

The soul — the more it will have faith, so much the more will it be united to God. The act of faith is concentrated upon Jesus Christ. We find Christ in the Church, Spouse and Mother. "Therefore," the saint writes, "we must let ourselves be guided in all things . . . by the law of Christ made man, of His Church and of His ministers." Man of today, anxious for meaning in existence, sometimes indifferent to the Church's preaching, perhaps skeptical toward mediations of the Revelation of God — John of the Cross offers him an invitation to honest search. He persuades him to set aside everything that might be an obstacle to the faith and sets him in front of Christ.

In the silence of prayer, encounter with God is actuated.

December 15

Come, Christ, Come!

Advent Prayer

We are awaiting the moment of the new birth of Christ. Chris is He who "shows sinners the way. He guides the humble to Justice, he teaches the humble his way" *(Ps* 25:8–9). So, it is toward Him who is to come — toward Christ — that we turn with full confidence and conviction. And we say to Him: Guide us! Guide us in the truth!

Guide, O Christ, fathers and mothers of families in the truth . . . spurred on and strengthened by the sacramental grace of Matrimony and conscious of being the visible sign on earth of Your unfailing love for the Church, we know how to be calm and resolute in facing with evangelical coherence the responsibility of married life and the Christian education of children.

Guide, O Christ, the young in the truth . . . that they may not let themselves be drawn to new idols, such as conspicuous consumption, wellbeing at any cost, moral permissiveness, violent protest, but may live your message in joy, which is the message of the Beatitudes, the message of love for God and one's neighbor, the message of moral commitment to the authentic transformation of society.

Guide, O Christ, all the faithful in the truth . . . so that the Christian faith may inspire all their lives and make them become courageous testifiers to the world of your mission of salvation and aware and dynamic members of the Church, sure of being children of God and brethren, with You and with all people! Guide us, O Christ, in the truth, always!

December 16

Advent Prepares for the Birth of God

All Advent lies in the perspective of Birth. Above all, that birth at Bethlehem represents the culminating point of the history of salvation. From the moment of that birth on, the expectation was transformed into reality. The "Come!" of Advent meets with the "Here I am" of Bethlehem.

However, this primary perspective of birth is transformed into a further one. Advent not only prepares us for the birth of God who becomes man. It also prepares man for his own *birth from God.* Man must, in fact, constantly be born of God. His aspiration toward the truth, the good, the beautiful, the absolute, is actuated in this birth. When the night of Bethlehem comes, then Christmas day, the Church will say, at the sight of the Newborn, who will show weakness and insignificance, like every newborn child, "Any who did accept him *he empowered to become children of God*" (*Jn* 1:12).

Advent prepares man for this "power," for his own birth from God. This birth is our vocation. It is our inheritance in Christ. Birth, which endures and is renewed. Man must *always* be born anew in Christ from God. He must *come to life again from God.*

Man journeys toward God so as to reach Him himself, to reach the Living God, the Father, the Son and the Holy Spirit. And he reaches there when *God himself comes to him.* This is the Advent of Christ. Advent, which surpasses the perspective of human transcendence, surpasses the measure of the human advent.

The Advent of Christ is accomplished in the fact that God becomes man, that God is born as man. It is accomplished at the same time in the fact that man is born of God, that man is reborn constantly from God.

December 17

Walking toward God

Once, at the beginning of his story, man, male and female, heard the voice of temptation: "You will be like gods who know what is good and what is bad" (*Gen* 3:5). Man yielded to that temptation. He continues to follow it constantly.

Against man's perennial temptation, we must set the Advent of Christ; we must be born of God and incessantly be reborn of Him.

The progress of culture and the sciences unrolls vast perspectives to us. This arouses rightful joy and leads to the development of a civilization of production and consumption, together with the development of a civilization of menace and violence. If, in the midst of such prospects, I have some particular proposal to put to you this Advent, it is as follows: *Do not give up living, being born from God constantly, and being reborn from God!*

The Advent of Christ throbs in man's nostalgia for the truth, for the good and the beautiful, for justice, for love and peace. *Christ's Coming throbs in the Church's sacraments,* which enable us to be born and reborn from God.

Long live Christmas, regenerated in Christ in the Sacrament of Reconciliation! Long live Christmas, absorbing the deepest content of the mystery of God. Towards Him, after all, all man's advent opens!

O Radix Iesse . . . evni ad liberandum nos, iam noli tardare!

— O Root of Jesse, . . . *come to free us,* now do not linger!"

December 18

Walking in God's Gaze

Man not only walks toward God (often unknowingly and even while denying Him) *through his own advent,* through the cry of his humanity Man goes toward God, walking in the history of salvation, in God's gaze, before the Lord, as we hear in the Gospel in regard to John the Baptist. He was to walk before the Lord with spirit and power.

This new direction of the way of the advent of man is linked in a particular way with the Advent of Christ. However, man walks "before the Lord" *from the beginning,* and will walk before Him until the end, because he is simply *God's image.*

He walks before the Lord, filling up his humanity and his early store with the content of his work, with the content of his culture and science, with the content of incessant search after the truth, the good, the beautiful, justice, love, peace. And he walks before the Lord while often enveloping himself in everything which is negation of the truth, of the good and the beautiful, negation of justice, of love, of peace.

> "O Root of Jesse, a sign for all peoples . . .
> come to free us, linger no more."

Christ's Advent is indispensable for man to find it in the certainty that, while walking through the world, living day after day and year after year, loving and suffering, he is walking before the Lord, whose image he is in the world. He renders testimony of Him to all creation.

December 19

The Culmination of Advent

We are by now at the culmination of Advent! During these days of grace, the Church has made us reflect, through her liturgy, on the mystery of the twofold coming of Christ: in the lowliness of our human nature and in the final coming of his Parousia.

We Christians are called to meditate during this period on the Incarnation of the Son of Man . . . on the moving reality of a Child, wrapped in swaddling clothes and laid in a manger.

But it is exactly this Child who guides, orients, marks the behavior, the choices and the lives of persons standing by Him and involved in His appearance among them. There is the aged Elizabeth. She has felt the life of a child flower miraculously in her womb, after having been awaited for years as a grace of the Lord: John the Baptist, he who was to be the precursor of the Messiah! There is her husband Zachary, whose tongue was loosed for him to sing the great deeds of God toward His people. There are the shepherds, who are enabled to contemplate the Savior. There are the Wise Men, the Magi, who had been searching for years for the secret of the skies and the stars and who prostrated themselves in adoration before the Newborn. There is old Simeon, who had also long awaited the Messiah, "a revealing light to the Gentiles and the glory of your people Israel" (Lk 2:32). There is Anne, the venerable prophetess, who jubilated for "the deliverance of Jersualem" (Lk 2:38). And Joseph, the silent, vigilant, attentive, tender, paternal custodian and protector of the Child's frailty.

And, above all, there is the Mother, Mary Most Holy.

In the face of God's inexpressible design, she sank into her insufficiency, called herself the "servant" of the Lord, and entered into the divine project with full readiness.

December 20

The Interior Advent

Before the manger at Bethlehem — as later before the cross on Golgotha — mankind makes a basic choice in regard to Jesus. In the last analysis, this is the choice which man is called upon to make unavoidably day after day, in regard to God, the Creator and Father. And this is done, before all and above all, within the depths of the personal conscience. It is there that the encounter between God and man takes place.

This is the *third coming* of which the Fathers speak. It is the "interior Advent," which was analyzed theologically and ascetically by St. Bernard: "In the first coming, the Word was seen on earth and mingled with mankind, when, as He Himself affirmed, they saw Him and hated Him. It the last coming every person shall see the salvation of God, and they shall look on him whom they pierced. But the intermediate coming is occult, in it only the elect see Him within themselves, and their souls are thereby saved" (*De medio adventu et triplici innovatione*)

This Interior Advent is brought to life through constant meditation on and assimilation of the Word of God. It is rendered fruitful and animated by *prayer of adoration and praise of God.* It is reinforced by constant reception of the *Sacraments, those of Reconciliation and the Eucharist in particular, for they cleanse and enrich us with the grace of Christ and make us "new," in accordance with Jesus' pressing call:* "Be converted" (*cf. Mt* 3:2; 4:17; *Lk* 5:32; *Mk* 1:15).

In view of this, every day can and ought become Advent for us Christians. It can and ought become Christmas! For, the more we purify our souls, the more shall we make room for God's love in our hearts, the more Christ will be able to come and be born in us!

December 21

Sharing with Others

The path to God is not covered with interior joy alone. Man desires to *bring others* to Him too. He therefore becomes a messenger and apostle of the love of God: "Give thanks to the Lord, acclaim his name; among the nations make known his deeds (*Is* 12:4).

Man obedient to God's grace discovers the world of God's works, which are hidden to the eyes of the sinner. Man guided by divine grace also desires *to share the nearness to God, which he experiences, with others.*

Well, I want to tell you, in Christ's name:

Have humble and courageous awareness of what the Father has given you.

Let this awareness be your strength, your light, your hope.

Give the world what the Father has given you: the kingdom of God.

Do not weary . . . from continually seeking even the slightest occasions for widening prudent and sincere contacts with that great human and social reality in which you are immersed as leaven, so as to conduct and carry forward that work of promotion, based on truth, justice and respect for the dignity of the person, which constitutes the necessary premise for the world to have knowledge of Christ in the faith and in the Church. . . . May the experience of the approach of our God in the time of Advent prepare the hearts of all for the joy of Christmas!

December 22

Not a Consumer Christmas

We must not transform and debase Christmas into a festivity of useless wastefulness, in a manifestation of facile consumerism. Christmas is the feast of the humility, of the poverty, of the nakedness, of the lowliness of the Son of God, who came to give us His infinite love. It ought therefore to be celebrated in an authentic spirit of sharing, of participation together *with the brethren who have need of our affectionate aid.* It ought to be a fundamental stage in meditation on our behavior in regard to "the God who comes." And we can meet this God who comes in a defenseless, crying child. In a sick person, who feels the strength of his body inexorably leaving him. In an old man or woman who has worked for the whole of life and is now made marginal and barely tolerated in our modern society, based on productivity and success.

O Christ, King of the Peoples, awaited and desired for centuries by mankind, wounded and scattered by sin, You who are the cornerstone upon which mankind can reconstruct itself and regain a definite and enlightening guide for its path through history, You who reunited the divided peoples by means of your sacrificial gift to the Father, come and save man. He is pitiable and great, he was made by You "with dust of the earth," and he bears Your image and likeness in Him!

December 23

Christmas Is upon Us

The solemnity of the Holy Feast of Christmas is near. In it we commemorate the birth of the Divine Redeemer Jesus at Bethlehem. This leads me. . .to meditate with you on this historically determining event and to suggest a few practical guidelines.

Faith, based on the Gospel story, tells us that God became man. That is, He entered into human history, not so much to challenge it as to *enlighten* it, to *orient* it, *to save* it, by redeeming every single soul. This is the meaning of the Incarnation of the Word; this is the authentic meaning of Christmas, the feast of true joy and true hope.

Comprehending and accepting the message of Christmas means living the perennial contemporaneity of Christ. In our history as intelligent, free men and women, Jesus remains salvation for ever and for all. That is, he remains the answer to the supreme questions tormenting man and the grace for rising out of evil and living in the perspective of eternity. Bring this meaning of Christmas in your minds, in your life, in your human and Christian ideals! Man of today is bewildered by so many contrasting ideologies and shocked by so many dramatic and dolorous phenomena. He has need to know *with certainty* that, in spite of all, there is hope and joy, because God became man, Christ was really incarnated for us, the Savior announced by the Prophets came, and has remained with us!

We must *believe in Christmas,* strongly, deeply!

December 24

Christmas Eve

The imminence of Christmas finds us gathered for the customary welcome exchange of good wishes. Our hearts pour out with mutual joy: *Dominus prope est!* The Lord is near! (*Phil* 4:5). Expectation of the earthly birth of the Son of God made man in these days polarizes our attention, our vigilance and our prayer, sharpens it, makes it more intense and humble. We thank you, therefore, for this your presence, which enables us to foretaste, in communion of spirit, the wealth of the mystery which we are about to relive.

Let us go together to meet the Redeemer who is coming; the liturgy of Advent has already fully disposed us for this spiritual journey, which goes to meet the expectation of the peoples. We have so far followed it in company of *Isaiah*, the "type" of messianic expectation. We have followed it in the tracks of the Baptist. He has once again made his voice resound for us: "Prepare the way" (*cf. Mt* 3:3; *Lk* 3:4). Above all, we have followed it with Mary, the listening Virgin. She has been by us with her example and with her intercession because, where Jesus is awaited, there Mary always is, she, the "morning star," who prepares the advent of the "sun of justice" (*Mal* 3:20).

And now the days are about to be completed (*cf. Lk* 2:6) of that blessed Nativity which we shall see again in the Divine Mysteries of the Holy Night. Jesus is born to ransom, *He comes to redeem us.*

He comes to reconcile us with God. As St. Augustine well emphasizes, with his usual expressiveness, "By means of our Head we are reconciled with God, since in Him the divinity of the Only Begotten became a sharer in our mortality, so that we should be sharers in his immortality."

Christmas is the beginning of that "marvelous exchange" which unites us to God. *It is the beginning of the Redemption.*

December 25

You Are with Us, Emmanuel

Puer natus est nobis, Filius datus est nobis . . .
"A child is born to us, a son is given us . . ." *(Is 9:5).*

These words of the prophet Isaiah, uttered at midnight, initiated the feast of the Nativity. They were proclaimed to all who gathered in St. Peter's Basilica and to all who heard them in any other part of the world. They once more became the message of the Good News, *the word of Light and Joy.*

My brothers and sisters! All you for whom this Nativity is the sign of hope! I invite you to such spiritual union! Let us surround the place where God was made man with a vast — so extensive! — crown of hearts! Let us form a circle and court about this Virgin, who gave Him human life on the night of the Birth of God! Let us form a court about the Holy Family!

Emmanuel, You are among us! Together with us, You have condescended to the extreme consequences of that Alliance which has been concluded from the beginning with man, even though it had been so often violated and infringed. . . .

You are with us, Emmanuel! O truly admirable! God Almighty in the feebleness of a child.

December 26

St. Stephen

Today also, Christmas goes on exerting its salutary and bracing influence.

I wish to venerate St. Stephen together with you, as the Church honors him, the first Christian martyr on the day after the solemnity of the Nativity.

"Yesterday we celebrated the birth in time of our eternal King. Today we celebrate the glorious passion of one of his soldiers. Yesterday indeed, our King, vested in the noble robe of his flesh, came out from his royal dwelling in the womb of the Virgin and deigned to visit the world. Today, one of his soldiers leaves the tent of his body and ascends in triumph to heaven." These moving words are those of a saint of the ancient Church, St. Fulgentius. They keep their meaning intact because they give not only the core of a relationship of liturgical continuity between the feast of the Nativity and that of the Protomartyr but also and above all a relationship of intrinsic linking in the order of sanctity and grace. *Christ, King of history and Redeemer of man*, puts himself at the center of that itinerary toward perfection to which he calls every human being.

We venerate Saint Stephen and imitate his example as the testifier for Christ he showed himself to be, with his spirited words, his concern in service to the poor, his constancy during his trial and, above all, with his heroic death. While we do so, we see that his figure is lit up and rendered giantlike in the light of his Lord and Master, whom he willed to follow in the supreme sacrifice.

A valuable lesson comes from that for us. As we look at Stephen in the light of the Nativity, we ought to take up his example and teaching. We are called to live as children of God; we too shall be crowned as was Stephen above, in the homeland, if we are faithful.

December 27

St. John the Evangelist

Before our eyes, above all, lies that scene so graphically described by the evangelist John. We are on Mount Calvary, a cross is there, and Jesus is nailed to it. And there, nearby, is the mother of Jesus, surrounded by a number of women. The beloved disciple, John, is there. The Dying Man speaks, with the troubled breath of the last agony: "Woman, there is your son." Then, addressing the disciple, "There is your mother." The intention is clear: Jesus wills to entrust the mother to the care of the beloved disciple.

Is that all? The ancient Fathers of the Church discerned a more profound theological significance behind that apparently so simple occurrence. Origen identified the apostle John with every Christian. Since him, more and more recourse has been made to this text to justify *the universal motherhood of Mary*.

This conviction has a precise basis in the revealed fact. How can we fail, in fact, to think, as we read this passage, of the mysterious words which Jesus uttered during the marriage feast at Cana? When Mary made her request to Him, He answered, addressing her as "woman" — as above — and postponed the beginning of His collaboration with her for man's sake to the moment of the Passion, His "hour," in fact, as He was accustomed to call it.

December 28

Christmas Raises Man Up

"For a child is born to us, a son is given us; upon his shoulders dominion rests."

What happened on the night of Bethlehem cannot really be contained within a framework like that of a news report. Although this description is outlined in the readings of today's liturgy in a quite detailed way, it still does not tell all. To learn all about it, we have to enter into development of events in the light of the words of the prophet Isaisah, which we quoted at the beginning.

What power is on the shoulders of this Child, who did not have even a simple roof over his head at the moment of his entry into the world? Who had a manger for animals as his first crib?

We ask ourselves about this "power" during the night of Bethlehem, the power which this Newborn bears with Him into the world.

Well, we hear that, together with that angel who announced the birth of the Savior to the shepherds, "a multitude of the heavenly host, praising God and saying, Glory to God in high heaven and peace on earth *to those upon whom His favor rests."*

We find an answer to our question in that announcement at Bethlehem.

What power rested on the shoulders of Christ on that night? *A unique power.* The power which only He possesses. He alone has power to penetrate the soul of every human with the peace of the *Divine Pleasure.*

He alone has power to cause men to become children of God.

He alone is able to raise the history of man to the heights of the glory of God.

Only He.

Let us greet Him with thankfulness and joy on this radiant night.

Venite, adoremus! — "Come, let us adore!"

December 29

Christmas, the Feast Day of Man

Christmas is the feast day of man.

One of the billions of human beings who have been born and will be born on earth . . .

And, at the same time, one, unique and irrepeatable.

If we celebrate the birth of Jesus so solemnly, we do it so as to testify that every human is someone, unique and irrepeatable. . .

God assures him of that.

Through Him and in His eyes, man is always unique and irrepeatable; someone eternally thought and eternally preselected; someone called and denominated with his own name, as that first man, Adam; and like that new Adam, who was born of the Virgin Mary in the grotto of Bethlehem: "You . . . shall give him the name Jesus" (*Lk* 1:31).

It is humanity which is raised up in God's earthly birth. Humanity, human "nature," is assumed in the unity of the Divine Person of the Son, in the unity of the Eternal Word. . . . The birth of the Incarnate Word is the beginning of a new strength for mankind itself; the capacity open to every human being, to whom, according to St. John, "he empowered to become children of God" (*Jn* 1:12).

Accept the great truth on man. Accept this dimension of man, which has opened to all mankind . . . Accept the mystery in which everyone lives since Christ was born . . . God was pleased with man through Christ.

Man . . . it is not permissible to humiliate him; it is not permitted to hate him.

Happy Christmas to each and every man and woman!

Happy Christmas, in the peace and joy of Christ.

December 30

God's Presence in Time

Before the Crib, with adoring souls, let us reflect first of all on time that passes, flows on inexorably and bears our brief existences away with it. With his divine words, Jesus relieves us of the anxiety of senseless vacuity and tells us that, on the gigantic and mysterious curve of time, all human history is simply a return to the Father's house, a return to the homeland. Therefore, every single existence forms part of this journey toward the Father. Living means covering a stretch of the way on the return home, every day and in every hour.

As we think particularly of this troubled year which we have lived through, let us remember that the Christmas message affirms with absolute certainty that *God is always present,* even in the contradictions of human history. By creating man intelligent and free, He willed this history spangled with sublime peaks and tragic abysses, and He does not abandon mankind. The Nativity is the guaranty that we are loved by the Most High, that His Omnipotence is interwoven with His Providence in a manner almost always obscure and unfathomable to us.

This is why we have to remember St. Paul's words to the Corinthians: "The Lord is the one to judge me, so stop passing judgment before the time of his return. He will bring to light what is hidden in darkness and manifest the intentions of hearts. At that time, everyone will receive his praise from God."

A great thinker of the last century, Cardinal Newman, said in a sermon: "God's hand is always upon those who belong to Him, and leads them by unknown paths. The most they can do is to believe what they cannot yet manage to see but will see later on, and, remaining firm in their faith, work with God in that direction."

December 31

The Last Day of the Year

"Children, it is *the final hour*"(*1 Jn* 2:18).

How topical these words are! How they fit in well with what we are all living today, December 31!

The last day of the year. . .let us live it so as to participate in the Eucharistic liturgy, the Sacrifice of Christ . . . so as to *express God in the fullest way that our hearts and our consciences feel and to make manifest our thanksgiving and request for forgiveness.*

"It is truly right and just, and dutiful . . . *to give thanks* to You!" To You. Exactly to You, Father, Son and Holy Spirit. To thank You for all the abundance of the mystery of the Birth of God, in whose light the old year is passing and the new one is coming to birth. How eloquent it is, that the day which humanly tells us above all of "passing," with the precise content of the Church's liturgy, should also testify to Birth: God's birth in a human body. And, at the same time, of man's birth from God: "Any who did accept Him he empowered to become children of God" (*Jn* 1:12).

Together with this thanksgiving, let all the *words of propitiation* become the content of our participation in the Holy Mass today, beginning with the initial *Confiteor* through the *Kyrie Eleison* to the *Agnus Dei,* "Lamb of God who takes away the sins of the world." Then to our "Lord, I am not worthy. . . ."

Let us put everything which our consciences live into these words, what weighs upon them, what God alone knows how to judge and remit. And let us not avoid standing here before God, with consciousness of guilt, the attitude of the publican in the Gospel. Let us take up such an attitude. It actually corresponds to man's inner truth. It brings liberation. It, exactly it, links up with hope.

January

January 1

Mary, Mother of Peace
Solemnity of the Holy Mother of God

Implore peace with us.

Mary's motherhood . . . is like a final message from the Octave of the Nativity of the Lord.

Birth always speaks of the Mother, of Her who gives life. . . . The first day of the New Year is the day of the Mother. There is no image . . . of the mystery of the birth of the Lord simpler than the image of the Mother with Jesus in her arms.

Is not this image the source of our singular confidence?

But there is another image of the Mother with the Son in her arms: the "Pietà," Mary holding Jesus taken down from the cross. With Jesus, who expired before her eyes . . . and, after death, He returned to those arms in which at Bethlehem He was offered as Savior of the world.

I would therefore join our prayer for peace with this twofold image: "Mother, you who know what it is to hold the corpse of Your Son in your arms, . . . spare all mothers the death of their sons, torments, slavery, the destructions of war, persecutions, concentration camps, prisons! Preserve the joy of birth to them, of nourishment, of development of man and of his life.

In the name . . . of the birth of the Lord, implore peace together with us, with all the beauty and majesty of Your motherhood, which the Church exalts and the world admires. We beg you: be with us at every moment! Make this New Year a year of peace by virtue of the birth and death of Your Son! Amen.

January 2

To Be in Peace

I desire to indicate a number of privileged lines of commitment, for an educational and apostolic project. You must above all seek peace as harmony and cohesion in your personal, vital structures: *peace in you,* the fruit of interior struggle, of sincere commitment to a life in insistence with your faith, of constant effort to restore man to the integrity, the harmony, the beauty of his divine origin.

Yes, there is need to work — as I am insistingly repeating in the Wednesday catechesis — as chaste people, in coherence with oneself and one's own responsibilities, without obscuring anything. And, in peace, to accept the vocation which God assigns us, whatever it may be, even the most demanding.

You must "insofar as it be within your power, *live in peace with all,*" beginning with the family, and gradually extend your peace initiative to the personal level, that of the group and that of the association.

You more than anyone, because you are young, have to overcome evil with good, even the most inveterate evil, the most hardened. For your part as well, open breaches in the wall of hate, do not let yourselves be drawn into it. Promote overcoming every sort of rancor, rivalry, envy!

Through you, *let there be peace in the spheres of cultures* which are harbored in the hearts of mankind. If all really wish an end to violence, let there be courage enough for disarmament of ideological hatred and a review of one's own aims on the record of peace.

You must also *work for peace in the international sphere.* And not only by reason of the inevitable linkage between personal initiative and community or collective initiative but specifically for an action which is possible for you all.

To Catholic Action Youth.

January 3

Being Peacemakers

Following Christ is following peace, in peace, Peace in accepting the message of His Love: peace in accepting His Spirit, peace in living His grace, in intimacy with Him, through the Sacraments and, above all, the Eucharist.

Now, it is up to you to go and *make the announcement of the Gospel of peace.* You are actually lay evangelizers of peace, promotors of works of peace: bearers of words and deeds of peace, of lived examples and explicit acts of peace, in close consequence of your existence.

You are then asked to be persuaded that peace is the other name of life; that life and peace have the same name. You are expected to have the conviction that announcing peace means in concrete taking historical man as the starting point, together with the fabric of his existence from the first moment, the fabric of his relationships with the environment and with others.

Peace is service to life and promotion of life, development, progress for each and all. "Our 'yes' to peace extends to a 'yes' to life," Paul VI said in his message for Peace Day, 1978.

Why conceal this from all those who are capable of hearing it? It is on the peace front that one commits oneself for the beliefs of life. It is illusory and, in the end, contradictory to affirm we want peace and then fail to do honor to every human life that is born. This is where the problems on the local, national and international levels link up with each other and the perspective of peace becomes a vector of radical transformation. It is at this point that the various humanitarian cultures ought to face up to each other and decide what development to imprint upon the movement of hearts toward peace. "The aspirations of the *spirit* — let it not be forgotten — lead to *life* and to *peace*."

January 4

Peace, the Fruit of Fraternity

The Word became flesh . . . in time.

The years which pass end on December 31 and begin again on January 1. They really pass by bearing a comparison with the fullness coming from God. They pass under the gaze of Eternity and the Word.

At the Beginning of the New Year, we desire to re-read the message of peace in the depths of that mystery, the message which was revealed once for all in the night at Bethlehem: peace to men of good will! Peace on earth! This is what the mystery of the Birth of God means to tell us every year; this is what the Church brings out today as well. . . .

All mankind ardently desires peace and sees war as the greatest peril in earthly existence. The Church is totally conscious of these desires and, at the same time, of the fears and worries troubling all people, manifesting these sentiments at the beginning of the New Year especially. *What is peace?* What can peace on earth be, peace among people and peoples? What can it be if not the fruit of fraternity, showing itself to be stronger than that which divides men and sets them against one another? St. Paul speaks of such fraternity when he writes to the Galatians, "You are sons." And, if sons, sons of God in Christ, then you are also brethren.

He goes on to write, "You are no longer a slave but a son." It is in this context that the theme of the message. . . belongs, "To save peace, respect liberty."

January 5

Free Us from Evil

It is not possible to utter a more fundamental wish on this day opening the New Year than: "FREE US FROM EVIL!"

As we recite these words from Christ's prayer, it is very difficult to give them a meaning different from opposition to what is against peace, destroys it, threatens it. So let us pray:

Free us from war, from hatred, from destruction of human lives!

Do not let us slay! Do not permit the use of means which are at the service of death and destruction. . . .

FREE US FROM EVIL!

Father in heaven, Father of life and Giver of peace. . . .How meaningful are Jesus Christ's words: "'Peace' is my farewell to you, peace is my gift to you; I do not give it to you as the world gives peace" (*Jn* 14:27).

It is this dimension of peace, the deepest dimension, which Christ alone can give to man.

It is fullness of peace rooted in reconciliation with God himself. . . .

We implore this peace for the world. . . for all men, for all nations, of differing languages, cultures and races. For all continents. . . .

Peace is indispensable.

January 6

The Holy Bishop: John N. Neumann

Saint John Neumann. . . now and forever a saint of the universal Church.

His message and his example of holiness must continually be transmitted to *every new generation*. . . . And, if we listen carefully today, we can hear Saint John Neumann speaking to all of us in the words of the Letter to the Hebrews: "Remember your leaders who spoke the word of God to you; consider how their lives ended, and imitate their faith. Jesus Christ is the same yesterday, today, and forever" *(Heb* 13:8).

I am reminded of the one thing which motivated Saint John Neumann throughout his life: *his love for Christ.* His own prayers show us this love; for from the time he was a child he used to say: "Jesus, for you I want to live; for you I want to die; I want to be all yours in life; I want to be all yours in death."

And at the First Mass he celebrated as a priest, he prayed in these words: "Lord, give me holiness." My brothers and sisters in Christ: this is the lesson we learn from the life of Saint John Neumann, and the message which I leave with you today: what really matters in life is that we are loved by Christ and that we love him in return. In comparison with the love of Jesus, everything else is secondary. And without the love of Jesus, everything else is useless. May Mary, our Mother of Perpetual Help, intercede for us.

January 7

Offer Our Gifts to the Divine Child with the Magi

I want to draw your attention briefly to the attitude of the Magi. When, through the guidance given by the mysterious star, they found Mary with the Child Jesus, "they prostrated themselves and did him homage. Then they ... presented Him with gifts of gold, frankincense, and myrrh."

Modern man, too ... meets with God when he opens up to Him with the interior gift of his human "ego," to accept and exchange the immense gifts which He presented to him first: the gift of existence, the gift of the Redemption, the gift of faith.

And that Child, who accepted the gift of the Wise Men, is still always He before whom people and entire peoples "open their coffers," that is, their treasures.

The gifts of the human spirit take on a particular value in the act of this opening to the incarnate God; they become the treasures of the various cultures, the spiritual wealth of the peoples, and of the nations, the common patrimony of all mankind.

The center of this exchange is Christ: the same who accepted the gifts of the Magi.

He himself, the same who is the invisible and incarnate Gift, *causes opening up of souls to that exchange of gifts.* Not only individuals live by them, but peoples, nations, the whole of mankind.

January 8

God's Epiphany in Modern Man

Above all, the divine epiphany is proclaimed in today's solemnity: "We observed his star at its rising and have come to pay him homage."

On the night of the Nativity of the Lord, the shepherds in the fields at Bethlehem saw the light and came to adore Him.

Today the Magi from the East come. They are led by a star. *They come and adore*. Whom do they adore? The Child. The Newborn man. The man who is a particular epiphany of God.

They made a long journey to reach that place, where the star had guided them.

In the Child born at Bethlehem they recognized the latest Gift which the Eternal Father had made to man. In this Gift, *man* appears in the world as *a particular epiphany of God*.

He was so from the beginning, created in the image and likeness of God. He knew that none of the creatures around Him in the world were of his stature. None is really like him. He alone, man, had that particular resemblance to God from the beginning. He was His image.

He darkened this likeness in himself with sin. He disfigured the image. But he did not destroy it.

Man walked toward the Messiah in the tracks of that likeness. He followed the star of his divine destinies, just like those Magi who came from the East. And so history entered a further development. Christ came so that man might recognize a particular epiphany of God in himself.

January 9

Response to the Epiphany of God

The Magi of the East "prostrated themselves and did him homage . . . they opened their coffers and presented him with gifts of gold, frankincense, and myrrh." *The gifts are a response to the Gift.*

In Christ, born on the night of Bethlehem, the Magi of the East recognized that definitive Gift which the Eternal Father makes to man. The gift of His Son, the gift of the Eternal Son: "God so loved the world that he gave his only Son. . . ."

Through this Gift, man rediscovers the epiphany of the Living God and bears it within himself. The Eternal Son has given mankind the power "to become children of God." He has given this power as a Brother to brethren. He has revealed and He continually reveals the Father in those whom "the Father has given Him for an inheritance."

Man who bears the epiphany of the Living God in himself *lives a new life.* He knows that he has to produce fruits. He knows that he must respond to the Gift with a gift. So he brings gold, incense and myrrh.

In this gift from man, which is a response to the Gift from on high, is enclosed the full significance of human life, and the pre-announcement of the call to glory together with it. In this, man and the world are reconfirmed as epiphany of God, who extends *beyond* the bounds of temporality and destructibility.

Do everything you can, so that the people to whom you are sent may believe that they are epiphany of the Living God.

Do all you can that they may respond with a gift for the Gift, that they may bring gold, incense and myrrh.

Do everything, for the pre-announcement of the call to glory to grow and be strengthened in human hearts.

January 10

Baptism Raises Up Children in the Son, Monstrances of God

"This is my beloved Son. My favor rests on him" *(Mt 3:17).*

The words of the Gospel . . . are . . . verified also for . . . children, to whom I . . . administer Baptism.

Jesus is the firstborn of many others *(cf. Rom 8:29).* What happened in Him is repeated mysteriously in each of us. . . .

"This is my beloved Son; my favor rests on him." [The Father] delights in these little ones, because He will see the immortal stamp of his Fatherhood impressed in their spirit, the interior and true likeness to His Son: children in the Son.

And, at the same time, *the Holy Spirit* will descend, invisible, but present as then, to fill these little souls with the riches of his gifts, to make them his dwellings, his temples, his monstrances, which will have to radiate His presence through the whole course of their lives. We do not know how their lives will be, but He already sees them in their fullness.

We . . . lay the foundations of New Christian lives: in these beloved of the Father, redeemed by Christ, signed with the seal of the Spirit, the object of eternal preference which already projects itself into the future, and into the whole of eternity, in a love without end. . . . These dearest children . . . bright with the total innocence of grace . . . holy in God's own holiness . . . remain always faithful to this, our common, stupendous Christian vocation, for the whole of their lives.

January 11

With Baptism, Walk in a New Life

[Baptism] finds its deepest meaning in the fact that we are bringing a new and extraordinary relationship of grace into being between God and these creatures. . . .

With this Sacrament, God's Fatherhood is imparted in a new way, and whoever receives it acquires a fresh relationship of preference in His regard.

A condition of intimate communion with Him is actually set up, in that this communion represents the overcoming of all interior alienation because of sin and, as St. Paul writes, formation of a "new creation" *(2 Cor* 5:17). Baptism. . . is truly *a new birth, a rebirth*. . . We rejoice keenly, with profound spiritual delight. Ours is the joy of the divine family. . . a number of new members enter to become part of the family of God, and while they acquire a new Father in Him, they also find new brethren in us, ready to receive them, with concern and exultation, into the great community of the children of God.

After His Baptism, Jesus "went about doing good works and healing all" *(Acts* 10:38). Baptism must be made *manifest in concrete living,* with luminous and adequate testimony. . . .

"Through baptism into his death, we were buried with him so that, just as Christ was raised from the dead . . . we too might live a new life" *(Rom* 6:4). Let us ask the Lord to "strengthen" us "inwardly through the working of his Spirit" *(Eph* 3:16) so as to live always for his greater glory. Amen.

January 12

On Making Disciples

Our Lord Jesus Christ said: "Go, therefore, make disciples of all the nations. Baptize them in the name 'of the Father, and of the Son, and of the Holy Spirit. Teach them to carry out everything I have commanded you." *(Mt* 28:19–20).

Since then . . . there has been ceaseless organizational or communal response from those who believe and are baptized. The Acts of the Apostles tells us: "Those who accepted his message . . . devoted themselves to the apostles' instruction and the communal life . . . *(Acts* 2:41–42). Here we already see the Church's communitarian nature. . . .

"This is how all men will know you for my disciples: your love for one another" *(Jn* 13:35). . . . The communal dimension of your Christian vocation was strongly emphasized by the liturgical reform of the Second Vatican Council. Every liturgical act is . . . an act of the entire Body of Christ . . . and every Mass . . . is an act of Christ in his Body. Every good deed done by a member is to the advantage of all the members together, and every sin is not only an offense against God but is also a wound inflicted on Christ's Body. . . So it is clear that it is not even thinkable that a Christian should live solely for himself.

A Christian who has not learned to see and love Christ in his neighbor is not fully Christian. We are our brothers' keepers; we are bound to each other by the bond of love. . . .

This communal or organizational nature of our vocation ought to be directed toward the universal Church. We are a local Church instituted by Christ the Lord only to the degree in which we are part of the universal Church.

January 13

The Holy Family of Nazareth

The birth of the Child in the night of Bethlehem gave rise to the Family. Hence the Sunday during the Octave of Christmas is the Feast of the Holy Family of Nazareth. This is the Holy Family, because, shaped by birth of Him whom even His adversary was constrained one day to call "the Holy One of God" (*Mk* 1:24). The *Holy Family*, because the sanctity of Him who was born became the source of a singular sanctification, both that of the Virgin Mother and that of her Spouse, who in the eyes of mankind, as lawful consort, was considered to be the father of the child born during the census at Bethlehem.

This Family is at the same time a *human Family*. The Church, therefore, addresses every human family through the Holy Family in the Christmas season. Sanctity impresses a unique, exceptional, irrepeatable, supernatural character upon this Family, in which the Son of God came to the world. At the same time, everything that we can say about every human family, of its nature, of its duties, of its difficulties, we can say as well about this Sacred Family. In fact, the Holy Family was truly poor. It was without a roof over its head at the moment when Jesus was born and was forced into exile. When the danger was over, it remained a family living *modestly*, in poverty, through the labor of its hands.

Its circumstances were similar to those of so many other human families. It is the place where our solidarity meets up with every family, with every union of man and woman, in which a new human being is born.

It takes upon itself those profound, beautiful and generally difficult problems which married and family life brings.

January 14

Jesus at the Marriage Feast of Cana

The Lord Jesus was invited to take part in a marriage being celebrated at Cana of Galilee.

With Jesus, at Cana of Galilee was His Mother. It even seems that it was she who was invited, for we read: "There was a wedding at Cana in Galilee, and the mother of Jesus was there. Jesus and his disciples had likewise been invited to the celebration." We may therefore conclude that Jesus was invited with His Mother, and perhaps through regard for her. The disciples were invited together with Him.

Jesus was to be invited by men and women many more times during the course of his teaching activity. He would accept their invitations, He would relate to them, sit down at table and talk.

It is well to insist on this line of events: Jesus Christ is continually *invited* by individuals and by various communities. Perhaps there is no one in the world who has had so many invitations. He went to such individuals, and passed time in the midst of human communities. He necessarily had to subject Himself to the conditions of the time and place in the course of his earthly life and activity. Contrariwise, after the Resurrection and the Ascension, and after institution of the Eucharist and the Church, Jesus Christ *can be contemporaneously the Guest of all persons and all communities* inviting Him, in a new way, that is, a sacramental and mystical way. He himself said, "If someone loves me, he will keep my word and My Father will love him, and we shall come to him and take up our dwelling in him."

January 15

Mary, Present at the Marriage Feast of Cana

At Cana, Mary was also revealed in the full simplicity and truth of Her Motherhood. *Motherhood* is always open toward the child, open toward the man. It shares even in their most hidden worries. It takes up such worries and tries to find remedies for them. So it was during the marriage feast at Cana. When wine ran out, the master of ceremonies and the bridal couple certainly felt very embarrassed. It was then that the Mother of Jesus said, "They have no more wine." The subsequent developments of the occurrence are well known.

At the same time Mary revealed herself at Cana of Galilee as *the Mother conscious of Her Son's mission, aware of His Power.*

It was exactly that knowledge which made her say to the servants, "Do whatever he tells you." And the servants followed the hint given by the Mother of Christ.

What else can I wish for you. . . married couples and families; for you, young people and children; you, sick and suffering, worn down by age; you, finally, dear shepherds of souls, religious, men and women, and all of you?

What can I wish for you but that you will always listen to these words of Mary, the Mother of Christ: "Do whatever he tells you"? And may you accept those words with your hearts, because they were uttered from the heart. From the heart of Mother. And that you will fulfill them: "God has chosen you . . . calling you to this/with our Gospel, for possession of the glory of our Lord/Jesus Christ.'

So accept this call with all your lives.

Realize the words of Jesus Christ. Be obedient to the Gospel. Amen.

January 16

The Family, Community of Love and Life

Jesus was invited to Cana of Galilee to take part in a wedding and marriage feast. We may rightly deduce from the evangelist's text that this episode in particular determined the beginning of his apostolic life, even though various other events are linked with the commencement of Jesus of Nazareth's public activity. It is important to note that Jesus began his work in the circumstances of a wedding.

At the very beginning of his *messianic mission,* Jesus Christ in a certain sense touches *human life at its fundamental point.* The starting point. Matrimony marks a new beginning every time, even though it is as ancient as humanity. This is above all the beginning of a new community bearing the name "family." The family is the community of love and life. So the mystery of human life was entrusted to it by the Creator. Matrimony is the beginning of the new community of love and life upon which man's future on earth depends.

The Lord Jesus set the beginning of his activity at Cana of Galilee in order to demonstrate this truth. His presence at the nuptial reception brought out the fundamental significance of matrimony and of the family for the Church and for society.

To what degree do spouses take up these duties together with the Sacrament which God and the Church put before them?

January 17

A Prayer for Every Family

God, from whom all fatherhood in heaven and earth descends, Father, who are Love and Life, ensure that every human family on earth shall become, through Your son, Jesus Christ, "born of woman," and through the Holy Spirit, the source of divine charity, a true shrine of life and love for the generations which are always renewing themselves.

Ensure that Your grace shall guide the thoughts and the works of spouses toward the good of their families and of all families in the world. Ensure that the young generations shall find firm support in the family for their humanity and their growth in truth and love. Ensure that love, reinforced by the grace of the Sacrament of Matrimony shall show itself to be stronger than any weakness and every crisis through which our families pass at times.

Ensure, finally, we ask You, through intercession of the Holy Family of Nazareth, that the Church, in the midst of all the nations of the earth, may fruitfully accomplish her mission in the family and through the family, through Christ Our Lord, who is the way, the truth and the life, for ever and ever. Amen.

January 18

Unity of Christians Is a Gift of God

This week of prayer comes around again punctually, to arouse the consciences of Christians to examine themselves under God's eyes on the question of regaining of full unity. It comes around again . . . to remind us that unity is a gift of God; therefore we must ask for it intensely from the Lord. The fact that . . . Christians of various confessions join in common prayer . . . takes on a quite special significance.

Christians are rediscovering with increasing lucidity how partial but true communion already exists, and, before God and with His help, they are moving toward unity. They are moving toward that goal by beginning with prayer to the Lord, to Him who purifies and liberates, who redeems and unites. . . . We must be very attentive and make sure that prayer does not lose that power of turning things upside down which ought to shake the consciences of all about the division of Christians, "which openly contradicts the will of Christ, provides a stumbling block to the world, and inflicts damage on the most holy cause of proclaiming the good news to every creature."

We ask You, O Lord, for the gifts of Your Spirit so that we can enter into the depths of the truth whole and entire. . . . Teach us to overcome divisions.

Send Us Your Spirit to lead all your children to full unity, in full charity, in obedience to Your will. Amen.

January 19

Unity of Christians, A Task for All

Many voices — those of Catholics, of Orthodox, of Protestants . . . *unanimously* rise to our Father who is in heaven, in concordant and fervent prayer. . . .

Unity of Christians is all the more urgent *in our time* so that the Church may perform her mission more effectively and render her testimony of full fidelity to the Lord and proclaim the Gospel.

All Christians ought . . . to strive and collaborate for recovery of unity, all Christians who wish to be consistent in their vocation and mission.

The prayer which is raised up throughout the world to God on the Sunday for Christian Unity will certainly strengthen everyone's commitment, according to each one's function and the gifts received, to make his and her own contribution to this search and will warm hearts and enliven hopes to go on in joy and confidence along the ways of the Lord. They certainly lead us to full unity and to His Kingdom. . . . Let us pray to the Theotokos, the Mother of God, who brought us Christ, true God and true Man, the Prince of Peace, Him who, together with His Spirit, realizes the Kingdom of God in us.

January 20

Fraternal Relationships among Christians

"Behold, how good it is, and how pleasant, where brethren dwell as one!" (*Ps* 133:1).

We are closely linked by fundamental common bonds in the Bible, God's Word, in the apostolic faith which we profess in the great creeds and which becomes our life in Baptism. Deepening of *baptismal sacramentality* opens up extraordinarily positive perspectives to us along the path of full unity.

And is not prayer for unity, raised up in each of our communities, or also, when possible, in fraternal union of hearts, the best means for drawing down the Spirit of concord upon the ecumenical enterprise, He who transforms our wills and renders them docile to His inspirations?. . . . It is very important for all efforts . . . for *relationships* among all those bearing the name of Christian to be *fraternal*. . . .

It is suitable to go on purifying the memory of the past so as to launch a future of reciprocal comprehension and collaboration. . . . Various forms of collaboration do exist . . . between the Catholic Church and the other Churches and Communities. . . .

It is necessary to go on making efforts for the accomplishment of the Lord's desire, manifested at the Last Supper: "That all may be one . . . that the world may believe. . . ." (*Jn* 17:21). That all are firm in unity of spirit and exerting ourselves with one accord for the faith of the Gospel" (*Phil* 1:27), to the glory of the Holy Trinity, Father, Son and Holy Spirit.

January 21

St. Agnes, Virgin and Martyr

With her story of virginity and martyrdom, Saint Agnes aroused . . . a wave of emotion and admiration in the world. . . . In her we are struck by her mature judgment in spite of her youth, the firmness of her decision notwithstanding her woman's impressionability, her fearless courage, notwithstanding the judges' threats and the harshness of the torments.

Agnes gave the supreme testimony to Christ through the bloody holocaust of her young life. The image of that heroic maiden takes us back in mind to the words spoken by Jesus, "Father, Lord of heaven and earth, to you I offer praise; for what you have hidden from the learned and the clever, you have revealed to the merest children" (*Mt* 11:25–26).

We feel almost a quiver of exultation pass through these solemn words. Jesus saw far. He saw the innumerable ranks of men and women over the centuries, of all ages and circumstances, who would adhere joyously to His message. And Agnes was among them.

A characteristic links them in common. They are little, that is, simple, humble. . . . They are people who know that they do not know anything and are not worth anything; they know they need help and forgiveness. Therefore [He] finds in them hearts open to understand him.

Not so the "learned" and the "clever". . . . Christ does not ask man to give up his reason. Only he who accepts his intellectual and moral *limits* and recognizes that he *needs* salvation can attain to faith and in faith meet, in Christ, his Redeemer.

January 22

To All Christians

Among Christians today there exists a deep awareness of the necessity to be perfectly united in Christ and in His Church: to be one thing only, according to Christ's prayer. . . .

The work of reconciliation, the path towards unity may be long and difficult. But, as on the road to Emmaus, the Lord himself is with us on the way. . . . He will be with us until the much awaited moment comes when we shall be able to rejoice together in acknowledgment of Him in the Sacred Scriptures and in "the breaking of bread" (*Lk* 24:35). . . . Internal renewal of the Catholic Church, in full fidelity to the Second Vatican Council, is in itself an indispensable contribution to the work of the unity of Christians.

While, in our respective churches, we make progress . . . in sanctity and . . . authenticity of Christian life, we must also become more and more united with Christ, therefore more united among ourselves in Christ. He alone . . . can bring our hopes to fulfillment. . . . "Things that are impossible for men are possible for God" (*Lk* 18:27).

Let us go on . . . examining together . . . the necessity for common service to a world which needs it. . . . All Christians ought to rise together in defense of spiritual and moral values against the pressure of materialism and moral permissiveness. Christians ought to unite in promoting justice and defending the rights and dignity of every human person. . . .

We must urge citizens, communities and politicians towards the paths of tolerance, cooperation and love.

January 23

Unity of Christians — Patient Expectation, Not Inert Acceptance

It is important that every Christian man and every Christian woman seek individually in his and her own heart for what might hold back achievement of full union among Christians. Complete unity in faith is still lacking among us and must be won before being able to celebrate the Eucharist together in truth. The very desire for complete unity in faith is itself a gift of the Holy Spirit, and we humbly give thanks to God for it. . . .

Fidelity to the Holy Spirit requires interior conversion and fervent prayer. And let us pray that rightful patience in awaiting God's hour shall not turn into inert acceptance of the status quo of division in the faith. Through God's grace, may such patience never take the place of the definite and generous response which God demands to His call to perfect unity in Christ. . . .

Let us remember that we have been called to demonstrate *utmost fidelity to the Will of Christ.*

Let us persevere in asking the Holy Spirit to remove all divisions from our faith, to give us that perfect unity in truth and love for which Christ prayed; for which Christ died — to bring together the children of God who were scattered.

January 24

To Catholics

"Favor and peace be yours in abundance" (*1 Pt* 1:2).

Like Peter, I would first of all give thanks for the lively hope that is in you and which comes from the risen Christ. I would exhort each of you to be grateful to God and firm in faith, as "children of obedience," also keeping your souls *in obedience to the truth,* in a sincere fraternity, with honorable behavior among the peoples, so that, seeing your good works, they may glorify God. . . .

Yes, I would invite you to consider this letter as particularly yours . . . read it carefully and meditate on every statement. . . .

I would draw your attention to one of its exhortations: "Should anyone ask you the reason for this hope of yours, be ever ready to reply, but speak gently and respectfully. Keep your conscience clear" *(2 Pt* 3:15–16). These words are the golden rule for relationships and contacts which the Christian has to have with his fellow citizen of a different faith. . . .

Always have the courage and pride of your faith. Deepen it. *Get close to Christ, ceaselessly,* as living stones in the cornerstone, sure of reaching the goal of your faith, the salvation of your souls. . . . Draw with joy upon the gushing fount of the Eucharist.

May He fill you with His charity!

.

January 25

St. Paul's Conversion — The Call of Christ

Today we celebrate the appearance of the Risen Jesus to Saul of Tarsus. The apparition was a revelation of the mystery of the Church and bore Saul to conversion. It conferred a mission of unique importance on him for the future of the Church.

The persecutor responded to the revelation with faith. But we should not forget what that cost Paul. His vocation was no easy one. To begin with, many Christians were afraid of him and did not believe that he was a true disciple (*cf. Acts* 9:26) Subsequently, Paul was to vaunt the sufferings borne and the weakness experienced, because it was through them that God's glorious power was made manifest. His conversion on the road to Damascus was immediate and radical, but he had to live it in faith and perseverance for long years of apostolate; from that moment on his life had to be an *incessant conversion,* a *continual renewal:* "Our inner being is renewed each day. . . ." *(2 Cor* 4:16).

When God calls, when God converts, He also gives a mission. The mission received by Paul was that of being "a witness before all men" of the things which he had seen and heard *(Acts* 22:15). So, Paul received from the risen Christ the same command which all the Apostles received, "Go into the whole world and proclaim the good news to all creation" *(Mk* 16:15). In this specific mission given to Paul, however, Christ revealed and realized in a particular way the Church's mission to all nations, the mission, that is, to be truly universal, truly catholic, "a testifier to all mankind."

Paul's mission had incalculable effect on all the work

of evangelization and for the universality of the Church. In a prayer meeting for unity toward the end of the Second Vatican Council, Pope Paul VI said that the Church sees the "apostle of her ecumenicism" in St. Paul.

January 26

Saul's Response — Conversion and Unity

The conversion of Saul of Tarsus makes us relive the dramatic mode of his personal encounter with Christ the Lord, when the fiery disciple ... struck down as by lightning on the road to Damascus by the unmistakable voice of ... Jesus ... opened himself up immediately to hearing His word, and at the very moment when he docilely received the heartfelt reproach of the Divine Master, was established as "the instrument chosen ... to bring my name to the Gentiles ... and to people. ..." (*Acts* 9:15), in his quality of being a "witness" (*Acts* 22:15).

The central element of the whole occurrence was ... CONVERSION. Saul, destined to evangelize the peoples ... was called by Christ to work above all a radical conversion in himself. Christ appealed to him inwardly ... calling him by name, in a strictly personal tone which left no room for misunderstandings or evasions: "Saul, Saul, why do you persecute me? It is hard for you to kick against the goad. ... Get up now and stand on your feet" (*Acts* 26:14–16). And Saul began his laborious path of conversion, which was to last all his life, beginning from that humble "What must I do, Lord?"

This fact ... makes us aware of a demand: unity cannot but be the fruit of a conversion to Christ, who is Head of the Body which is the Church. ... We must ask ourselves ceaselessly how ... the various dimensions of our efforts at Christian living and our ecumenical path manifest the search for unity with regard to *conversion to*

Christ. . . . The example of Paul of Tarsus, who became
Saint Paul . . . lets us see . . . that conversion, hence unity,
is possible "to God," even though it may seem impossible
"to men."

January 27

Spiritual Communion with the Orthodox

Credo in Spiritum Sanctum Dominum et vivicantem. . . .

I believe in the Holy Spirit, Lord and lifegiver. . . .

This faith of the Apostles and the Fathers was solemnly professed and taught to be professed by the
Council of Constantinople in the year 381. We . . . in
spiritual unity with our Brethren, who celebrate the
jubilee liturgy in the Cathedral of the Ecumenical Pat-
riarchate at Constantinople, desire to profess it, by teaching it with the same purity and power in this year . . . as
it was professed and taught by that venerable Council
sixteen centuries ago.

We also desire to renew the teaching of the Second
Vatican Council in its light, the teaching of that Council
of our times which gave evidence so generously of the
work of the Holy Spirit, Lord and giver of life, in the
whole mission of the Church.

We therefore desire to put this Council into practice
in life, this Council which has become *the voice and commitment* of our generations, and to understand the teachings of the ancient Councils more profoundly, in particular that which was held one thousand six hundred years
ago at Constantinople.

We fix our gaze on the mystery of the one Body which

is made up of various members; in this light, we express the desire with fresh fervor that *that unity may be accomplished,* the unity in Christ to which are called — according to St. Paul's words — all those who are "baptized" in a single Spirit to form one sole Body"; all those who "have drunken of the one sole Spirit."

We express this wish with fresh fervor particularly on this day when we recall the times when the Church was undivided. We therefore cry out, "O most blessed light/enter deeply/into the hearts of your faithful."

January 28

The Genius of St. Thomas Aquinas

His realistic and historical method, a fundamentally optimistic and open-minded one, not only makes St. Thomas *Doctor Communis Ecclesiae,* "Common Doctor of the Church," as Paul VI called him ... but also makes him *Doctor Humanitatis,* because he was always prompt and disposed to receive the human values of all cultures. The Angelic Doctor, Thomas, may well affirm, *"Veritas in seipsa fortis est et nulla impugnatione convellitur* — Truth is strong in itself, and no assault weakens it." Truth, like Jesus Christ, may always be denied, persecuted, combatted, wounded, martyred, crucified; but it always lives again and rises again and cannot be wrenched out of the human heart. St. Thomas put all the power of his genius at the exclusive service of the truth. He seems to wish to disappear behind it, almost through fear of troubling its brightness, so that it, and not he, should shine forth in all its radiance.

According to St. Thomas, to fidelity to the voice of things, in philosophy, there corresponds in theology fidelity to the voice of the Church. His rule, from which he never departed, was the principle: *"Magis standum est auctoritati Ecclesiae . . . quam cuiuscumque Doctoris"* — "More assent must be given to the authority of the Church than to that of any Doctor." So, the truth propounded by the authority of the Church assisted by the Holy Spirit is the gauge of the truth expressed by all theologians and doctors, past, present and to come. The authority of the doctrine of Aquinas here resolves and is made good in the authority of the doctrine of the Church. This is why the Church has set him up as exemplar and model for theological research.

January 29

Spiritual Communion with the Anglicans

Roman Catholics and . . . Anglicans of the whole world . . . desire to grow in reciprocal comprehension, in fraternal love and in common testimony of the Gospel. . . .

We address the bishops, clergy and faithful of our two communions in every country, diocese and parish where our faithful live side by side.

We recommend that all pray for this work and do their best to obtain better results, through their collaboration toward increasing fidelity to Christ and testimony of Him to the whole world. Only through such collaboration and prayer can the memory of the enmities of the past be cancelled and an end be put to our antagonism. . . .

We recognize a new challenge to abandon ourselves completely to the truth of the Gospel in the . . . accords which we may come to and the difficulties we may meet

... We turn ... in prayer to Jesus, the Good Shepherd
... that He may lead us toward the complete unity to
which we are called. Trusting in the power of this same
Holy Spirit, we pledge ourselves anew to work for unity
with firm faith, renewed Hope, and ever deeper Love.

This love of God has appeared over us in the person
of the Holy Spirit, the spirit of truth and unity. Love
grows through truth; truth reaches men through love.

Christ, look down upon us; see the desire of so many
hearts! You who are Lord of history and Lord of human
hearts, be with us! Jesus Christ, eternal Son of God, be
with us!

January 30

Spiritual Communion with the Lutherans

Unity, penance, prayer.

In the school of the Apostle of the Gentiles we can
gain consciousness that we are all in need of conversion.

There is no Christian life without penance.

"There is no true ecumenicism without interior
conversion."

"Who are you to pass judgment on another. . . .
(Rom 14:4). Let us rather recognize our faults together.
This holds good as well for the grace of unity: "All have
sinned." We ought to see and say this in all seriousness
and draw our conclusions. . . .

Jesus Christ is the salvation of us all . . . "We are at
peace with God through our Lord Jesus Christ" *(Rom*
5:1) and among ourselves . . . we believe and together
profess all that. . . .

All our gratitude for what remains in common to us

and unites us must not blind us to what still divides us. . . .
We are called to go forward together, *in dialogue of truth
and love,* to *full* unity of the faith . . . We must not leave
anything untried. We must do everything to unite ourselves. We owe this to God and to the world. . . .

The will of Christ and the signs of the times urge us to
common testimony of the increasing fullness of truth
and love. . . . The tasks awaiting us are great and
grave. . . . "The Spirit helps us in our weakness"
(Rom 8:26). Trusting in Him, we can go on with our
dialogue, facing up to the work required of us.

Let us begin with the most important dialogue, *let us
pray!*

January 31

St. John Bosco

St. John Bosco was one of those who, in the Church's
history, best understood Christ's words on the kingdom
of heaven as exemplified by means of a child. He was
one of the most understanding of *the child's soul,* one of
the greatest educators of youth.

The saint comprehended that in every young human
being, in a boy, in a girl, the kingdom of God is proposed
in a particular manner as a task for man. It is necessary
to receive it in this sense, in such a perspective, if we
desire, after all, to enter it. The Lord says, "Whoever
welcomes one such child for my sake welcomes me"
(Mt 18:5). Jesus Himself is given to us and is assigned as
a task to the child's soul because, through Jesus, and only
by virtue of Him, the kingdom of God makes a beginning in man and develops.

John Bosco grasped this truth in an extraordinary way, as only a saint could grasp it. He found the principal grace of his priestly life in it, his own special vocation. He drew vigorous, actually incomprehensible, energies from it. He loved the kingdom of God present in the child's soul.

Such evangelical love not only made that simple priest an educator of genius but a sage educator of educators as well. He became in this way the creator of many modern centers for youth and the enlightened Founder of that Congregation which cultivates his spirituality and his grace, transmitting them from generation to generation, over more than a century now.

"Be wholly directed to all that is true, all that deserves respect, all that is honest, pure, admirable, decent, virtuous, or worthy of praise. . . . Live according to what you have learned and accepted, what you have heard me say and seen me do. Then will the God of peace be with you" *(Phil* 4:8–9).

February

February 1

According to Your Word

Fiat mihi secundum verbum tuum – "Let it be done to me as you say."

These words of Mary's were uttered by her during the Annunciation. We repeat them with our lips and meditate on them in our hearts when we pray with these words. They take on particular eloquence in the light of tomorrow's feast, the feast of the Presentation of the Lord in the temple. The liturgy renews remembrance of the event every year forty days after Christmas. It took place forty days after Jesus' birth at Bethlehem.

Here is what we read in St. Luke: "When the day came to purify them according to the law of Moses, the couple brought him up to Jerusalem so that he could be presented to the Lord, for it is written in the law of the Lord, 'Every first-born male shall be consecrated to the Lord.' They came to offer in sacrifice 'a pair of turtledoves or two young pigeons,' in accord with the dictate in the law of the Lord" *(Lk* 2:22–24).

It was on the occasion of this blessing and presentation that Mary heard the following prophetical words from the mouth of Simeon: "This child is destined to be the downfall and the rise of many in Israel, a sign that will be opposed — and you yourself will be pierced with a sword — so that the thoughts of many hearts may be laid bare" *(Lk* 2:34–35).

Let us meditate as we pray on the answer which Mary gave to the Annunciation, *"Fiat mihi secundum verbum tuum"* — "Let it be done unto me as you say."

February 2

The Presentation of the Lord

Lumen ad revelationem gentium — a revealing light to the Gentiles.

These words resounded for the first time at the place in the Temple at Jerusalem where the rite of purification of mothers after birth of their firstborn was being performed. They were pronounced by the aged Simeon, who was a prophet. He uttered them to Mary and Joseph, who had brought the child born at Bethlehem to the Temple.

Although these words were spoken in one place only, the truth which they proclaimed resounded throughout the Temple — the entire space dedicated to the God of Israel in expectation of the Messiah. These words filled the Temple at Jerusalem with the light of its destinies, conceived from all eternity: "a revealing light to the Gentiles, the glory of your people Israel" (*Lk* 2:32).

Let us walk in procession, bearing these candles, *the sign of the light* "which gives light to every man" (*Jn* 1:9). The sign of Christ born at Bethlehem. The sign of Christ presented in the Temple. *The sign of contradiction (cf. Lk* 2:34). Let us confess Christ in this sign. Were not His contemporaries to contradict it? The children of the people to whom He had been sent? Yes. So, it was, they contradicted him. So as to extinguish the light, they inflicted death upon Him. Simeon prophesied that death when he said to His Mother, "You yourself shall be pierced with a sword" (*Lk* 2:35).

Death on the cross did not put out Christ's light. He was not crushed by the tomb slab . . . So, we enter . . . bearing light, the sign of Christ crucified and risen again. Simeon's prophecy was to be confirmed to the end on the cross and in the resurrection: a sign of *contradiction* — a sign of *light*.

February 3

Christ, Light of Human Life

Did not Christ enter into the story of man through this sign? Does He not thus emerge toward us out of the various eras of human history? An era has never existed where He was not contradicted. And He has revealed Himself anew every time as the light to enlighten man, in that contradiction.

Is not our era also one of manifold contradiction in regard to Christ? And does He not reveal Himself anew in this century too as the light to enlighten people and peoples? Today we profess Christ by means of a sign which is light, as Son of Mary, Christ born at Bethlehem, presented in the Temple, Christ crucified and arisen again. It is a simple sign and a rich one at the same time. As rich as life, for, in fact, the life was the light of man (*Jn* 1:4).

Christ is the light of human life. He is the light because he scatters the darkness of human life. He is the light because He clarifies its mysteries. Because He answers the fundamental questions with definitive answers. He is the light because He gives meaning to life. Light, because He convinces man of his great dignity . . .

Let us live in Christ with the light of the Presentation. Does not the whole world turn into a gigantic temple of the cosmos through the heart of man, where man offers up "spiritual sacrifices"? Does it not become a great Christocentric space of the created spirit, where the Holy Spirit operates, the more the *little human heart* lets itself be penetrated by the light of Christ and becomes the temple of the Presentation!

February 4

Dialogue with the Jews

Shalom! "Whoever meets Jesus Christ, meets Judaism"
Declaration on the Church's relationship with Judaism issued by
the Bishops of the German Federal Republic, April 1980.

Faith in the Church of Jesus Christ, son of David and
son of Abraham (*cf. Mt* 1:1), actually . . . contains "the
spiritual heritage of Israel for the Church." A living heritage, which ought to be understood and preserved in its
depths and riches by us Catholic Christians. . . . The profundity and richness of our common inheritance open us
up to each other in a particular manner, in amical
dialogue, in confident collaboration. . . .

The *first* dimension of this dialogue, that is, the meeting between the People of God of the Old Testament,
never denounced by God (*cf. Rom* 11:29) and the people
of the New Testament, is at the same time a dialogue
within our Church, as it were, between the first and the
second part of her Bible. . . .

A *second* dimension of our dialogue — the true and
central dimension — is the encounter between the Christian Churches of today and the people of today who are
the people of the Alliance concluded with Moses. . . .

A *third* dimension of our dialogue: Jews and Christians, as children of Abraham, are called to be a blessing
to the world (*cf. Gen* 12:2), inasmuch as they pledge
themselves together for peace and justice among all men
and all peoples, and do so in plenitude and profundity,
as God Himself conceived them for us, and with the
readiness to sacrifice which this high intent, however,
demands. . . .

February 5

Fraternity between Christians and Moslems

I deliberately address you [Moslems] as brethren. It is certain that we are this, because we are members of the same human family, whose strivings — whether men are aware of it or not — tend toward God and the truth coming from Him. But we are brethren especially in God who created us and whom we try to reach, each along his own way, through faith, power, worship, fidelity to His law, and submission to His will.

Your well-being, that of your Christian brothers and sisters, calls for an atmosphere of mutual esteem and confidence. You know as I do that such an atmosphere has been too often let deteriorate in the past, to the detriment of all relations.

But, dear friends, we know all too well that there is no positive reason why that past should live again today. If at all, we ought to look back at the past with sorrow so as to ensure stability for a better future.

You have been hearing for some years of the urgent necessity to sit down together, face our problems, and re-establish mutual esteem and confidence. A fruitful dialogue has thus begun, and since then not a year has passed without your meeting your Christian fellow citizens, under the auspices of government organs and private institutions.

Dear Moslems, my friends: I would like to add that we Christians, like you, seek the basis and model of mercy in God Himself, the God to whom your Book gives the most beautiful name of al-Rahman, whereas the Bible calls Him al-Rahum, the Merciful. Only within this structure of religion and its common promises of faith, may one actually speak of *mutual respect, opening,* and *collaboration* between Christians and Moslems. Then comes the will to work together, to construct a more fraternal society.

February 6

The Holy Martyrs of Nagasaki

Dear Friends: Today I would be one of the many pilgrims who come here to this Hill of the Martyrs at Nagasaki, the place where Christians sealed their fidelity to Christ with the sacrifice of their lives. They triumphed over death with an insuperable act of praise to the Lord. In an attitude of prayer before the monument to the Martyrs, I wish to penetrate the mystery of their lives, I would that they spoke to me and the whole of the Church, I wish to hear their message, which is still alive after hundreds of years. Like Christ, they were taken to a place where common criminals were put to death. Like Christ, they gave their lives so that all of us might believe in the love of the Father, in the salvific mission of the Son, in the infallible guidance of the Holy Spirit.

At Nishizaka, on February 5, 1597, twenty-six Martyrs testified to *the power of the Cross.* They were the first of a rich harvest of Martyrs, because many subsequently consecrated this soil with their sufferings and death. Christians died at Nagasaki, but *the Church in Nagasaki did not die.*

I come today to this place as a pilgrim, to thank God for the life and death of the Martyrs of Nagasaki. I thank God for the lives of all those who, wherever they be, suffer for their faith in God, for their loyalty to Christ

the Savior, for their fidelity to the Church. Every epoch
— past, present, and to come — produces shining examples of the power which is in Jesus Christ for the edification of all.

I come to the Hill of the Martyrs today *to give testimony
of the primacy of love in the world.*

February 7

To Representatives of Buddhism and Shinto

Venerable friends, representatives of Buddhism and
Shinto in Japan, I am very happy to welcome you today.
I greet you first of all as sons of the noble and industri-
ous people of Japan. Your country has made outstanding progress in many fields. At the same time it has remained attached to its own lifestyle, with emphasis on
respect, harmony and art.

The Catholic Church expresses her esteem for your
religions and for your high spiritual values, such as purity, detachment of heart, love for the beauty of nature,
and benevolence and compassion for everything that
lives.

It gives great joy to know that you have come here to
carry forward your dialogue and collaboration. . . . The
themes you are discussing . . . each from the standpoint
of his own religion, are the relationship between man
and nature and the relationship between religion and
culture. I am deeply convinced that these are themes of
great importance for the future of our world. Indeed,
this conviction of mine is reflected in my first Encyclical
Letter, *Redemptor Hominis.* Be assured, then, that I shall
follow this dialogue and subsequent ones with interest
and appreciation.

On this earth we are all pilgrims to the Absolute and Eternal, who alone can save and satisfy the heart of the human person. *Let us seek His will together for the good of all humanity.*

February 8

Knowing How to Accept Christ

"He came among His own people." Think of those who shut their interior doors to Him, and let us ask why. There are so many, many, many answers, objections, causes.

Our human conscience is not up to embracing them. It does not feel qualified to judge. The Almighty alone searches the hearts and consciences of every person to the depths. He alone. Only He, the eternally Born; only the Son. In fact, the Father has made all judgement over to the Son, Christ, "the real light which gives light to every man" (*Jn* 1:9). How much man loses when he meets Him and will not see the Father in Him. God actually revealed Himself to man in Christ as the Father.

And how much man loses when he does not see his own humanity in Him. Christ actually came into the world so as to reveal man fully to man and make his most lofty vocation known to him. "Any who did accept Him, he empowered to become children of God" (*Jn* 1:12). Hence rises a warm wish and desire, a humble prayer: that the people of our century may accept Christ. That people of the various countries and continents, the various languages, cultures and civilizations may accept Him, find Him again, that there may be given to them the Power — coming only from Him, because it is in Him alone.

February 9

Christ Becomes Light and Salvation

Christ, at the beginning of His public life, historically became the light and salvation of the people to whom He was sent.

The glory of the Lord had already enveloped the shepherds in light during the night (*cf. Lk* 2:9) of the birth of Jesus Christ, but this is the first time that the Gospel speaks of a light shown to all. When Jesus quit Nazareth, was baptized in the Jordan, and then went to Capernaum so as to make a beginning of his public ministry, it was as if *a second birth* of him occurred, consisting in abandonment of private life and hidden life in order to give himself to the total and irrevocable commitment of a life spent for all, even unto the supreme sacrifice of Himself.

However, Matthew also tells us that Jesus at once enlightened other men, while He walked by the sea of Galilee, that is, by the shores of the Lake of Gennesaret. That was the summons to the first disciples, the brothers Simon and Andrew, then the other two brothers, James and John, all toiling fishermen. They immediately . . . abandoned boat and father to follow Him. They certainly felt the fascination of the secret light emanating from Him, they followed Him without delay, so that the path of their lives should be brightened by his effulgence. But the light of Jesus shines for all. He made Himself known to His Galilean fellow countrymen, as the evangelist says, "taught in their synagogues, preached the good news of the kingdom, and healed the people of every disease and illness."

As may be seen, His is a light which *illuminates* but also *warms,* for it is not limited to clearning mind but also intervenes to redeem situations of material want.

February 10

St. Scholastica

Today is also the liturgical feast day of St. Scholastica, Virgin, and sister of St. Benedict. They were both born 1,500 years ago at Norcia . . . *two saints,* to whom not only the Church but medieval and modern Europe as well owe so much . . . Norcia — that most ancient city, rich in history and art, cradle of the Benedictine Order . . . made mankind the magnificent gift of *those two great personalities."*

I look with sincere admiration on all monasteries of Benedictine nuns — it is with lively satisfaction that I apply to them the image so dear to St. Benedict, who considered them "schools of service to God."

How can I not recall in this regard that intense day passed by the holy brother and sister in praise of God and holy conversation, as St. Gregory the Great relates. That day was followed by the famous nightlong vigil which St. Scholastica obtained through her prayer. They spent that whole night sating themselves with sweet colloquies and telling each other — that holy brother and sister — of experiences of their spiritual life.

February 11

Lourdes, Suffering, Sanctified and Sanctifying

The reality of faith, of hope and of charity. The reality of suffering sanctified and sanctifying. The reality of the presence of the Mother of God in the mystery of Christ and His Church on earth: a presence which is particularly alive in that elect portion of the Church which consists of the sick and the suffering.

These persons, if animated by faith, turn to Lourdes. Why? Because they know that there, as at Cana, "there is the Mother of Jesus" and where She is, Her Son cannot be absent. Sick of all sorts go on pilgrimage to Lourdes, borne up by hope that, through Mary, Christ's saving power may be manifested in them. . . . Christ's saving power . . . reveals itself in the *spiritual sphere* above all.

It is in the hearts of the sick that Mary makes Her Son's wonderworking voice heard, a voice which prodigiously resolves the rigidity of sourness of heart and rebellion and gives the soul back eyes with which to see the world, others, one's own destiny in a new light. . . .

At Lourdes the sick discover the inestimable value of their suffering . . . the meaning that pain may have . . . in their lives, when interiorily renewed by that flame which consumes and transforms . . . in the life of the Church. . . .

Upright by the Cross of Her Son on Calvary, the Most Holy Virgin courageously shared in His Passion and knows how to convince ever fresh souls to unite their sufferings with Christ's sacrifice, in a joint "offertory," which surpasses time and space and embraces the whole of mankind and saves it.

February 12

The Pope Speaks to the Sick

Although God allows suffering to exist in the world, he does not enjoy it. Indeed, our Lord Jesus Christ, the Son of God made man, *loved the sick;* he devoted a great part of his earthly ministry to healing the sick and comforting

87

the afflicted.

Our God is a God of compassion and consolation. And he expects us to take the ordinary means to prevent, relieve and remove suffering and sickness. Therefore we have preventive health-care programs; we have doctors, nurses, paramedicals and medical institutions of many kinds. Medical science has made much progress. We should take advantage of all this.

But even after all these efforts, suffering and sickness still exist. A Christian sees *meaning in suffering*.

He bears such suffering with patience, love of God and generosity. He offers it all to God, through Christ, especially during the Sacrifice of the Mass. When the sick person receives Holy Communion he unites himself with Christ the Victim.

When suffering is associated with Christ's Passion and redemptive death, then it has great value for the individual, for the Church and for society. This is the meaning of those wonderful words of Saint Paul on which we must meditate over and over again: "Now I find my joy in the suffering I endure for you. In my own flesh I fill up what is lacking in the sufferings of Christ for the sake of his body, the church."

I also know personally what it means to be sick and to stay in the hospital for a long time, and how it is possible to comfort and support others who share the same lot of confinement and suffering, and how necessary it is to pray for the sick and to show them one's loving concern.

February 13

The Sick and the Holy Father

We have gathered . . . to honor and celebrate Mary Most Holy through remembrance of Her apparition to the humble Bernadette, there, at the grotto of Massabielle, to entrust her with a special message of mercy and grace. And who could assert that that message does not keep its full value *in our days* as well?

By making use of that unknown girl, Mary intended to call sinners above all to conversion, by asking for the common commitment of all Christian faithful for them and for their salvation. It is a fact that the appeal aroused a fervent movement of prayer and charity in the Church, in service to the infirm and the poor above all. . . . Please . . . Brothers and Sisters . . . accompany me with your thoughts and affection, but above all with the charity of a special entreaty, so that the Lord — who alone can give it — will give me the indispensable aid, for God gives the increase *(cf. 1 Cor 3:6–7).*

You especially who are tried by sickness, please unite the oblation of your sufferings and follow me closely in that way during my journeys. You can do much for me. Once again, you are capable of communicating to me that strength which I spoke of already the day after my appointment to the see of Rome, and the interior power which I experienced also during the days of my illness.

February 14

SS. Cyril and Methodius

Saints Cyril and Methodius were brothers in blood but even more so in faith. They were proclaimed by me on 31 December 1980 heavenly patrons of the whole of Europe, side by side with Saint Benedict. . . .

These intrepid followers of Christ and untiring preachers of the Word of God, were natives of Thessalonica, the city where Paul performed part of his apostolic task and to the first faithful of which he addressed two letters. The brothers entered into spiritual and cultural contact with the patriarchal church of Constantinople, which was then flourishing with theological culture and missionary activity. They knew how to unite the demands and commitments of the religious vocation with missionary service. The first witnesses of their apostolic ardor were the Kazars of the Crimea. But their most important evangelizing work was done in the mission to Greater Moravia, undertaken after Rastislav, prince of Moravia, had made request to the Emperor and Church of Constantinople.

The apostolic and missionary work of Saints Cyril and Methodius was very complex and varied. Considered today at a distance of eleven centuries and from many points of view, it is seen to have been of extraordinary fruitfulness and also had exceptional theological, cultural and ecumenical importance. These aspects not only concern the history of the Church, but they concern the civil history and political history of a part of the continent of Europe as well.

A translation of the Sacred Books into the vernacular for liturgical purpose and catechetical purposes made Saints Cyril and Methodius not only the Apostles of the Slav peoples but the Fathers of their culture as well.

Their untiring missionary service was accomplished in union with the Church of Constantinople, by which they had been sent out, and with the Roman See of Peter, by whom they were confirmed. It manifests their indomitable love for the Church, One, Holy, Catholic. It acts as a spur to us for that unity to be fully lived in faith and charity.

February 15

The Evangelizing Work of SS. Cyril and Methodius

Cyril and Methodius were two authentic "workers" in God's harvest. . . . The Church extols their meritorious apostolic action and is reminded that she has even greater need today of Christians capable of making their contribution to the announcement of Christ Jesus' message of salvation — through their commitment, their energies, their enthusiasm. But the Church is equally aware that she needs souls totally and exclusively consecrated to preaching of the Gospel, to missionary action. She needs priests, religious men and women, men and women missionaries who will generously and gladly quit family, homeland, human affections and dedicate their whole lives to suffering for the Gospel (*cf. Mk* 8:35).

Seeing the historical importance of the evangelizing work accomplished by the two holy brothers, the Church becomes even more profoundly conscious *that evangelization is the grace and vocation proper to her, her deepest identity.* She exists in order to evangelize — Paul VI wrote — that is to say, to preach and teach, to be the channel of the gift of grace, to reconcile sinners with God, perpetuate

Christ's sacrifice in the Holy Mass, which is the remembrance of His death and of His glorious resurrection.

For Saints Cyril and Methodius that meant making the announcement of the Gospel preeminent. That announcement did not mortify, destroy or eliminate the authentic human and cultural values typical of the genius of the countries evangelized, but elevated and exalted them, and so contributed to an openness and a solidarity which were capable of overcoming antagonisms and creating a common spiritual and cultural patrimony, which laid a solid basis for justice and peace.

February 16

Prayer to SS. Cyril and Methodius

Let us raise our humble and fervent prayer to the two holy brothers, Patrons of Europe, to ask their powerful intercession with the Most Blessed Trinity.

O Saints Cyril and Methodius, who brought the faith with admirable dedication to Peoples thirsting for the truth and light of the faith: ensure that the whole Church shall always proclaim Christ, crucified and risen again, Redeemer of mankind!

O Saints Cyril and Methodius, who always remained deeply bound to the Church of Constantinople and the Roman See of Peter, in your difficult and harsh missionary apostolate: ensure that two sister Churches, the Catholic Church and the Orthodox, may overcome the elements of division in charity and truth and soon reach the desired full union!

O Saints Cyril and Methodius, who, with sincere spirit of fraternity, went out to the various Peoples to bring them all the message of universal love preached by

Christ: ensure that the peoples of the continent of Europe, conscious of their common Christian patrimony, may live in reciprocal respect of lawful rights and in solidarity and be peacemakers among all the nations of the world!

O Saints Cyril and Methodius, who, driven on by love for Christ, abandoned all so as to serve the Gospel: protect the Church of God, me, Successor of Peter in the Roman See, the bishops, priests, religious, men and women, missionaries, men and women, fathers, mothers, the young of both sexes, children, the poor, the sick, the suffering, that each one of us, wherever Divine Providence has set him and her, may be a worthy "worker" in the Lord's harvest! Amen!

February 17

Creation Is a Gift

In Christ's mouth the words "he created" contain the same truth which we find in the Book of Genesis. The first account of creation repeats the words several times, from Genesis 1:1 ("In the beginning when God created the heavens and the earth") down to Genesis 1:27 ("God created man in his image"), and in it God reveals Himself above all as Creator.

Christ referred back to that fundamental revelation enclosed in the Book of Genesis. The concept of creation has all its profundity there, not only profundity metaphysical but also fully theological. A creator is he who "calls into existence out of nothing" and establishes the world in existence and man in the world, *because He is "love."* To tell the truth, we do not find this word "love"

(God is love) in the story of creation. However, the story often repeats "God saw how good it was." We are led through these words to see love as the divine motivation of creation, almost the source from which it flowed: in fact *only love gives rise to good and delights in the good (cf. 1 Cor* 13).

Therefore, as God's action, creation not only signifies calling from nothing into existence and establishing the existence of the world and man in the world, but it also means, according to the first story, *beresit bara* — "donation," a fundamental, radical giving, that is to say, a giving wherein the gift arises exactly from nothing.

Creation is a gift, because man appears in it, and he, as "the image of God," is capable of comprehending the very meaning of the gift in the calling out of nothing into existence. And he is capable of responding to the Creator with the language of this comprehension.

February 18

Creation, the Gift of Love

The reality of the gift, and the act of giving, is outlined in the early chapters of Genesis as the constitutive content of the mystery of creation. It confirms that the radiance of Love is an integrating part of this same mystery. Only Love creates Good, and, in the last analysis, it alone can be perceived in all its dimensions and profiles in created things and in man above all.

His presence is, as it were, the final outcome of that hermeneutic of giving which we are conducting here. The original happiness, the beatifying "principle" of man, whom God created "male and female" *(Gen* 1:27), the spousal meaning of the body in its original nudity, all express rooting in Love.

This coherent giving goes back to the deepest roots of the conscience and the subconscious, to the ultimate strata of subjective existence in both of them, man and woman. It is reflected in their reciprocal "experience of the body," it *testifies to their being rooted in Love.*

The first verses of the Bible speak of it so much as to remove all doubt. They not only speak of the creation of the world and of man in the world but also of grace, that is, of communication of holiness, of radiance of the Spirit, which produced a special state of "spiritualization" in that man who was actually the first. In Biblical language, that is, in the language of Revelation, the term *"first" actually means "of God":* "Adam, son of God" *(cf. Lk 3:38).*

February 19

The Mystery of Creation

"Come, let us bow down in worship; let us kneel before the Lord who made us, for He is our God, and we are the people he shepherds, the flock he guides" (Ps 95:II). Venite adoremus! Come, let us adore!

This prayer contains an invitation addressed to the human intellect and to the will and the heart as well.

It is the most fundamental invitation: come out and go to meet God, who is the Creator!

Your Creator!

With God, to whom everything which is owes its existence.

With God, who, as Creator, stands "above" all creation, above the cosmos, and at the same time embraces and penetrates this cosmos to the farthest depths, to the essence of all things.

Come out to meet God, who is the Creator!

This is the prime, fundamental call to understanding enlightened by faith; indeed it is the prime invitation to understanding sincerely seeking the Truth along the paths of science and philosophical reflection.

Confirmation of this might be found in the declarations of men of science over the centuries and in our own age as well. Newton, for example, affirmed, and I quote, that "an intelligent and powerful Being . . . governs all things, not as the soul of the world, but as Lord of the universe, and because of his dominion He is usually called Lord God, Pantocrator." Einstein for his part maintained that "science without religion is lame, and religion without science is blind." He said: "I desire to know how God created the world. I am not interested in this or that other phenomenon, nor in the spectre of a chemical element. I wish to know God's thought — the rest is a detail."

February 20

Fear Born of the Death of God

"The doors were shut . . . through fear."

This means *that fear* was stronger *in them* over those days than other feelings. Rather, they did not expect anything good from the fact that the tomb was found to be empty. They did expect further molestation, vexations on the part of the representatives of the Jewish authorities. That was a simple human fear, arising from the immediate threat.

However, *there was a deeper fear* underneath that immediate fear and timidity for themselves. The deeper fear was caused by the events of the recent days. It had begun during the Thursday night and had reached its peak during Good Friday. It endured after Jesus had been taken down from the cross and laid in the tomb; it paralyzed all initiative. It was *fear born of the death of Christ.*

One day, in fact, Christ asked the disciples, "Who do people say that the Son of Man is?" *(Mt* 16:13). They mentioned various rumors and opinions concerning Christ. He then asked them directly, "Who do you say that I am?" *(Mt* 16:15). Then they heard, and accepted in silence, as their own, these words of Simon Peter's, "You are the Messiah, the Son of the Living God" *(Mt* 16:16).

So, on the cross died the Son of the Living God.

The fear with which the hearts of the apostles were seized had deep roots in that death: *fear born, as it were, from the death of God.*

Fear travails the present generation of mankind too. People feel it in an emphatic way. It is perhaps felt more deeply by those who are more conscious of the whole situation of man and have at the same time accepted the death of God in the human world.

February 21

Consumer Society

This fear in the present generation does not lie on the *surface* of human life. It is *compensated* at the surface by the various means exerted by modern civilization and technology. These permit man to free himself from his depths, to live in the dimension of *homo oeconomicus,* economic man; of *homo technicus;* of *homo politicus;* and, to a certain degree, in the dimension of *homo ludens,* playing man, as well.

Man, with his planetary dimension, was never so much aware of all the forces which he is capable of putting to use and setting to his own service, never has he made such use of them. From this point of view, and in this dimension, conviction concerning the progress of mankind is fully justified.

In countries and circles with greater technical progress and greater material well-being, side by side with this conviction, goes an attitude which we usually describe as consumer-oriented. This testifies to the fact that the conviction of the progress of man is only partly justified. Indeed, it testifies that the direction taken by progress can kill what is most profoundly and most essentially human in man.

The consumer attitude does not take all the truth about man into consideration. Neither the historical truth, nor the social truth, nor the interior and the metaphysical truth. Rather it is a flight from that reality. Man is created for happiness. Yes! But man's happiness is not identified with enjoyment! In such enjoyment the consumer-oriented man loses the full dimension of his humanity, he loses deeper feeling and meaning of life. So, such a direction of progress kills what is most deeply and essentially human in man.

February 22

The Feast of the Chair of St. Peter

The feast of the Chair of Saint Peter by a happy coincidence is also the birthday of George Washington . . . *I once again greet the people of America.*

If you sometimes wonder why . . . the Catholic faithful of the United States for over a century have given financial support and have sacrificed of themselves to provide for . . . many . . . the opportunity to prepare for the priesthood in Rome, the answer is found in the words of Peter at Caesarea Philippi; it is linked to the mystery of Peter's mission in the universal Church. Here in Rome the universality and rich diversity of the Church are seen more clearly than elsewhere; here the apostolic tradition of the Church as *a living reality* and not merely as a relic of the past becomes a conscious part of your vision of faith; and here in Rome you encounter the Successor of Peter as he endeavors to show fidelity to Christ by confirming all his brethren in the faith.

February 23

Fear of Death Today

Progress has been achieved by generations of men, with great difficulty, with waste of great energies and with great expense. However, it contains *a potent coefficient of death* within its complexity. It even conceals a gigantic *potential for death* in itself. Is it necessary to test this for oneself in society, which is conscious of what possibilities of destruction exist in the military and nuclear arsenals of today?

Man of today is therefore afraid. The superpowers are afraid, they possess those arsenals and others have fear — continents, nations, cities. . . .

This *fear is justified*. Not only do possibilities of destruction and slaughter exist which were once unknown, but *men are slaying other men abundantly already today!* They kill in homes, in offices, in universities. Men armed with modern weapons kill defenseless and innocent people.

Incidents of that sort have always occurred, but today it has become a system. If men assert that it is necessary to slay other men for the purpose of changing and improving man and society, then we must ask ourselves whether, together with this gigantic material progress which our age shares, we have not reached the point at the same time of *wiping out man himself, who is such a fundamental and elementary Value!* Have we not arrived at negation of that fundamental and elementary principle which the ancient Christian thinker expressed with the phrase, "Must man live"? (St. Irenaeus).

So, therefore, a justified fear upsets the present generation of men. Will this direction of gigantic progress, which has become the exponent of our civilization, not become the beginning of a gigantic, programmed death of man?

February 24

Liberation from Religious Alienation

Is not the fear which upsets modern man also something which, *in its deepest roots, has arisen from "the death of God?"*

Not that death on the cross, which became the beginning of the Resurrection and the source of glorification of the Son of God, at the same time the foundation of human hope and the sign of salvation. No, not from that death. But from the death whereby man makes God die in himself, particularly in the course of the last stage of his story, in his thought, in his conscience, in his workings.

This is like a common denominator of many initiatives of human thought and will. Man takes himself and the world away from God, thinking that only in this way will he be able to enter into full possession of the same, become master of the world and his own destiny. So man "makes God die" in himself and others. Of what use are entire philosophical systems, social, economic and political programs? We live, therefore, in an epoch of gigantic material progress, which is also the epoch of a negation of God previously unknown. Such is the image of our society.

But why is man afraid? Perhaps exactly because, in consequence of this negation of his, he remains alone in the last analysis, metaphysically alone . . . interiorly alone.

Or maybe? Maybe because man, who makes God die, will not find any other decisive restraint against slaying man. This decisive restraint is in God. The ultimate reason why man should live, respect and protect the life of man *is in God.* The ultimate foundation of the value and dignity of man, of the meaning of his life, is the fact that he is God's image and likeness!

February 25

Knowing the Identity of Jesus Christ

In the seventh chapter of the Fourth Gospel, the evangelist John accurately notes the perplexity of many persons in Jerusalem about Jesus' identity.

It was the Feast of Tabernacles which recorded the Hebrews' life in the desert. There was great movement of people in the Holy City, and Jesus was teaching in the Temple. Some said: "Is this not the one they want to kill? Here he is, speaking in public, and they don't say a word to him. Perhaps even the authorities have decided that this is the Messiah. Still, we know where this man is from. When the Messiah comes, no one is supposed to know his origins."

Such statements indicate the perplexity of the Jews in that Temple; they awaited the Messiah; they knew that the Messiah would have something arcane and mysterious about him. They even thought that Jesus might be he, given the prodigies that He performed and the doctrines He taught. But they were not sure of it, because the official religious authority was against Him and would even eliminate Him.

Jesus then explained the reason for their perplexity, or their lack of knowledge of His real identity; they based themselves solely on external, civil and family data and *did not go beyond his human nature;* they did not penetrate the outside layer of his appearance. "So you know me, and you know my origins? The truth is, I have not come of myself. I was sent by One who has the right to send, and him you do not know. I know him, because it is from him I come: he sent me."

February 26

Jesus Christ, the Unknown

It is an historical fact, related by the Gospel, and it is also the symbol of a perennial reality: many do not know and do not want to know who Jesus Christ is. They remain perplexed and disconcerted. More, as in those days they tried to arrest Him after His discourse in the Temple, so certain people impugn and combat Him today.

But you know who Jesus is. You know where He came from and why He came. You know that Jesus is the Incarnate Word, He is the Second Person of the Most Holy Trinity, Who took a human body. He is the Son of God made man, who died for our salvation on the cross, rose again gloriously, and is always present with us in the Eucharist.

What Jesus said to the Apostles at the Last Supper holds good also for all Christians enlightened by the magisterium of the Church: "Eternal life is this, to know you, the only true God, and him whom you have sent, Jesus Christ. I have given you glory on earth by finishing the work you gave me to do. Do you now, Father, give me glory at your side, a glory I had with you before the world began. I have made your name known to those you gave me out of the world. These men you gave me were yours; they have kept your word. Now they realize that all you gave me comes from you. I entrusted to them the message you entrusted to me, and they received it. They have known that in truth I came from you.... Just Father, the world has not known you, but I have known you; and these men have known that you sent me" (*Jn* 17:3– 25).

The great tragedy of history is that Jesus is not known, is consequently not loved, not followed.

You know Christ! You know who He is! Yours is a great privilege! Know how to be always worthy and conscious of it!

February 27

Having Knowledge of Jesus Christ

Having knowledge of God! Having God for Father! These are enormous assertions; they put philosophers into a state of crisis! But the Christian gives himself to them confidently.

The life of the just is different from that of others, and his paths are quite different; so he ends by being a reproach and condemnation to those who do not live rightly, who are blinded by malice and do not want to know "the secrets of God."

The Christian is in the world but not of the world (*cf. Jn* 17:16). His life must necessarily be different from that of someone without faith. His conduct, his habits of life, his way of thinking, of making choices, of evaluating things and situations, are different, because they happen in the light of Christ's words, which are a message of everlasting life.

Finally, to cite the Book of Wisdom again, the just man affirms his death to be blessed, whereas the malicious do not "count on a recompense of holiness nor discern the innocent soul's reward" (*Wis* 2:22).

The Christian ought to live in the perspective of eternity. Sometimes his authentically Christian life may even arouse persecution, open or insidious: "Let us see

whether his words be true; . . . with revilement and tor-
ture let us put him to the test that we may have proof of
his gentleness, and try his patience" (*Wis* 2:17).

Certainty of the eternal salvation awaiting us renders
the Christian strong against temptations and patient in
tribulations: "They will harry you," the Divine Master
said, "as they harried me" (*Jn* 15:20): a great honor.

February 28

The World Is Thirsty for Mercy

Man has deep need to *meet with the mercy of God, today*
more than ever. To feel himself radically understood, in
the weakness of his wounded nature, above all to have
spiritual experience of that Love which receives, enlivens
and resuscitates to new life. In the various forms of your
apostolate, in acceptance of all poverty, spiritual and material, you desire to promote and favor such a meeting
between modern man and the Lord's goodness —
exactly by virtue of the charism of your religious profession. Your work in favor of the clergy embraces concrete
forms of assistance and cultural promotion and training. In this work too you are led by this basic spirit, by
this birthmark, I would say, that of helping others to
have the experience of the divine goodness, to be fervent
spreaders of it. For the priest, that which holds good for
every man is even more true; "he, finding mercy, is he
who manifests it at the same time."

You have several times repeated your exaltation at the
recent encyclical, which you have found almost a proof
and confirmation of your vocation to be the Family of
the Merciful Love.

Courage, dearest brothers and sisters. *The world is thirsty,* even without knowing it, *for the Divine Mercy,* and you are called to proffer this prodigious water, healing to soul and body. You venerate the Mother of Mercy under the particular title of "Mary Mediatrix." May she make you ever more conscious of her motherhood, "which endures without cease from the moment of the consent faithfully given to the Annunciation," and may she make you all apostles, workers and servers of the Divine Goodness and Mercy. I accompany you with my blessing.

March

March 1

Lent, Remember That You Are Dust

Never, perhaps, does God's word resound so directly for us. Never does He address each in this way, without exceptions: *Remember that you are dust and you shall return to dust.*

And each accepts these words. They are so obvious! Their truth is confirmed with so much accuracy in the story of man! These words speak of death, with which the life of every man and woman on earth ends. At the same time, they call each of us back to "the origin." They were uttered to the first Adam as the fruit of sin: ... the tree of knowledge of good and bad. From that tree you shall not eat; the moment you eat from it, you are surely doomed to die" (*Gen* 2:17).

Death as the fruit of the tree of knowledge of good and evil. The fruit of sin. Those words were spoken by God-Yahweh. The Creator God, He who called and constantly calls the world and man out of nothing. And He created man "of the clay of the ground" (*Gen* 2:7); He fashioned him with the same material of which the whole of the visible world. is made.

When God says, "For you are dirt, and to dirt you shall return" (*Gen* 3:19), His words sound like *a severe sentence upon man.* God, who pronounced them, reveals himself in them as Creator and Judge.

However, those words are of suffering at the same time. A forewarning of Good Friday is expressed in them. The suffering of the Son of God is expressed in them, for He was to say, *"Abba* (O Father) ... take this cup away from me" (*Mk* 14:36). Yes, those severe words *conceal God's pain and sorrow in them*. He foretold them to man whom He had created in His own image and likeness. God's image and likeness must return to dust?

"Then the Lord was stirred to concern for his land and took pity on His people," says the prophet Joel (2:18).

March 2

The Life and Mission of Blessed Agnes of Bohemia

Seven hundres years have elapsed since the holy death of Blessed Agnes of Bohemia. Like St. Clare, she walked faithfully in the footsteps of St. Francis; like him, she quit home, brothers and sisters, father and mother, for love of Christ and to give testimony of His Gospel (*cf. Mk* 10:29). She lived and died at Prague, but the fame of her holiness spread throughout Europe, even in her lifetime. I would therefore give honor to this blessed one and so follow the example of my predecessors, particularly Pope Gregory IX who was her contemporary. She has been invoked for centuries by the people of Prague and the Czech people as their patroness with God, at the same time as one of the noblest of . . . personages. . . .

Thanks to Agnes's example, the monastery of Poor Clares at Prague became the source and origin of further monasteries of the same order in Bohemia, Poland, and other countries. . . .

The charity burning in her heart did not permit her, however, to shut herself up in sterile solitude but drove her to put herself at the service of all. She assisted sick nuns, she looked after lepers and those afflicted with other contagious maladies, she washed their garments and patched them during the night, thus showing that the edifice of her spiritual life rested on foundations of humility. She became the mother of the poor in that way and won a place in the hearts of the indigent and humble of Prague which she kept for centuries.

Her charity was fed by prayer *centered on the sufferings of Christ*. Christ suffering was the expression of supreme love for her, and His cross comforted her during her last years of life, especially when, with heroic patience, without ever complaining, she bore misfortunes, injustices, want and illness, and so followed Christ to the very end.

March 3

Blessed Agnes of Bohemia, a Model for Our Time

What says Your Blessed Agnes to you who live . . . today? Above all, she remains the model of the perfect woman (*cf. Prov* 31:10). Such a woman knows how to realize her femininity in generous, disinterested service, which in her case embraced the whole nation, from the royal family to those most humble and marginal. In her, consecrated virginity rendered her heart free and enkindled it more with charity toward God and all people. She thus testified that "the Kingdom of God and His justice are that precious pearl which is to be preferred to every other value, however great, and is to be sought as the sole definitive value."

She was foundress of the Crossbearers of the Red

Star, which still exists, and of the first monastery of Poor Clares on Bohemian soil. She thus showed *the value of the religious institute,* in which brothers and sisters follow the example of the early Church where the multitude of believers "are of one heart and of one mind" *(cf. Acts* 4:32) and lived life in common, "persevering in prayer and communion in the same spirit" *(Acts* 2:42). As a true daughter of St. Francis, Agnes knew how "to use earthly goods well, in continual search for eternal goods," by feeding the poor, caring for the sick, assisting the aged, encouraging the distraught, and in that way becoming able to bring peace and reconciliation and give comfort and new hope. . . .

Is there not need for this generous and disinterested service in our day? Even when there are no hungry in the material sense, how many feel alone and abandoned, sad and desperate, without the warmth of sincere affection and the light of an ideal which is not deceptive? Do they not need to meet an Agnes in their lives, who will bring them peace and joy, a smile and hope?

Blessed Agnes' secret was her union with the Divine Bridegroom, and her prayer.

March 4

The Time of Truth

The Christian is actually called by the Church to prayer, penitence and fasting, to interior and exterior shedding of oneself. He stands before God and recognizes what he is. He rediscovers himself.

Remember, man, that you are called to other things besides these earthly and material goods, which threaten to divert you from the essential. Remember, man, your fundamental vocation; you come from God, you return to God with the prospect of the Resurrection, the path blazed by Christ.

"Anyone who does not take up his cross and follow me cannot be my disciple" *(Lk* 14:27).

So it is a time of deep truth, truth which converts, restores hope, puts everything in its place, reconciles and lets optimism arise.

It is a time which makes us think about our relations with "Our Father." It is a time which reestablishes the order that ought to reign among brothers and sisters. It is a time which makes us responsible for one another and frees us from our egoisms, our pettinesses, our mean-nesses, our pride. It is a time which enlightens us and lets us understand better that we also must serve, like Christ. "I give you a new commandment: love one another" *(Jn* 13:34). "And who is my neighbor?" *(Lk* 10:29).

It is a time of Truth. Like the Good Samaritan, it makes us halt on the way and recognize our brother, put our time and goods at his service in daily sharing. The Good Samaritan is the Church! The Good Samaritan is each of us! Through vocation! Through duty! The Good Samaritan lives charity. St. Paul says, "This makes us ambassadors for Christ" *(2 Cor* 5:20).

And this is our responsibility! We are called to others, to our brethren.

Where is our love in it? Where is our Truth?

March 5

Believing in God Is the First Truth

"I believe in God, Father Almighty, Creator of Heaven and Earth." This *the first truth of the faith,* the first article of our Creed. Creatures give testimony of God the Creator. The more man lets himself be carried away by the eloquence of creatures, their richness and beauty, the more need to adore the Creator grows in him and ought to grow in him. On our knees before the Lord, let us prostrate ourselves and adore.

These are not extravagant words. They confirm the perennial ways of the fundamental logic of the Faith, and of the fundamental logic of thought about the cosmos as well, about the macrocosmos and the microcosmos. Here indeed the Faith confirms itself in a particular way as *rationale obsequium,* "reasonable worship."

I ask you to think about this disproportion which really exists in gigantic areas of contemporary civilization; the better man knows the cosmos, the less he seems to feel obliged to "bend the knee" and "prostrate himself" before the Creator.

Need we ask why?

Do people think that knowledge of the world and enjoyment of the effects deriving from it make man master of creation? But should men not think, rather, that what man knows — the astonishing richnesses of the microcosmos and the dimensions of the macrocosmos — he finds, as it were, "ready-made," and that what he produces on that basis he owes to the wealth of raw materials which he finds in the created world? . . .

But, is it possible that contemporary man actually does not think that there may be a fundamental "injustice" toward the Creator in the entire direction of the development of his civilization and his mentality?

"Come let us go down on bended knees before Him who has created this."

March 6

A Path of Faith

Lent is presented . . . *in the likeness of a path,* like that to which God called Abraham: "Go forth from the land of your kinsfolk and from your father's house to a land that I will show you" (*Gen* 12:1). And Abraham set off, without lingering, and without any support other than the divine promise.

Well, Lent is a journey for us too. We are called to face it with determination and to entrust ourselves to the projects which God has for us.

Even though the journey may be full of trials, St. Paul assures us that, like Timothy, each of us is helped by "the strength which comes from God" (*2 Tim* 1:8). And the country toward which we are heading is *the Christian's new life.* It is a paschal Life, which can be realized only through the "power" and the "grace" of God — a mysterious power, "the grace held out to us in Christ Jesus before the world began but now made manifest by the appearance of our Savior. He has robbed death of its power and has brought life and immortality into clear light through the gospel" (*2 Tim* 1:9–10).

The letter to Timothy also points out that the bread of new life is given to us because of a mysterious calling and assignment on God's part "not because of any merit of ours but according to His own design"(*2 Tim* 1:9). So we ought to be men and women of faith, like Abraham; men and women, that is, who do not count so much on themselves as on the word, the grace and the power of God.

The Lord Jesus, while living on earth, personally revealed this way to His disciples.

March 7

Remembrance and Challenge

Lent is remembrance.

It reminds us of the way pointed out to us by the Lord with His forty days' fast at the beginning of his messianic mission. It also reminds us that — at whatever point one may be on his earthly path — one must detach oneself from the "threefold desires" (*cf. 1 Jn* 2:16), "works of the flesh" (*Gal* 5:19), which "oppose the Holy Spirit" (*Acts* 7:51), and so leave room for "the fruit of the spirit" (*Gal* 5:22), by following Christ in prayer and fasting, so far as one is capable.

If, therefore, we feel ourselves to be in that unity with Christ which makes us remember the very name of Christian, we cannot admit that this exceptional period in the Church's life does not stand out in some way in our lives. . . . Let us live the spirit of penitence better.

Let us remember that the Christ of Lent is above all the Christ who awaits us in every suffering person, He who urges us to love and judges according to what we have done for even one only of our weaker brethren.

Lent is therefore not only remembrance, but it is also continual *challenge*. Entering into this period and living it in the spirit which the oldest and everliving tradition of the Church transmits to us, means: *opening up our consciences;* letting Christ Himself open them for us with the word of His Gospel, above all with the eloquence of His Cross.

Lent is thus an exceptional occasion for saving "the inward man" in each of us (*Eph* 3:16). He is often forgotten, yet he is created "in justice and holiness" (*Eph* 4:24) through the operation of the Sufferings and the Resurrection of Christ.

March 8

Your Grace Be upon Us

The Lord Jesus took the path of Lent together with His disciples during His life on earth. He continues to follow it together with His Church. Lent is the period of a particularly intense presence of Christ in the life of the Church. So we ought to try to get closer to Christ in a more special way during this season.

We must live in intimacy with Him, open up our hearts to Him, our consciences: "Lord, may your grace be upon us, because we hope in You." Lent is especially a time when grace ought to be "over us" in a particular fashion. Hence it necessary for us simply to open up to it.

God's grace is actually not so much something to be won as something available, calling for joyous acceptance, like a gift, without impediments being raised. This is concretely possible, first of all, through an attitude of deep prayer, which exactly entails weaving a dialogue with the Lord. Then it is possible also through an attitude of sincere humility, because faith is precisely adherence of heart and mind to the Word of God. Finally, through practice of authentic charity, which should let shine out all that love of which the Lord has already made us the object.

Just as the Lord commanded Abraham to set out on his path, so we too set out once again along this path of Lent at the end of which is the Resurrection. We see that Christ overcomes death and causes life and immortality to shine forth by means of the Gospel. Therefore, borne up by the power of God, we ought to take fatigue and disappointment, bearing them for the sake of the Gospel.

March 9

The Temptation of Jesus in The Desert

We have entered Lent in order to follow Jesus' example. "For forty days . . . He was tempted by the devil" (*Lk* 4:1) as he entered upon his messianic activity in Israel, and, "During that time He ate nothing" (*Lk* 4:2). The evangelist Luke tells us that Christ "was tempted by the devil" (*Lk* 4:2) and gives a detailed account of the temptation. We behold an event which touches us deeply. The temptation in the desert has constituted a fruitful theme for reflection and creativity for many people, saints, theologians, writers and painters. So profound is the content of this occurrence! It tells us so much about Christ: the Son of God who became true Man. This gives everyone much food for meditation.

The description of Jesus' temptation has particular eloquence. In this period, more than in any other, man must make himself aware that his life runs on in the world between good and evil. Temptation is nothing else but directing toward evil everything which man can and ought put to good use.

Temptation draws us away from God and directs us in a disordered way toward ourselves and the world. Let everyone enter into himself, now above all, in this period of Lent, let him renew his faith in Jesus Christ Crucified and Risen. Let him meditate on the teaching of the faith! Meditate on its divine truths! And, above all, with your faith, your heart and your life ("we believe with the heart to obtain justice").

Profess this faith with mind and heart, in word and deed.

March 10

Our Temptations

The number and manifold character of our temptations have their basis in that threefold concupiscence of which the First Letter of St. John tells us: "For nothing that the world affords comes from the Father. Carnal allurements, enticement for the eye, and life of empty show — all these are from the world" (*1 Jn* 2:16).

As is well known, in St. John's mind, the "world" from which the Christian should keep away is not creation, the work of God which was entrusted to the dominion of man, but the symbol and sign of everything which separates from God, that is, the opposite of "God's kingdom." There are three aspects of the world from which the Christian should keep his distance, so as to be faithful to Jesus' message. They are sensual appetites, excessive hunger for earthly goods — on which man deludes himself that he can build all his life — and prideful self-sufficiency in regard to God ... the "three concupiscences" are the three great temptations to which the Christian will be subjected in the course of his earthly life.

But behind this threefold temptation, we find the earliest and all-embracing temptation, addressed directly by Satan himself to our first parents: "You will be like gods who know what is good and what is bad" (*cf. Gen* 3:5).

The first Adam chose himself instead of God; he yielded to the temptation and found himself poor, frail, weak, "naked," "the slave of sin" (*cf. Jn* 8:34).

However, the second Adam, Christ, confirmed the fundamental structural and ontological dependence of man upon God, against Satan. Christ tells us that man is not humiliated, but is exalted in his own dignity whenever he prostrates himself and adores the Infinite Being, his Creator and Father: "You shall do homage to the Lord your God; him alone shall you adore." (*Mt* 4:10).

March 11

Unbounded Liberty, the Same as Slavery

Creating God's kingdom means being with Christ.

Creating the unity which ought to exist in us and among us means gathering (accumulating) together with Him. This is the basic program of God's kingdom. In His statements, Christ sets it in opposition to the evil spirit's activity in us and among us. This activity stakes its program on apparently unbounded liberty for man. It flatters man with a liberty which is not his own. It flatters entire social groups, societies, generations. It flatters, to make clear in the end that this liberty is nothing else than adaptation to manifold constraints: constraint of the senses and instincts, constriction of the situation, constriction of information and the various means of communication, constriction coming from current ways of thinking, of evaluating, of behaving, in which silence is imposed upon the fundamental question — is such and such a way of behaving good or bad, worthy or unworthy of man?

Can man awaken? Can he say to himself clearly that in the end this unlimited liberty becomes slavery?

Christ does not flatter His hearers. He does not flatter man with the semblance of "unrestricted" liberty. He says, "Know the truth, and the truth will set you free" (*Jn* 8:32). In this way, He shows that liberty was not given to man only as a gift but also as a duty. It is a duty which I and each of you is given as a task for himself and herself. It is the duty which measures life. It is not a property, which we may make use of in any way whatever and squander as well.

March 12

The Truth, Source of True Liberty

This task of liberty is a marvelous task. It is accomplished according to Christ's program and His kingdom *on the terrain of truth.* Being free means achieving the fruits of liberty, acting in the truth. Being free also means knowing how to yield, how to submit to the truth, not to subject truth to oneself, to one's fancies and will, to one's interests at the present time. Being free, according to Christ's program and His Kingdom, does not mean passive enjoyment, but effort, the labor of liberty. At the price of such effort, man does not "waste," but together with Christ "gathers" and "accumulates."

At the price of that effort, man also obtains that unity in himself which is proper to the Kingdom of God. At the same price, again, marriages, families, social groups, societies, achieve similar unity. The unity of truth with liberty. And the unity of liberty with truth.

My dear friends! This unity is your particular task, unless you wish to give in, unless you want to surrender to the unity of that other program, that which seeks to accomplish itself in the world, in mankind, in our generation and in each of us, the program of him whom Holy Scripture also calls "the father of lies" (*Jn* 8:44).

The call of Lent is therefore a call "to gather together with Christ." Do not permit destruction of this interior unity, which, through the Holy Spirit, Christ constructs in the conscience of every one of you. Unity, where liberty grows out of truth, and truth is the measure of liberty.

Learn to think, to speak and to act according to the principles of evangelical simplicity and clarity: "Yes, yes; no, no." Learn to call white white and black black — bad bad and good good.

March 13

Liberty Means Acting in Truth

Christ did not stake his Kingdom's program on appearances. He builds it up on truth. The liturgy of Lent reminds us of the truth of sin and the truth of conversion, day after day, through the words of the Prophet. What ardent words! They call to mind the truth of sin and the truth of conversion.

Today's liturgy does so as well. It begins with words of Jeremiah, the most tragic of the prophets, then adds an invitation to penance in the words of the prophet Joel: "Return to the Lord your God. For gracious and merciful is he. . . ." (*Joel* 2:13).

The right to conversion corresponds to the truth on man. It corresponds to the inner truth of man as well. What the Church ardently implores during Lent particularly is that man shall not let this truth in him be stifled and shall not deprive himself of his interior truth. That he shall not let this truth be snatched from him under the appearance of "unlimited liberty." That he shall not cease to hear the cry of conscience in himself as the cry of Truth, the Truth which surpasses him, but which decides about him at the same time, which makes him man and decides about his humanity.

The Church prays that man, each man and woman—in particular, the young, but everyone! — may not take the semblance of liberty and the semblance of liberation for true liberty and liberation built on truth, for liberation in Jesus Christ. The Church prays for this every day.

"Oh, that today you would hear His voice: Harden not your hearts as at Meribah, as in the day of Massah in the desert, where your fathers tempted me; they tested me though they had seen my works" (*Ps* 95:8–9).

Yes, May man, witness of creation, man — the Chris-

121

tian, witness of the Cross and of the Resurrection (a witness is one who has looked and seen) keep his heart open and his conscience clear. May he have in him that liberty for which Christ has liberated him (*cf. Gal* 5:1).

March 14

We Need Christ the Liberator

The spirit of penitence and the practice of it stimulates us to detach ourselves sincerely from everything superfluous that we have, sometimes even what is necessary to us, and hinders us from being truly what God wishes us to be: "Where your treasure is, there your heart is also" (*Mt* 6:21).

Are our hearts holding on to material riches? To power over others? To egoistically subtle ways of domineering? Then we have need of Christ the Liberator. If we wish, He can loose us from these sinful links which are tripping us up. Let us be ready to let ourselves be enriched by the grace of the Resurrection by freeing ourselves from every false treasure. Those material goods which are often not necessary to us, for millions of human beings constitute the essential conditions for survival.

But hundreds of millions of people, in need of the minimum necessary for their subsistence, look to us to be helped, to find the indispensable means for integral human promotion as well as for the economic and cultural development of their countries. But declarations of good intention to make a simple gift are not enough to alter man's heart. There is need *for conversion of spirit*, which can push us to a meeting of hearts and sharing of our lives with the least-favored members of our society, with those deprived of everything, sometimes their dignity as men and women, as boys or girls.

It is there that we meet and more intimately live the mystery of the suffering and redemptive death of the Lord. Real sharing is going out to meet the others; that is what helps us to free ourselves from bonds enslaving us.

March 15

Christ Is the Liberator

"He will liberate you" . . . "You who dwell in the shelter of the Most High." At the moment when he was tempting Christ, the tempter made reference to the words of a psalm, with its praise for the merciful providence of God. As he sought to convince the Messiah, to persuade him to throw himself down from the highest pinnacle of the Temple at Jerusalem, he reminded Him: "He will bid His angels take care of you; with their hands they will support you that you may never stumble on a stone" (*Mt* 4:6).

Then, as we know, Christ rebuked the tempter, saying, "You shall not put the Lord your God to the test" (*Mt* 4:7). He rebuked him for misusing the divine words, for interpreting them perversely and falsifying the truth contained in them. *"Ipse liberabit te"* — "He will liberate you." The Church reminds us every day during Lent of the proper meaning of liberation of man, that which God accomplished and goes on accomplishing in Christ: liberation from sin, liberation from the desires of the flesh, the concupiscence of the eyes, the pride of life (*cf. 1 Jn* 2:16), liberation from what coerces man most, even though it may permit him to preserve the appearance of autonomy.

Man saves these appearances at the cost of possession and use of things, at the price of a service which he does not understand as service but as making others serve him, often by using force, at his neighbor's expense. True liberation of man, that which is brought to him by Christ, is also liberation from the semblance of liberation, from appearance of liberty which is not true liberty. *"Ipse liberabit te. . . ."*

During Lent, the Church calls upon us to bow our heads to God. When we raise our heads, we see Christ, Redeemer of Man. He teaches us, by means of the whole of His life, then definitively through His suffering and death, what "being free" means.

March 16

Father, I Have Sinned

"Father, I have sinned against you . . ." *(Lk* 15:18).

In the period of Lent, the Church ponders these words with particular emotion, since this is the time when the Church more profoundly desires to convert herself to Christ — and *without these words there is no conversion in all its interior meaning.*

Without these words, "Father, I have sinned," man cannot truly enter into the Mystery and the Resurrection of Christ, so as to obtain the fruits of Redemption and Grace from them. Those are key words. They, above all, show man's great interior openness to God: "Father, I have sinned against you."

If it is true that sin in a certain sense shuts man off

from God, it is likewise true that *remorse* for sins opens up all the greatness and majesty of God, his fatherhood above all, to man's conscience.

Man remains shut to God so long as the words, "Father, I have sinned against you," are absent from his lips, above all while they are absent from his *conscience,* from his *"heart."*

Being converted to Christ, finding the interior power of His Cross and His Resurrection, finding the full truth of human existence in Him, "in Christ," is possible only with the form of these words: "Father, I have sinned." And only at the cost of them.

In Lent, the Church labors above all that every man and woman may blame himself or herself for sins before God alone and that they may consequently accept the salvific power of the pardon contained in Christ's Suffering and Resurrection.

March 17

St. Patrick

Patrick was a witness to Jesus Christ, from the days which he spent as a shepherd boy at Slemish to the day of his death at Saul. He lit the Paschal fire for the first time in Ireland on the hill of Slane, so that the light of Christ might shine through all Ireland and unite the whole of its people in love for the unique Jesus Christ. It is a cause of great joy for me to find myself . . . in sight of the hill of Slane, and to proclaim . . . that same Jesus, the Incarnate Word of God, the Savior of the world.

Let us greet Christ today in the words of the Paschal Liturgy, which was celebrated by Patrick for the first time in Ireland on the hill of Slane: Christ is the Alpha and Omega, the beginning and the end of everything. All times and ages belong to him. To Him be glory forevermore. May the light of Christ, the light of the faith, continue to shine out from Ireland. May no darkness ever extinguish it!

St. Patrick prayed for himself, that he might be faithful until death to the light of Christ. He prayed that the people of Ireland might ever remain loyal to the light of Christ; *he prayed constantly for the Irish.* He wrote in his *Confession*: "May God never permit that it happen to me to lose the people which He has reconquered in the extreme parts of the world. I pray God that He give me perseverance, and deign to make me be a faithful witness to Him until the end of my life for God. . . . From the time when I first knew him in my youth, love of God and fear of Him have grown in me, and until now, by virtue of God's grace, I have kept the faith."

March 18

The Remembrance of the Servant of God, Pius XII

I desire today to commemorate the great Pope Pius XII. He was called to the See of Peter . . . at the beginning of the month of March 1939. It was almost at the beginning of the Second World War. . . .

I shall never forget the profound impression made upon me when the occasion was offered to see him at close quarters for the first time. It happened during an audience granted to young priests and seminarians of the Belgian College. Pius XII went up to each of those present. When he came to me, the Rector of the College (now Cardinal de Fürstenberg) said that I came from Poland. The Pope halted for a moment, with evident emotion, and repeated *"From Poland."* He then said in Polish, "Praised be Jesus Christ." That happened in the early months of 1947, little less than two years after the end of the Second World War, which was a terrible trial for Europe and for Poland.

On this fortieth anniversary of the beginning of that significant pontificate, we cannot forget how much Pius XII *contributed to the theological preparation of the Second Vatican Council.* Above all, as regards doctrine on the Church, the first liturgical reforms, the fresh drive given to Biblical studies, the great attention devoted to the problems of the contemporary world.

So we have a natural debt, a duty to recall the memory of that great soul, in today's prayer to Mary, to whom he was so devoted, as we all well know.

March 19

St. Joseph Hears God's Word

St. Joseph is great in the spirit. He is great in faith, not because he uttered any words of his own but above all *because he heard the words of the living God.*

He listened in silence. And . . . he became . . . a witness of the Divine Mystery. . . .

The Word of the living God fell deeply into the soul of that man — that Upright Man.

And we, do we know how to listen to God's word?

Do we know how to absorb it in the depths of our human "ego"?

Do we open our consciences to this word? . . .

Do we read Sacred Scripture?

Do we take part in catechesis?

We have so much need of faith!

Great faith is so necessary to men of our time, the difficult modern age.

Great faith is necessary today to individuals, families, communities, the Church.

People of God! . . .

Fear not to accept Mary, together with Joseph of Nazareth.

Fear not to accept Jesus Christ, his Son, all your lives.

Fear not to accept Him with faith like Joseph's.

Fear not to accept Him under the roofs of your houses. . . .

Fear not to accept Christ in your daily work.

Fear not to accept Him in your "world."

Then this world will be really human. It will become ever more human. Only the God-Man can make our "human world" fully human.

March 20

St. Joseph, Spouse of Mary the Virgin

The Word was made flesh and came to dwell in the Virgin, who, while remaining a virgin, became a mother. *This was the mystery of Mary. Joseph did not know that mystery.* He did not know that in Her whose spouse he was had been accomplished the promise of faith made to Abraham. That is, he did not know that the prophecy which the prophet Nathan had made to David had been achieved in her, Mary of the stock of David. The prophecy and the promise of the faith, accomplishment of which was awaited by the whole people, by Israel, chosen by God, and all mankind.

This was the mystery of Mary. Joseph did not know that mystery. She could not convey it to him, because it was a mystery above the capacity of human understanding and the human tongue's possibility of expression. It could not be conveyed by any human means. It could only be accepted from God, and be believed. And Mary believed.

Joseph did not know this mystery and suffered a very great deal inwardly because of it. We read: "Joseph her husband, an upright man unwilling to expose her to the law, decided to divorce her quietly."

But there came a certain night when Joseph also believed. God's word was addressed to him and the mystery of Mary, his spouse and wife, became clear to him. He believed that the promise of faith made to Abraham and the prophecy heard by King David, had been accomplished in her. "Joseph, son of David, have no fear about taking Mary as your wife. It is by the Holy Spirit that she has conceived this child. She is to have a son and you are to name him Jesus because he will save his people from their sins."

"Joseph awoke," the Evangelist concludes. "He did as the angel of the Lord had directed him."

March 21

Conversion, God's Gift

Conversion is fundamentally a turning away from sin and a turning toward, a return to the Living God, to the God of the Alliance: "Come, let us return to the Lord, for it is he who has rent, but he will heal us; he has struck us, but He will bind our wounds" (*Hos* 6:1) is the invitation of the prophet Hosea. He insists on the interior character of true conversion. It should always be inspired and moved by love and knowledge of God. And the prophet Jeremiah, the great master of interior religion, foresaw an extraordinary spiritual transformation of the members of the People of God, through the action of God: "I will give them a heart with which to understand that I am the Lord. They shall be my people and I will be their God, for they shall return to me with their whole heart" (*Jer* 24:7).

Conversion is a gift from God which man must ask for with fervent prayer and which was merited for us by Christ, "the new Adam." Sin and death entered into the world through the disobedience of the first Adam and dominate man. But, "If death began its reign through one man because of his offense, much more shall those who receive the overflowing grace and gift of justice live and reign through the one man, Jesus Christ" (*Rom* 5:17).

The Christian, strong with the strength which comes to him from Christ, moves farther and farther from sin, that is, from the sad reality of the original disobedience. This occurs to the degree to which Grace abounds in us more and more; Grace, God's gift, granted through the merits "of one man, Jesus Christ" (*cf. Rom* 5:15). Conversion is thus an almost gradual, effective and continuous transition from the "old" Adam to the "new" one, who is Christ.

March 22

Harden Not Your Hearts

Hear His voice today: "Harden not your hearts (*Ps* 95:8).

This prayer is relevant and necessary, but it is particularly recommended in the course of these forty days *that we hear the voice of the living God.* It is a penetrating voice, when we consider how God speaks in Lent not only with the exceptional richness of His Word in the liturgy and in the Church's life but above all with the paschal eloquence of the Passion and Death of His own Son. He speaks with His cross and with His sacrifice. In a certain sense, this is the last discourse in His dialogue with man, lasting centuries, a dialogue with his mind and with his heart, with his conscience and his conduct. The heart means man in his inner spirituality, the very center, so to say, of his likeness with God. The interior man. *The man of conscience.*

Our prayer during Lent aims at awakening of consciences, arousing them to the voice of God. In fact, the diseases of consciences, their indifference to good and evil, their errors, are a great danger to man. They are indirectly a menace to society as well, because the level of society's morals depends in the ultimate analysis on the human conscience.

A man who has a hardened heart and a degenerate conscience is *spiritually a sick man,* even though he may enjoy the fullness of his powers and physical capacities. Everything must be done to bring him back to having a healthy soul. "Hear today his voice . . . harden not your heart."

March 23

Conversion Is, above All, Acceptance

"Return to me . . . I will return to you" (*Zech* 1:3).

Here is another invocation from the Lenten liturgy, introducing us to the whole reality of conversion. We convert to God, who awaits us. He awaits in order to turn to us, "to convert to us." We journey toward God, He desires to come to meet us. Let us open up to God, who desires to open to us.

Conversion is not a one-way process, a unilateral expression. Being converted means believing in God who loved us first, who has loved us eternally in His Son, and through His Son gives us grace and truth in the Holy Spirit. That Son was crucified, so as to speak to us with His arms spread as widely as God is open to us. How incessantly God "converts to us," through the Cross of His Son!

Our conversion is in this way not a unilateral aspiration at all. It is not only an effort on the part of the human will, understanding and heart. It is not only a commitment to directing our humanity upwards, when it so heavily tends downwards.

Conversion is above all *acceptance*. It is the effort to accept God in all the wealth of His "conversion" (*convertar*" — "I shall be converted") to man. This conversion is a Grace.

An effort of understanding, of heart and of will, is also indispensable for accepting Grace. It is indispensable for not losing the Divine dimension of life in the human dimension; for persevering in it.

March 24

Conversion, God's Gift to the Church

"Be converted to me . . . I will turn to you."

The Church converts to Christ to renew consciousness and certainty of all His gifts, those gifts with which she was endowed by him through the Cross and Resurrection. Christ is at the same time the Church's Redeemer and her Spouse. As Redeemer and Spouse, Christ established the Church among weak, sinful and fallible men, but He established her at the same time strong, holy and infallible. She is so, not through the work of men but through the power of Christ.

Believing in the Church's strength does not mean believing in the strength of the people who constitute her, but it means believing in the gift of Christ: in that power which "in weakness reaches perfection" (2 Cor 12:9).

Believing in the Church's holiness does not mean believing in the natural perfection of man, but it means believing in the gift of Christ: in that gift which makes us heirs of sin, heirs of the divine holiness.

Believing in the Church's infallibility does not mean — in any way — believing in the infallibility of man, but it means believing in Christ's gift: in that gift which permits fallible men to proclaim infallibly and infallibly confess the truth revealed for our salvation.

The Church of our time — this difficult, perilous age in which we live, this critical epoch — ought to have *particular certainty regarding Christ's gift,* the gift of strength, the gift of holiness, the gift of infallibility.

The more she is conscious of the weakness, sinfulness,

fallibility of man, the more she should maintain her certainty of those gifts, coming from Her Redeemer and Her Spouse.

This is also an essential way of Lenten conversion for the Church of Christ.

March 25

Annunciation of the Lord: Fear Not

"Non temere — Fear not." This is the constituent element of the vocation. For man fears. He fears, not only to be called to the priesthood, he also fears to be called to life, to his duties, to a profession, to marriage. He fears. This fear also reveals a sense of responsibility, but not of mature responsibility.

One must accept the call, one must listen, one must receive, one must measure one's strength, and answer, "Yes, yes." Fear not, fear not because you have found grace, do not fear life, do not fear your maternity, do not fear your marriage, do not fear your priesthood, for you have found grace. This certainty, this consciousness, helps us as it helped Mary.

"Earth and paradise await your "yes," O Virgin most pure." These are words of St. Bernard, famous, most beautiful words. They await your "yes," Mary. They await your "yes," O mother who must give birth. A man who must take on a personal, family, social responsibility awaits your "yes". . . .

Here is Mary's response, here is the answer given by a mother, here is the reply of a young woman: a "yes" which suffices for a whole life.

March 26

Annunciation of the Lord: Mary's Yes and Our Yes

Maybe there is another point: for all people are born at your "yes." This must be understood: such a yes in imitation of Mary, such a yes creates joy, a new life, a breath, a blessing. *A yes like Mary's:* what a blessing! What fullness of good in the world! A yes from Mary: how much blessing! What joy, what felicity! What salvation! What hope. . . .

So, this is how I have contemplated the mystery of the Annunciation and, together withit, the mystery of the Christian vocation and especially of the priestly vocation. . . .

Here, in this chapel, the image of Our Lady stands over all: Our Lady of Confidence. This image in a certain way sums up the mystery of the Annunciation and the vocation. Behold Her who found confidence in the Lord. If the Lord says to you you must be a priest; if the Lord says this to you, it means that the Lord has confidence in you. Can you then fear? It is not enough to fear, it is necessary to mature, so as to assume responsibility, for Our Lady of Confidence means her who had immense confidence in God. With this confidence, she was capable of becoming the Mother of God. . . .

It is a good thing that we find the gaze of Our Lady of Confidence in this chapel of the Roman Seminary, because we can prepare ourselves with confidence under this gaze for what the Lord calls us to do.

March 27

Let Yourselves Be Reconciled with God

In this particular season of the spirit, which Lent is, the call to reconciliation ought to have particular resonance and force in our hearts and consciences. If we are really disciples and confessors of Christ — who reconciled man with God — we cannot live without seeking such interior reconciliation for our part too. We must not remain in sin and fail to make efforts at finding the way again which leads to the Father's house, where He is always waiting for us to return.

The Church calls us during Lent to look for such a way: "We implore you, in Christ's name be reconciled with God" (2 Cor 5:20). Only through being reconciled with God in Christ's name can we taste "how good the Lord is" (Ps 34:9), by trying for ourselves, experimentally, as it were.

It is not of God's severity that confessors throughout the world, those where men and women reveal their sins, speak; they speak rather of his merciful bounty. And how many approach the confessional, sometimes after many years' absence, bearing the weight of mortal sins and, as they depart from it, find the desired relief. They find joy and peace of conscience, which they could not find anywhere else. No one actually has the power to free us from our sin; God alone has that power. And the person who obtains such remission receives the grace of a new life of the spirit, which God alone can grant us in his infinite goodness.

"When the afflicted called out, the Lord heard, and from all his distress he saved him" (Ps 34:7).

March 28

The Return to the Father's House

Lent is the time for a particularly loving meeting on our Father's part with each and every one of us, so that even the most prodigal son may still take account of the waste which he has perpetrated, call his sin by its name, and finally make his way with complete sincerity back to God. Such a man must go back to the Father's house. The way back leads through *examination of conscience, repentance, and resolve to improve; need for confession* arises in him.

Our reconciliation with God, the return to the Father's house, is accomplished through Christ. His suffering and death on the cross stand between every human conscience, every human sin, and the Father's boundless Love. Such Love is prompt to raise up and pardon; it is nothing else than Mercy. In personal conversion, in repentance, in firm resolve to reform, and finally in confession, each of us agrees to perform a personal spiritual labor. This labor is an extension and prolonged reverberation of that labor of salvation which our Redeemer undertook. This is what the Apostle of reconciliation with God has to say: "For our sakes God made him who did not know sin, to be sin, so that in him we might become the very holiness of God" (*2 Cor* 5:21).

So let us undertake our labor of conversion and penitence for Him, with Him and in Him. Unless we undertake it, we are not worthy of the name of Christ, we are not worthy of the inheritance of the Redemption.

"If anyone is in Christ, he is a new creation. The old order has passed away; now all is new! All this has been done by God, who has reconciled us to himself through Christ, and has given us the ministry of reconciliation" (*2 Cor* 5:17–18).

March 29

Conversion Goes by Way of the Cross

To be converted to God, in an essential and radical way, we must return to that "principle" which is: at the beginning is human sin and death, which results from it. We must regain consciousness of sin, which has become the beginning of every sin on earth, which has become the lasting foundation and the source of man's sinfulness.

That original sin actually remains in the whole human race. It is the inheritance of the first Adam in us. And even though cancelled by Baptism through the operation of Christ, "the final Adam" (1 Cor 15:45), it leaves its effects in each of us.

Being converted to God, as the Church desires in the period of the forty days of Lent, means getting to the roots of the tree, which, as the Lord says, "is not fruitful" (Mt 3:10). There is no other way of healing man. So, to "be converted" in the way the Church expects of us today during the Lenten season, we need to return to that "principle," that "beginning," which is "you are dust, and you shall return to dust," so as to find ourselves again in the "new Beginning" of Christ's Resurrection and Grace.

So the way passes through Good Friday. It passes beneath the Cross. There is no other way of full "conversion." Upon this unique road, we are awaited by Him whom the Father, through Love, "made him . . . to be sin" (2 Cor 5:21) — although He had not known sin — "so that in him we might become the very holiness of God."

Let us take the road of such conversion and reconciliation with God, by collaborating in a particular fashion in this period of forty days, with Christ, through *prayer, almsgiving and fasting.*

"A clean heart create for me, O God, and a steadfast spirit renew within me" (Ps 51:12).

March 30

The Struggle Goes On

God's kingdom has its beginning in the history of creation together with man. It has a long history. At the summit of this history stands Christ. "The reign of God is at hand" *(Mk* 1:15). He spoke of it from the beginning of his messianic teaching and he perseveringly, tirelessly, announced this Kingdom to be chosen people.

Conversion is necessary for being able to regain the full truth of the Kingdom of God. After all, He gave His life for that truth. . . . Good Friday closed with a controversy over God's Kingdom.

On the Day of the Resurrection the truth of Christ's words was confirmed, the Truth that the Kingdom of God has come to us, the Truth of the whole of His messianic mission.

The struggle between the kingdom of evil, of the evil spirit, and the Kingdom of God has not ceased, however; it is not over. It has only entered upon a new stage, actually the definitive stage. In this stage the struggle goes on in ever new generations of human history.

Do we really have to demonstrate that this struggle goes on in our day as well? Yes. It certainly goes on. Indeed, it develops together with human history in single peoples and nations.

It goes on in each of us. And, by following the history, including our own contemporary history, we can also define in what way the kingdom of the malign spirit is not divided but seeks unity of action in the world and, by various paths, tries to have its effects upon man, on groups, on families, on society.

As at the beginning, so also now, it stakes its program on *human liberty* . . . on man's apparently unlimited liberty.

March 31

Entering into Ourselves

Lent is the time for entering into oneself. It is the period of particular intimacy with God in the secrecy of one's own heart and conscience.

The essential work of Lent, the work of conversion, is performed in such interior intimacy with God. Words resound in that interior privacy and intimacy with God himself, in all the truth of one's own heart and conscience. Words such as those of the Psalmist, one of the profoundest confessions which man has ever made to God: "Have mercy on me, O God, in your goodness; in the greatness of your compassion wipe out my offense. Thoroughly wash me from my guilt and of my sin cleanse me. For I acknowledge my offense and my sin is before me always: Against you only have I sinned, and done what is evil in your sight" *(Ps* 51:1–6).

Those are purifying words. Transforming words. They transform man within and are a testimony of transformation. Let us recite them often during Lent. Let us above all seek to renew this spirit which enlivens them; that interior breath of life which has linked the power of conversion exactly with these words.

Lent is essentially an invitation to conversion. The "works of mercy" spoken of in the Gospel open the way to it. Let us do such works as far as we can. But first of all, let us make use of them for an interior meeting with God lasting the whole of our lives, in everything constituting our lives and, in view of the profundity of this conversion to Him, radiating from the penitential psalm of today's Liturgy.

"We implore you in Christ's name: let yourselves be reconciled with Go." So speaks the Church, our mother, to all her children. Let it be so over the whole of this period.

"Let yourselves be reconciled with God," for He has done much for this reconciliation.

April

April 1

The Cross, a Living Call to Conversion

During Lent, the Church desires to enliven herself by taking up with particular commitment the mission of her Lord and Master in all its salvific value. She therefore listens to Christ's words with the greatest attention. He unchangingly announces the Kingdom of God, independently of the mutations of temporal events in the various fields of human life. And his last word is *the cross on Mount Calvary,* that is, the sacrifice offered by his love to reconcile man with God.

In the season of Lent, we should all look at the Cross with special attention in order to comprehend its eloquence anew. We should not see it only as a memorial of events which occurred two thousand years ago. We have to grasp the teaching of the Cross as it speaks to our time, to man of today: "Jesus Christ is the same yesterday, today, and forever" *(Heb* 13:8)

In the Cross of Jesus Christ a living call to *metanoia,* to conversion, is expressed: "Reform your lives and believe in the gospel" *(Mk* 1:15). We have to accept this call as being addressed to each and all of us in a particular manner on the occasion of the season of Lent. Living the season of Lent means being converted to God through Jesus Christ.

Christ himself indicates the rich program of conversion to us in the gospel. Christ — and the Church, after him — also offers us the means in Lent useful for such conversion. It is a question of *prayer,* above all, then of *almsgiving,* then of *fasting.* We must accept these means and bring them into our lives in proportion with the needs and possibilities of a Christian of our time.

April 2

The Program of Conversion

Prayer remains always the prime and fundamental condition for approaching God. During Lent, we must pray, we must try to pray more, to find the time and the place for praying. It is chiefly prayer which gets us away from indifference and makes us sensitive to the things of God and the soul. Prayer also educates our consciences. Lent is a particularly apt time for arousing and educating the conscience. The Church reminds us especially in this season of the indispensable necessity of sacramental confession, so that we may all live Christ's resurrection, not only in the liturgy but also in our own souls.

Almsgiving and fasting are closely linked with each other as means of conversion and Christian penance. *Fasting* means some mastery over ourselves. It means being demanding toward ourselves, being ready to give up something — food, enjoyment and various pleasures. In its broadest and most essential meaning, *almsgiving* is readiness to share joys and sadnesses with others, to give to one's neighbor, to the needy in particular; to divide not only material goods with others, but also the gifts of the spirit.

So, therefore, turning to God through prayer goes along with turning to mankind. By being demanding with ourselves and generous with others, we give expression to our conversion in both a concrete and a social way. Through fuller solidarity with mankind, with the suffering and especially with the needy, we unite with Christ, suffering and crucified.

April 3

Not Momentary Practices
but Constant Attitudes

During Lent we often hear directed at us these words: prayer, fasting, almsgiving.

We are accustomed to think of these things as good, pious works, which every Christian ought to do at this time above all. This is a correct, but not a complete way of thinking. Prayer, almsgiving and fasting require to be more deeply understood, if we wish to bring them more into our lives, and not regard them simply as passing practices, calling for something momentary from us, depriving us of something only for a short while. This way of thinking will not yet get us to the real meaning and real power which prayer, fasting and almsgiving have in the process of *conversion to God* and *spiritual maturation.* One goes along with the other: we mature spiritually by converting to God, and conversion is effected through prayer as well as through fasting and almsgiving, properly understood.

It would perhaps be well to point out at once here that it is not a matter of momentary "practices" but of *constant attitudes of mind*, which give lasting form to our conversion to God. As a liturgical season, Lent lasts only forty days in each year. But we have to stretch out to God always. That means that we have to be converted continually.

Lent ought to leave a strong and indelible imprint on our lives. It ought to renew the knowledge in us of our union with Jesus Christ, who makes us see the need for conversion and shows us the way to accomplish it. Prayer, fasting and almsgiving are exactly the way pointed out to us by Christ.

April 4

Who Is My Neighbor?

"Who is my neighbor?" (*Lk* 10:29).

Do you remember? Was it not with the parable of the Good Samaritan that Jesus answered a question put by a doctor of the Law? The doctor had just quoted the Law: "Thou shalt love the Lord thy God with all thy heart, and with all thy soul, and with all thy strength, and all thy mind; and thy neighbor as thyself." *The Good Samaritan is Christ.* It is he who comes to us first, making us his neighbor, to succor us, heal us, save us. But if there be still some distance between God and us, that depends only on us, on the obstacles which we put up against such rapprochement.

The sin in our hearts, the injustices we commit, the hatred and divisions which we nourish — all these things cause us not to love God yet with all our souls, with all our strength. The season of Lent is the privileged time for *purification* and *penitence,* for letting the Lord make us his neighbor and save us with his love.

The second commandment is like the first (*cf. Mt* 22:39) and forms one whole with it. We must love others with the same love which God pours into our hearts and with which he himself loves us. Here, too, what obstacles stand in the way of making the other our neighbor: we do not love God and our brethren enough.

Why still so many difficulties, raised against leaving the important but insufficient stage of reflections, declarations and professions, to become emigrants with emigrants, refugees with refugees, poor with those lacking everything?

April 5

The Spirit of Love and Sharing

The time of Lent was given to us as the Church and through the Church, to purify us of the residues of egoism, of excessive attachment to goods, both material and other, which keep us far from those with the right to make claims upon us: chiefly those who, physically near or far from us, have no possibility of living their lives as men and women with dignity, as humans created in the image and likeness of God.

So let yourselves be permeated with the spirit of penitence and conversion, which is *the spirit of love* and *sharing*. In imitation of Christ, bring yourselves close to the poor and those whom the world rejects. Take part in everything being done in your local church, for Christians and all people of goodwill to be able to bring each of their brethren the means, even the material means, for living worthily, for undertaking their own human and spiritual promotion and that of their families.

May the Lenten collections — and this holds good for poor countries as well — give you the means to help local churches in even poorer lands through sharing, so that they may achieve their mission of being Good Samaritans to those for whom they are directly responsible: the poor, the hungry, victims of injustice and those who cannot yet be responsible for their own development and their own human communities.

Penance, conversion: this is the *path*, not a sad but a *liberating path, that of our time of Lent.*

And if you still ask yourselves, "Who is my neighbor?," you will read the answer on the face of Christ and hear it from his lips: "I assure you, as often as you did it for one of my least brothers, you did it for me" (*Mt* 25:40).

April 6

Be Artisans of the Charity of Christ

"Those who believed shared all things in common; they would sell their property and goods, dividing everything on the basis of each one's need" (*Acts* 2:44–45).

These words of St. Luke arouse a great echo in my heart, in this liturgical season of Lent. Lent is a period of precious weeks, offered by the Church to all Christians, to help them to reflect on their profound identity as children of the Heavenly Father and brethren of all mankind, and to find new vigor for concrete, generous sharing, because God himself has called upon us to base our lives on charity.

Our relationships with our neighbor are of capital importance. And when I say "neighbor," I obviously mean those who live beside us, in the family, in the neighborhood, in the town or village, in the city. But it also means those with whom we work, those who are suffering, are sick, know loneliness, are really poor. My neighbor is also all those who are geographically quite distant, or who are exiled from their own countries, are without, lack food and clothing, often lack liberty.

My neighbor is all those unfortunates who have been completely or almost ruined by unforeseeable and dramatic catastrophes, which have thrown them into physical and moral want, often enough also into the sadness of losing their dearest ones. Lent is truly a pressing appeal from the Lord for personal and communitarian interior renewal, in prayer and return to the sacraments, but in acts of charity as well, through personal and collective sacrifices of time, money and goods of all kinds, so as to meet the needs and succor the troubles of our brethren in the world.

Sharing is a duty which no one of goodwill, above all no disciple of Christ, can evade.

April 7

St. John Baptist de la Salle

A grateful thought rises spontaneously in our minds to God, the giver of all good things, for having given inspiration to the founder of the Brothers of the Institution of the Christian Schools.

Their primary concern to train good teachers, bringing pupils and parents into the work of education, a fraternal atmosphere in relations between teachers and pupils, based on respect, trust and love; true religious training nourished by catechesis and liturgical life; founding of schools diversified according to the diverse needs of the youth of his time: for poor boys, for the sons of artisans, for laborers, for teachers . . . also the use of the mother tongue. These are all a clear and concrete demonstration of the great attention that Saint John Baptist de la Salle gave to man and the signs of his time. They represent so many *happy pedagogical intuitions which were also prophetical and anticipatory.*

I would like on this occasion to point out his rich spirituality in his deep love for prayer and meditation on the Word, his filial devotion to Mary — for which he was known as "the priest of the Rosary" — and finally, *his unshakeable fidelity to the Roman Pontiff.* It was precisely by reason of this that he sent two brothers to Rome from the beginning of his institute, to put them at the Pope's disposal.

"You have to show the Church what love you have for her. You have to give her proof of your zeal, by working for the Church which is the body of Christ. You are ministers of the Church for the mission which God has given you as dispensers of his word." This is what . . . [the Saint] wrote in his testament to you, dear brothers, and I add my same exhortation.

April 8

Almsgiving: A Sign of Justice

The call to penance, to conversion, means a call to inward openness to others. Nothing can replace this call, in the history of the Church and in the history of man. This call has infinite destinations.

It is addressed to everyone and it is addressed to each one, for reasons concerning each one. Each should therefore look at himself under the twofold aspects of the destination of the call.

Christ requires an opening toward others from me. But toward what other? Toward the one who is by me, at this moment! This call of Christ's cannot be "put off" till an indefinite future when the "right" beggar will appear and put out his hand.

I ought to be open to every person, ready to "lend myself." To lend myself with what? It is well known that we can sometimes "make a gift" to another with a single word; but with a single word we can also strike him painfully, harm him, wound him. We can even "kill" him morally. So, there is need to take up this call of Christ's in those ordinary daily situations where each of us is always the one who can "give" to others and at the same time knows how to accept what others can offer him ... I must not be closed and ungrateful, I must not isolate myself.

Accepting Christ's call to open to others demands, as we see, *reworking of the whole style of our daily lives.*

We must accept this call within the real dimensions of life, not put it off till conditions and circumstances will be different, till the necessity presents itself. We must continually persevere in that interior attitude. Otherwise, when that "extraordinary" occasion occurs, it may happen that we shall lack the proper disposition.

April 9

Almsgiving, A Sign of Solidarity

Christ's command to open up "to the other," to one's "brother," yes, the brother, has an ever concrete and ever universal range. It concerns everyone, because it refers to all. The measure of this opening is not only the nearness of the other; it is also his need: I was hungry, I was thirsty, I was naked, in prison, sick. . . .

We respond to this call by looking for those who are suffering, and even following them *over* frontiers of states and countries. This is how, through the heart of every one of us, the *universal dimension of human solidarity is created. The Church's mission is to safeguard this dimension:* not to confine herself to any frontiers, any political tendencies, to any systems.

It means safeguarding universal human solidarity, above all with those who are suffering; it means safeguarding it in regard to Christ, who shaped that dimension of solidarity once for all: "The love of Christ impels us who have reached the conviction that since one died for all, all died. He died for all so that those who live might live no longer for themselves but for him who for their sakes died and was raised up" *(2 Cor* 5:14–15). And he gave it as a task once for all. He gave it as a task to the Church. He gave it to all. He gave it to each one.

Therefore, in our consciences, in the individual conscience of the Christian, in the social consciences of the various groups, nations, I would say that *particular zones of solidarity* need to be formed, exactly with those who suffer most. We have to work systematically for the zones of particular human needs, great sufferings, wrongs and injustices, to become zones of Christian solidarity on the part of the whole Church and, through the Church, single societies and all mankind.

April 10

The Charity of Good Example

Penitence is synonomous with conversion. Conversion means overcoming everything contrary to the dignity of the children of God; it is sincere return to the Heavenly Father, who is infinitely good and merciful. . . .

This return is the fruit of an act of love. It will be more expressive and pleasing to him the more it is accompanied by the sacrifice of something necessary and, above all, of superfluous things.

A very vast range of acts is open to our initiative, from assiduous, generous doing of our daily duties to humble, joyful acceptance of annoying disappointments which can be met with in the course of the day, up to renunciation of something very pleasant in order to be able to bring aid to someone in a state of need. But *the charity of good example* is above all most pleasing to the Lord. Good example is required by the fact that we belong to a family of faithful whose members are independent; each needs help and support from the others.

Good example does not affect only exterior action but goes deep and builds up the most precious and most active of gifts in the other, namely, adherence to one's own Christian vocation.

All these things are difficult to put into practice, for our weak powers need a supplement of energies. Where can we find them?

Let us recall the words of the Divine Savior: "Apart from me you can do nothing" (*Jn* 15:5). *We must turn to him.* You know, anyhow, that Christ is to be found in the personal dialogue of *prayer*, particularly in the *reality of the sacraments.* We reconcile ourselves to God and the brethren through the Sacrament of Penance; we receive Christ in the Eucharist, which sustains our weak and wavering wills.

April 11

St. Stanislaus, Bishop and Martyr

History proclaims St. Stanislaus "Patron of the Poles."
This fact, and the fact that he has been acknowledged by
the Polish episcopate as, above all, patron of moral order, has a reason. The reason is the *ethical eloquence of his
life and his death* and of the whole tradition which has
been expressed by generations in Poland, the Poland of
the Piast dynasty, that of the Jagellons, and that of the
elected kings, right down then to our own day.

The title of patron of moral order which we apply to
St. Stanislaus is linked above all to universal recognition
of the authority of the moral law, that is, the law of God.
This law obligates all, whether they be subjects or rulers.
It is the moral norm and an essential criterion of the
value of man. Only when we begin from *this law, that is,
the moral law,* can the dignity of the human person be
universally respected and acknowledged. Hence,
morality and law are the fundamental conditions for social order. States and nations are built upon law, without
which they perish.

The Polish episcopate has to add a particular concern
for the entire Polish cultural heritage to its present mission and ministry. We know to what degree that cultural
heritage is impregnated with the light of Christianity. It
is also well known that the culture is the prime and fundamental proof of the identity of the nation.

Inasmuch as it is continuation of the mission of St.
Stanislaus, the Polish episcopate's mission is distinguished in a certain way by his historical grace, and so
remains evident and irreplaceable in this field.

April 12

The Cross Reveals All of Christ

Glory to you, Word of God!

This greeting is repeated day by day in the liturgy of Lent. It precedes the reading of the Gospel and testifies that the season of Lent is a period in the Church of particular *concentration on the word of God.* Such concentration was — especially in the early centuries — linked with preparation for Baptism on the night of the eve of Easter. The catechumens prepared themselves for that with increasing intensity.

But it is not only in consideration of Baptism and the catechumenate that Lent raises us to such intense concentration on God's Word. The need arises from the very nature of the liturgical period, that is, from *the depth of the Mystery,* which the Church enters from the beginning of Lent. The mystery of God reaches hearts and minds above all through God's word. We are actually in the period of "initiation" to Easter, which is the central mystery of Christ as well as of the faith and life of those who confess Him.

Praise be to you, Word of God! This *word* in the penultimate week of Lent becomes *particularly intense;* I would say it becomes particularly *dramatic.* The readings taken from St. John's Gospel bring this out.

When talking with the Pharisees, Christ says, ever more clearly, who He is, who sent Him, and His words do not meet with welcome.

Who are you? "When you lift up the Son of Man, you will come to realize. . . ." (*Jn* 8:28): you will know, you will find the answer to this question which you put to Me now, without trusting to the words I say to you.

"Lifting up" by means of the Cross *in a certain sense* constitutes *the key to getting to know the whole truth,* which Christ proclaimed.

April 13

The Cross, Beginning of the Resurrection

"The One who sent me is with me. He has not deserted me since I always do what pleases Him" (*Jn* 8:29).

In these words the *unlimited solitude* which Christ had to experience on the cross in his "lifting up" is revealed to us. That solitude was to begin during the prayer in the garden of *Gethsemani*. This must have been a real spiritual death agony and was to be completed in the crucifixion. Then Christ cried, "My God, my God, why have you foresaken me?" (*Mt* 27:46).

But earlier, as if anticipating those hours of tremendous solitude, Christ says, "The One who sent me . . . *has not deserted me*. . . ." As if to say, first of all, even in this supreme abandonment, *I shall not be alone!* I will do at that time "what pleases Him," that which is the will of the Father! And I shall not be alone!

And, further: the Father will not leave me in the hands of death, because in the Cross is the beginning of the resurrection. Exactly for this reason, "the crucifixion" will become "the lifting up" by definition. "Then you shall know who I am." Then, too, you shall know that "I only tell the world what I have heard from him."

The crucifixion really becomes Christ's elevation. In the Cross is the beginning of the resurrection. Therefore, the Cross becomes the definitive measure of all things, those which stand between God and man. Christ measures them exactly with this yardstick. . . .

In a certain sense, the dimension of the world is set against the dimension of God. In his talk with Pilate, Christ was to say, "My kingdom does not belong to this world" (*Jn* 18:36).

The dimension of the world *meets with* the dimension of God exactly *in the Cross:* in the Cross and in the resurrection.

April 14

Jesus Foretells His Death

Three great holy days recall Christ's suffering, death and resurrection. The words which the Lord uses to announce his by now imminent end therefore make reference to glory. "The hour has come for the Son of Man to be glorified. . . . My soul is troubled now, yet what should I say — Father, save me from this hour?" (*Jn* 12:23, 27). He then utters the words which manifest the mystery of the redemptive death so profoundly: "Now has judgment come upon this world . . . and I — once I am lifted up from earth will draw all men to myself" (*Jn* 12:31–32). That elevation of Christ from the earth is anterior to his elevation into glory. It is elevation on the wood of the cross, the elevation of martyrdom, a mortal elevation.

Jesus foretells his death in these mysterious words as well: "I solemnly assure you, unless the grain of wheat falls to the earth and dies, it remains just a grain of wheat" (*Jn* 12:24). His death is the pledge of life; it is the source of life for all of us. The Eternal Father preordained that death in the order of grace and salvation, just as the death of the grain of wheat under the earth is ordained in the order of nature so that the seed may sprout and the ear bear much wheat. This then becomes daily bread, and man feeds himself on it.

The sacrifice accomplished in the death of Christ has also become food for our souls under the appearance of bread.

April 15

Christ, Son of the Living God

Christ, Son of the living God!

We are here, we, your Church: the Body from your Body and from your Blood. We are here, we are keeping watch.

We are by your sepulchre. We keep watch. We remain awake, so as to be before those women who "at dawn will come to the tomb, bringing the spices they had prepared" (cf. Lk 24:1) to anoint your body, in the tomb since the evening of the day before.

We keep watch in order to be near your tomb, before Peter, summoned by the words of the three women, comes too; before Peter comes, he who will bend down and see only the wrappings (Lk 24:12). He will go back to the Apostles, "full of amazement at what had occurred." At that moment, for the first time, in that empty tomb, where your body had been laid the day before, the words resounded, "He has been raised up!" (Lk 24:6).

"Why do you search for the Living One among the dead? He is not here; he has been raised up. Remember what he said to you while he was still in Galilee — that the Son of Man must be delivered into the hands of sinful men, and be crucified, and on the third day rise again" (Lk 24:5–7). . . .

That is why we watch. We wish to be before the women and the Apostles. . . . We wish to be with you, we, your Church, the body from your body and from your blood shed on the Cross.

We are your Body, we are your People. We are many. We gather in many parts of the world. . . . We are many, we are all united by the faith, born of your Easter, of your passage through death to new Life, the faith born of your Resurrection.

April 16

Christ Is Risen

I call you and invite you, wherever you may be, to render homage of veneration to the Risen Christ! To the Paschal Victim of the Church and of the world.

Let all the communities of the People of God, from the rising of the sun even to its going down, join together in this worship! Let all men of good will be with us! This is indeed the day that the Lord has made! *Agnus redemit oves* — the Lamb has ransomed the sheep. . . . This is the day on which the eternal battle was decided: *mors et vita duello conflixere mirando* — life and death have fought a marvelous duel! A struggle between life and death goes on even from the beginning. The battle between good and evil goes on in the world. Today the balance rises on one side: Life has got the upper hand! Good has got the better of it. Christ Crucified has risen from the tomb; he has shifted the balance in favor of Life.

Death has its limits. Christ has opened up a great hope: the hope of Life beyond the sphere of death.

Dux vitae mortuus regnat vivus — the lord of life, having died, reigns alive! Paschal Victim, you know all the names of evil better than anyone else can possibly mention and list them. You embrace all victims together with you!

Paschal Victim! Crucified Lamb! Redeemer! Even though, in the story of man, of individuals, of families, of society, finally of mankind as a whole, evil were disproportionately developed, the skyline of good were darkened, still it would not overcome You!

Christ Resurrected dies no more! Even though evil gained power in the history of man and the times in which we live; even though we could not see your return to the world, a world where man might live in peace and justice, a world of social love, even though, humanly, the transition were not to be seen, even though the powers of darkness and the forces of evil raged, You, Paschal Victim, Spotless Lamb, Redeemer, have already gained the victory. *And you have made it our victory!* The paschal content of the life of your people.

April 17

The Risen Christ, Conqueror of Death

Today we glorify Christ — the Paschal Victim — as *Conqueror of Death.* We glorify today that Power which gained victory over death and accomplished the Gospel of the works and Words of Christ with the definitive testimony of Life!

And today we glorify the Holy Spirit by virtue of whom He was conceived in the womb of the Virgin, with the power of whose unction He passed through the suffering, the death, and the descent into the netherworld, and with whose power he lives! "And death has no more power over him." Christ Risen was to pass through the locked door of the Cenacle, where the apostles were gathered; he was to stand among them and say, "Peace be with you. . . . Receive the Holy Spirit."

With these words, with this divine breath, he was to inaugurate the new age: the time of the descent of the Holy Spirit, the time of the birth of the Church. That was to be the time of Pentecost. It was, however, already inscribed, with all its fullness, in the paschal feast, and is rooted in it. . . .

May thoughts of peace win. May respect for life win. Easter brings the message of life liberated from death. May thought and programs for the safeguarding of human life against death win, and not the illusions of those who see progress for man in the right to inflict death on life just conceived.

April 18

Christ Risen Has Conquered Death

"You are looking for Jesus of Nazareth, the one who was crucified. He has been raised up, he is not here." (*Mk* 16:6). "The right hand of the Lord has struck with power" (*Ps* 118:16).

The centuries make pilgrimage to that place "where they laid him" (*Mk* 16:6). The generations halt before the empty tomb, as the first witnesses once did. This year more than ever, let us go on pilgrimage to Christ's tomb. Let us return to the earliest words proclaimed to the Pious Women, the words in which the paschal message was developed.

Redemption begins from the Cross and is achieved in the Resurrection. "*Agnus redemit oves, Christus innocens Patri reconciliavit peccatores*" — "The Lamb redeemed the sheep, Christ the innocent reconciled sinners to the Father."

So, *man was snatched from death* and restored to life.

So, *man is snatched from sin,* and restored to Love.

You all, who, everywhere, go on in the darkness of death, hear! Christ has conquered sin on his Cross and in his Resurrection. *Submit to his power!*

World of today! Submit yourself to his power! The more you find the old structures of sin in you, the more you see the horror of death rising on the horizon of your history, so much the more submit to his power!

O Christ, who heard our human world from the Cross, the world of yesterday, the world of tomorrow: the old world of sin, make it become new in your Resurrection; make it become new, through every heart of man visited by the power of the Resurrection.

April 19

In the Joy of the Risen Christ

Rejoice in this paschal season at Christ the Lord's victory over death.

The victory of life, the victory of good over evil. It is from this Christian certainty of the victory over every fear of death that your march toward a juster and more human future should take its steps: a future of liberty for God's children. In the joy of the Risen Christ, in the certainty of his victory — which is that of everyone who believes in him — you are called to set your thoughts going: on mature and lucid acceptance of reality, reconciliation and hence alliance among yourselves, with adults and with society in its manifold aspects.

Such an alliance with reality, such adherence to it, so as to improve it and alter it, causes a *new creativity* to be loosed from your minds, based on perspicacious analysis of situations, forces and mechanisms at work; and finally, on happy recovery of the commitment to liberate, to save, to promote.

As you accomplish this undertaking, it is necessary to bear in mind above all that the deepest level of the alliance with reality, its very foundation, is found in the Alliance with God, in reconciliation with him. If man finds in God that vital reunion with the roots of his own being, of his own harmony and his own unification, he holds the key to overcoming every form of fear, hence the key to liberation and fresh creation: "Behold, I make all things new."

Listen to "the words of this fundamental alliance with the Lord," in Christ Jesus and in the Church, his Mystical Body.

April 20

The Church, Witness of the Resurrection

O Risen Christ, in your glorified wounds receive all the painful wounds of contemporary man: those of which so much is said by the media; of social communications; also those which silently throb in secrecy hidden in hearts. May they be tended in the mystery of your Redemption. May they be cicatrized and closed up through Love, which is stronger than death.

In this Mystery: We are with you, who suffer want and hunger, sometimes witnessing the agony of children calling for food. We are with you, the ranks of millions of refugees, driven from your homes, exiles in your own countries.

We are with you, all you victims of terror, shut up in prisons or concentration camps, worn out by ill treatment or tortures. We are with you who have been abducted. We are with you, who live in the nightmare of daily threats of violence and civil wars. We are with you who are suffering unexpected calamities. . . .

We are with you, families who pay for your faith in Christ by suffering discrimination or having to give up studies and careers for your children. We are with you, parents trembling at the spiritual travail or certain errors of your children. We are with you, young people, who are discouraged at not finding work, housing and the social dignity to which you aspire.

We are with you, who suffer from ill health, age, solitude. We are with you who are bewildered by anguish and doubt, and ask light for your minds and peace for your hearts. We are with you who feel the weight of sin and call upon the grace of Christ the Redeemer.

April 21

The Church Shares Easter with All

In this Mystery of the Resurrection, we are with you. With you who have given fresh drive to resolves for Christian living, by throwing yourselves into the merciful arms of Christ. We are with you, the converted. the newly baptized, who have discovered the call of the Gospel.

We are with you, who are trying to get over barriers of distrust with gestures of goodness, reconciliation within families and societies. We are with you, men of labor and of culture, who wish to be evangelical leaven in the environments where you operate.

We are with you, souls consecrated to Christ, and especially with you who spend yourselves, in mission lands above all, to bring the brethren the good news of faith in Christ, you who, in the midst of oppression often concealed or ignored, enrich the Church by praying in silence, bearing with patience, invoking pardon and conversion for those who persecute you. We are with you, men of good will of every stock and every continent, who, in whatever way, feel the attraction of Christ and his teaching.

We are with all the dolorous wounds of contemporary humanity, and we are with all the expectations, the hopes, the joys of our brethren, to which Christ Risen gives meaning and value. . . .

The Church shares the Easter message with all brethren in Christ and all people in the world . . . in particular where oppression of conscience does not permit praying together and celebration. . . .

April 22

The Prayer to Our Lady of Jasna Gora

"Rejoice, O Queen of Heaven, enjoy, O angelic Lady! Today we all congratulate you, with joy we sing: Alleluia, for your Son has risen. . . ."

That is the *Regina coeli laetare"* . . . I join with you, dear compatriots, who are singing with your hearts to the Mother of Christ at Jasna Gora and in so many other places of our native land.

With this song I also express the joy of the Resurrection of the Lord, greater than any trial or suffering at all. It is difficult not to rejoice when we see that, even in the midst of suffering, many people share in this Good, find it again, or deepen their union with it.

I hear from many sides what is occurring now in the

hearts of many Poles. From among the many voices which reach me, I will quote that of the Polish episcopate: "The Bishops, together with the whole of society, expect that the state of war shall end as soon as possible, that the interned shall be released, that an amnesty be granted to those who were condemned by reason of the state of war, that those in hiding be assured of the possibility of showing themselves, and that no one be dismissed from work because enrolled in a union."

I quote these words, and I make them my own. . . .

I direct them to you, dear compatriots, before the Mother of the Risen One, together with the words of our *"Regina coeli. . . ."*

"Rejoice, and enjoy in heaven . . . *Pray the Lord for us in our need!"* Alleluia.

April 23

St. Adalbert, Bishop and Martyr

St. Adalbert was of Slav origin: his baptismal name was "Woitech," which means "a consolation to the army." His earliest training derived from the spirituality of Cyril and Methodius, was radiated in Bohemia from neighboring Greater Moravia. Subsequently, such spirituality was joined in his person with that of the West, represented in his time by the Cluniac movement, deriving from St. Benedict. These were "two differing forms of culture, but were profoundly complementary to each other at the same time." The Benedictine culture was "more logical and rational," that of the Holy Greek Brethren was "more mystic and intuitive." They went together then; they ought to go together now, in the form of that mutuality, for maintaining and reinforcing the spiritual and cultural unity of Europe.

St. Adalbert is the model of the intellectual become a bishop, evangelizer and reformer, who, in total giving of his own life, attains to martyrdom for Christ's sake. He was full of mercy for all, but he was also swift to defend with force the dignity and the rights of every man against the oppressions and vexations of the powerful. He is also an example of how to set oneself to true reconciliation among men and Christians.

Whence did he derive this grand light and spiritual strength? From two sources, which he could not separate: profound thirst for study, contemplation and austere living on the one hand and absolute fidelity to the Church and the Supreme Pontiff on the other. The moves which he made during his life are themselves clear testimony of this twofold movement of his spirit between missionary activity and contemplative quiet near the Vicar of Christ at Rome, where he lived several years, in a monastery on the Aventine.

Once back in Bohemia, he gave powerful drive to the radiation of Christianity toward the East.

April 24

The Resurrection Shows the Mission of Christians

"Jesus came and stood before them. 'Peace be with you,' he said. . . . *"As the Father has sent me, so I send you."* The apostles were sent out with the same mission with which Christ was sent to earth by the Father. They were sent out to all the world, to announce the Gospel of peace.

Only they? The Second Vatican Council teaches that the whole People of God is called *to participate in Christ's mission:* of Christ, Priest, Prophet, and King.

"As the Father has sent me, so I send you." He breathed on them and said, "Receive the Holy Spirit." Have you received the Holy Spirit? Have you "accepted" him? Do you know well what *receiving and accepting* the Spirit means? Remember particularly the Sacraments of Baptism, of Confirmation, of Penance, of the Eucharist, in which the gift of the Spirit is conferred or increased. You therefore have to bear in mind that they are exactly *paschal sacraments;* they take us back to the Cenacle to those words of Christ in particular. And remember again that the Spirit is a gift — prayer is always necessary for obtaining it. With prayer, too, we dispose ouselves to *accepting it properly.* The Spirit is actually given to us for active sharing in the Resurrection of Christ.

"Since you have been raised up in company with Christ, *set your hearts on what pertains to higher realms (Col* 3:1). At the very center of the mission which Christ received from the Father is found the new man: *the man open to the Father.* The man "open to the Father" means the man who lives in the full dimension of his humanity. That "set your hearts on . . . higher realms" is written in the very structure of man, who lives in the full dimension of his humanity only when he is capable of *surpassing himself with the power of truth and love.*

April 25

St. Mark the Evangelist

When we speak of "evangelical leaven," our thoughts turn of themselves toward St. Mark, whose feast it is today, and his Gospel. As we know, the Gospel which he wrote particularly brings out the contrast between Christ who pardons (2:10), overcomes demons (1:24–27), heals the sick (1:31), and those men who jeer at him (5:40) and desire his ruin (3:36). In this "scandalous" contrast Mark sees the guiding line of God's activity, for in that way he surprises people and induces them to question themselves about Christ's identity ("Who is he?" 4:41). That was how he prepared them, through the very experience of their humiliation, for the act of faith in his saving mission. "Truly this man was the Son of God" is the confession which the centurion came to at the foot of the Cross.

How can we fail to see all this as a clear indication for whoever wishes to follow Christ's footsteps and become *a testifier of him in the contemporary world*? Meekness in the face of opposition and clashes, dominion over the passions and the forces of evil, and commitment to alleviating every form of suffering — these are concrete modes whereby the Christian can himself provoke a query about Christ in people of today as well, for hearts to be disposed to accepting his message.

In that way he will be able to work effectively for the coming of God's kingdom and construction of the earthly City, in coherence with the Christian vision of the world and of history, which is not reconciliable with ideologies and movements inspired by materialism.

April 26

The Mother of Good Counsel

Mater Boni Consilii — Mother of Good Counsel. You who profess a special devotion to the Mother of God under the beautiful title by which you often call upon her . . . may you obtain help and comfort from her for your renewed resolves to tighten the bonds of the common life and, exactly by reason of that interior strengthening of roots, to project that life out to the whole ecclesiastical community, beyond it as well.

May we above all obtain from her that higher "counsel" which is discernment and sagacity in decisions, but even more the individualization of the increased spiritual needs of our age, vision of social and human reality in the light of the Gospel, and consequently courage to give adequate responses to these needs and that vision.

O Mother of Jasna Gora, I am, O Mother, all yours, and everything mine is yours! All that is mine, so also my homeland, my nation.

O Mother, I have been called to serve the Universal Church on the Chair of St. Peter at Rome. Thinking of this universal service, I constantly repeat, "*Totus tuus* — wholly yours." I desire to be the servant of all! At the same time, I am a son of this land and this nation. This is my nation. This is my fatherland.

Mother, everything that is mine is yours! What more can I say to you? In what other way entrust this land, this people, this heritage, to You? I confide them to you just as I can.

You are the Mother. You will understand and will accept.

April 27

The Resurrection Points to Transformation of Christians

It is exactly for this end that we receive the Holy Spirit, that the power of truth and love may form our interior life and make it radiate outwardly as well.

Formation of such a person is, at the same time, the prime task, the *prime mission* of each of us. To the gift, therefore, which comes from on high and calls us upward, there ought to be a response, that of our will, that is, our personal cooperation.

Other tasks follow from that. Only after we have had such "transformation" through the power of truth itself, and of love, should *transformation of the world* be attempted. This is a process beginning from the personal dimension and going toward the community dimension. Transforming the world means, for the Christian, being *open to the Father,* being *formed in the Spirit;* it means committing oneself responsibly to elevating and enriching, through one's own giving, all the reality and the communities with which one comes into contact: the family above all, then the world of our friends, the world of school, the world of work, the world of culture, social life, the life of the nation.

This is a hard task, certainly; it is a difficult task, but it is not beyond the energies of the young. In fact, the characteristics and qualities, that is, "the particular cultural, political and economic relief within the nation," then call for Christian values: loyalty to proverbial honesty, fidelity to pledges undertaken and the given word, the sacredness of the family, hard working and generosity toward the poor. These all objectively make up a precious heritage. . . . These were and are the characteristics of the parents; they have certainly passed to the children, spontaneously, as it were, by hereditary transmission.

It is the first positive response to the pledge to live according to the dimension of the Spirit and to contribute from the wealth of this gift to transformation of the world.

April 28

The Resurrection Points to the Real Humanism

Why did Christ speak of *remission of sins* immediately after uttering the words, "Receive the Holy Spirit"? He said, "If you forgive men's sins, they are forgiven them; if you hold them bound, they are held bound" (*Jn* 20:23). Remission of sins supposes knowledge and confession of sins. One and the other signify *the effort to live in truth and love*. It means the action of "the power of truth and love," which forms the new man and transforms the world.

The contradiction is *falsification* of the truth and *simulation* of love. Contradiction is obliteration of the line of demarcation between good and evil, it means calling humanism what is actually "sin." It would be far too easy, unfortunately, to give examples in this connection. Terrorism is rightly condemned today as an attack upon and violation of the elementary rights of man. Killing of man is condemned as something manifestly contrary to man's very existence. At the same time, however, depriving a human being *not yet born* of life is called "humanism"; it is considered to be a "proof of progress," of emancipation, even in conformity with human dignity!

Let us not deceive ourselves! We all have to take note of, denounce, overcome similar contradictions. Remember that only *"the truth will set you free"* (Jn 8:32). Only the truth has the power to *transform the world* in the direction of authentic progress and real "humanism." And let us not call the demands of truth, conscience and dignity a purely "political" choice. Those are supreme demands; therefore man may not renounce them.

My friends! Christ comes to the cenacles of our times too, and he says to you as well: Receive the Holy Spirit! What does that mean? It means, on one hand, that *we live in a risk situation.* But it also means, on the other hand, that *Christ has confidence in you.*

April 29

St. Catherine of Siena, Doctor of the Church

We look at St. Catherine today above all to admire in her what at once struck those who came close to her: *her extraordinarily rich humanity.* This was by no means obscured but rather was *increased and perfected by grace.* This made her, as it were, a living image of that veracious, healthy Christian "humanism," the fundamental law of which was formulated by St. Catherine's fellow Dominican and teacher, St. Thomas Aquinas. His aphorism is well known: "Grace does not suppress, but supposes and perfects nature." A human with complete dimensions is one who acts in the grace of Christ. . . .

So, our saint had a woman's nature, abundantly endowed with fantasy, intuition, sensibility, volitional and operative vigor, capacity for and power of communication, readiness to give herself in service. She was transfigured, not impoverished, in the light of Christ who called her to be his bride and to identify mystically with him in the depths of "interior knowledge," to commit herself likewise in charitable action, social, and even political action, among the great and the small, the rich and the poor, the learned and the ignorant. She, almost illiterate, became able to make herself heard, to read, to be held in consideration by rulers of cities and realms, by princes and prelates of the Church, by monks and theologians, by many of whom she was actually venerated, as "teacher" and "mother."

She was a prodigious woman. In that second half of the fourteenth century she showed of what a human creature is capable.

I insist — a woman, the daughter of humble dyers, showed how she could hearken to the voice of the one Shepherd and Teacher and nourish herself at the table of the Divine Spouse, to whom, as a "wise virgin," she generously consecrated her life.

This was a masterpiece of grace, renewing and elevating the creature to perfection of holiness, which is also full realization of the fundamental values of humanity. . . . If people of today, especially Christians, managed to rediscover the marvels to be known and enjoyed in the "interior cell," indeed in the heart of Christ! Then would man find himself again, and the reasons for his dignity, the basis of all his values, the height of his eternal vocation!

April 30

St. Pius V

Pius V . . . was born Antonio Ghislieri, and he sat upon the Chair of Saint Peter from 1566 till 1572. He is especially known as "the Pope of the Rosary" by reason of the impulse he gave through his example and teaching to the spread of this devotion, so dear to the heart of the Christian people. . . .

Dearly beloved, the truest and most sincere wish I can offer you is only this: "Turn yourselves into saints, make yourselves holy soon," and I repeat the words of St. Paul to the Thessalonians: "May the God of peace make you perfect in holiness. May he preserve you whole and entire, spirit, soul, and body irreproachable at the coming of our Lord Jesus Christ" (*1 Thes* 5:23).

Let us be glad to live in these times of ours, and let us courageously commit ourselves to the design which Providence is mysteriously accomplishing. . . .

John XXIII said that "the surpassing personage that was St. Pius V is linked with great trials that the Church had to bear in times much more difficult than ours."

St. Pius teaches us as well to have recourse to Mary Most Holy in our difficulties, for she is our heavenly Mother; she has overcome every error and every heresy. Let us pray to her always; let us pray to her especially with the Holy Rosary so that our sole and supreme ideal may ever be the salvation of souls.

May

May 1

St. Joseph the Worker

The Church venerates Joseph of Nazareth as a worker, an artisan, perhaps a carpenter by calling.

He was the one and only workingman among all those who have been on earth at whose workbench Jesus Christ, Son of God and Son of Man, labored every day.

Joseph himself had taught Him the work of his calling, set Him to it, showed Him how to overcome the difficulties arising from the resistance of the material, to draw works of human craftsmanship out from formless matter. *He, Joseph of Nazareth, linked the Son of God to human labor once and for all.*

Thanks to him, Christ Himself also belongs to the world of labor and He testifies to its most lofty dignity in God's eyes. . . .

The world entrusted by the Creator to man as a task always and everywhere on earth and in every society and nation is "the world of work."

"World of work" means at the same time *"human world."* The Church. . . . is sent to this world because "God so loved the world that He gave His only Son" (*Jn* 3:16). That happened and was accomplished over thirty years in Joseph's house at Nazareth.

May . . . the serenity of the modest workshop of Nazareth . . . ever reign in your workplaces . . . the serenity making human labor a factor for growth and giving it the dimension of a fruitful vocation. . . .

The Lord . . . is always with you at your workbenches, to give all the regnerative power of His Gospel, of His Grace and of His love.

Never ignore Him!

Never put Him aside!

May 2

To Jesus through Mary

Ad Iesum per Mariam.

When greeting Mary, Elizabeth in no way separated Mother and Son. Rather did she associate them intimately, for she added *"and blest is the fruit of your womb."* So, we too must address ourselves to the Lord Jesus with the readiness of lively faith, with the force of ardent love. The content of the expression, *"Ad Iesum per Mariam —* "to Jesus through Mary" — must be shown to be true for us too, that is, that it is really fact. . . .

Let us reflect: What is the meaning of Mary's presence in that house in the hill country of Judea? Was she there only through kindness and thoughtful concern for her kinswoman who had "conceived a son in her old age"? Was it a purely human act of assistance? No. That was a much more significant and spiritually fruitful presence, because Mary brought her cousin the incomparable gifts of grace, of joy and of light, associating the future Precursor with this bearing of gifts to his mother. The moment Mary's greeting sounded in her ears, the old woman not only felt the child leap in her womb but was also filled with the Holy Spirit and felt strengthened, indeed enthusiastic, in her reply to the greeting. Nor was that all: through illumination of that Spirit who had penetrated her, she above all acquired the superior capacity to see the very Mother of her Lord in her young cousin.

May 3

The Feast of Mary and Jasna Gora

Today's feast invites us to think . . . in a particular way. Jasna Gora is a particular sign of the presence, of the maternal presence of the Mother of God among us. We recall this today because it is the third of May . . . marking 600 years of Her presence among us in the image of Jasna Gora.

So we all make a pilgrimage to this image in our hearts and also try to make a pilgrimage there along the roads of our lives. I think of my pilgrimage to Jasna Gora; I have been thinking of it for some time. I desire to accomplish it. I consider this to be a duty for me, a duty of the heart, the duty of a son toward the Mother. Toward Her and my nation. I am morally committed to be with my compatriots at the feet of Our Lady of Jasna Gora. . . . I also think that adequate conditions for this ought to be created and I count upon it in the name of the prestige of Poland and in the name of the honor of a nation a thousand years old.

Dearest brothers and sisters . . . let us feel as if we were present spiritually at Jasna Gora and let us all live the mystery of the holy place, all the eloquence of that image, of that motherhood, which was given for defense of our nation. For maternity is always for life, in defense of life.

May 4

Mary, Queen of Poland

So it is that we look at events near and far through the prism of these eternal words, uttered from the height of the Cross. Through the prism of these words, a man was entrusted to the Mother of God as Her son. We all feel entrusted to Mary in that singular man. We therefore live with consciousness of this trust in the Mother of God, with the whole nation, not only each on his own but also as a great community.

We feel embraced by these words: "There is your son." We feel that we are children, and we consider her our Mother. And let us extend this maternity of Hers to all generations, to all occurrences, far and near. Let us read the signs of her motherhood in the development of those occurrences, which have never ceased to be full of hope for us, even with the difficulties involved. Such signs remain ours! They continue to be ours because we have the Mother. Motherhood is the source of identity for each of us. Man's first right is to be descended directly from motherhood.

And so, this singular motherhood of Mary's, transmitted one time to the Evangelist and Apostle John, then extended to so many people and to entire nations, to our nation above all, gives us *a particular sense of identity*.

May 5

The Virginal Maternity of Mary

The whole of Christ's life, from the beginning, was a discreet but clear separation from what so deeply determined the meaning of the body in the Old Testament. Almost in contradiction of all the expectations of the Old Testament tradition, Christ was born of Mary. She said clearly of herself at the moment of the Annunciation: "How can this be since I do not know man." That is, she professed her virginity.

And Mary's motherhood is virginal, even though Jesus was born of her as every other human being, like a son from his mother, even though this coming of His into the world was accompanied by the presence of a man who was the spouse of Mary and in the eyes of the law and of men, her husband. To this virginal motherhood of Mary corresponds the virginal mystery of Joseph, who followed the voice from on high, and did not hesitate to take Mary because "it is by the Holy Spirit that she has conceived this child." So the virginal conception and the birth to the world of Jesus were concealed from men. In the eyes of his fellow townsmen at Nazareth he was regarded as "the son of the carpenter" (*"ut putabatur filius Joseph"*) — as he was thought, the son of Joseph.

If spite of all that, the reality and essential truth of his conception and birth depart in themselves from what in the Old Testament was exclusively in favor of matrimony and rendered what actually happened incomprehensible and socially disfavored.

May 6

Mary's Maternity and Marriage

The story of the birth of Jesus is certainly in line with revelation of that "continence for the kingdom of heaven" of which Christ was one day to speak to His disciples. But that event remained concealed to men of those days and even to the disciples. Only gradually was it revealed to the eyes of the Church, on the basis of the testimonies and texts of the Gospels of Matthew and Luke. In the marriage of Mary and Joseph the Church honors Joseph as spouse of Mary and Mary as his spouse. The marriage at the same time holds concealed within itself the mystery of perfect communion of persons, of Man and of Woman, in the conjugal pact, together with the mystery of that *singular "continence for the kingdom of heaven."* In the history of the salvation, this continence has served to perfect *"the fecundity of the Holy Spirit."* Indeed, it was in a certain sense the absolute plenitude of that spiritual fecundity. This was because it was exactly in the conditions of the pact between Mary and Joseph at Nazareth, in matrimony and in continence, that the gift of the incarnation of the Eternal Word was realized. The Son of God, consubstantial with the Father, was conceived and was born as Man from the Virgin Mary. The grace of the Hypostatic Union is connected exactly with this, I would say, absolute plenitude of the supernatural fecundity, fruitfulness in the Holy Spirit, participated in by a human creature, Mary, in the order of "continence for the kingdom of heaven."

May 7

Virginal Maternity and Continence

A certain image was to be revealed gradually to the conscience of the Church through ever new generations of confessors of Christ, when — together with the infancy Gospel — certainty of the Virgin's divine motherhood was consolidated in them, that she had conceived through the Holy Spirit. Even if only in an indirect way — yet in an essential and fundamental way — such certainty was to help comprehension. On the one hand, comprehension of the holiness of matrimony and, on the other hand, of disinterest in prospect of "the kingdom of heaven," of which Christ had spoken to His disciples.

Nonetheless, when he spoke of it to them the first time (as the evangelist Matthew attests in chapter 19:10-12), that great mystery of his conception and his birth was completely unknown to them; it was hidden from them, as it was hidden from all hearers and questioners of Jesus of Nazareth. When Christ spoke of those who are made eunuchs for the kingdom of heaven, the disciples could understand it *only on the basis of personal example*. Such continence was to be imprinted on their consciences as a particular trait of likeness to Christ, because He had remained unmarried "for the sake of God's reign." In the tradition of the Old Alliance, matrimony and procreative fecundity "in the body" had been a religiously privileged condition. Detachment from such tradition was to be effected above all on the basis of the example of Christ Himself.

May 8

Blessed among Women

"Benedicte tu inter mulieres — blessed are you among women."

This stirring Marian greeting repeats and causes to re-echo through the centuries those words which Elizabeth uttered "filled with the Holy Spirit . . . in a loud voice" to the Virgin Mother of God. This greeting, dearest brothers and sisters, seems to me to be particularly appropriate . . . to honor and celebrate Mary Most Holy on the day which records the event of her apparition to the humble Bernadette, there at the grotto of Massabielle, to entrust her with a special message of mercy and grace. And who could affirm that that message does not keep its full value right down to our time?

Mary made use of that unknown little girl with the intention above all of bringing sinners to conversion, asking for them and for their salvation commitment on the part of the community of all faithful Christians. It is a fact that her appeal aroused a fervent movement of prayer and charity, in service to the infirm and the poor above all.

I have . . . many brothers and sisters . . . who are tried by pain and suffering. . . . You are in the front . . . dearest ill people, because an irreplaceable role has been assigned to you in the economy of salvation, in union with Him who is protagonist and artificer of salvation through His passion, death, and resurrection: Jesus Christ, our Redeemer and Lord.

May 9

My Being Proclaims the Greatness of the Lord

When the Virgin was proclaimed blessed together with "the fruit of your womb" and proclaimed blessed for having believed, she replied, "yes," but then *changed the person whom she addressed,* for she began to speak to the Lord, and raised a marvellous song of praise to Him in her lowliness of a servant. The *Magnificat* is the real Song of Songs of the New Testament, resounding on our lips daily, brethren. Let us try to intone it with particular fervor . . . so that, in spiritual union with Mary, we may repeat it with her word for word, almost syllable by syllable, and so learn from her how and why we too ought to bless the Lord.

She teaches us that God alone is great and therefore ought to be called magnificent by us. He alone saves us, therefore our spirits should exult in Him. He bows toward us with His mercy and raises us to Him through His power. Grand, indeed, and lofty is the lesson of the *Magnificat.* Each of us can and should make it his and her own, in all conditions of life, to attain comfort and serenity — beyond the gifts of grace and light — even in trials brought by tribulations and in the sufferings of the body itself.

May this be a source of consolation and peace also for you, sick brethren, and may it bear you up in your prayers and in oblation of your sufferings.

May 10

Entrusting the Church to Mary, Mother of God

"O Mother of men and peoples, You know all their sufferings and their hopes, You maternally feel all their struggles between good and evil, between the light and the darkness which shake the world. Receive our cry, directed in the Holy Spirit straight to Your Heart and, with the love of the Mother and Handmaid of the Lord, embrace the individuals and peoples which most look for this embrace, together with the individuals and peoples to whose trust You attend in a particular way. Take the entire human family under Your maternal protection. With outflows of affection, O Mother, we entrust it to You. May the time of peace and liberty approach for all, the time of truth, justice, and hope."

These words were uttered on Pentecost Day . . . in the Basilica of St. Mary Major, in connection with the anniversaries of the great ecumenical Councils of Constantinople and Ephesus. I repeated them once again on the solemnity of the Immaculate Conception.

The words quoted above are to be found in the act of entrustment of the Church to Mary, for the sake of her mission in the contemporary world.

May 11

Entrusting the World to Mary

The Second Vatican Council renewed in us consciousness of the Church and her mission and also consciousness of a particular relationship between the Church and the contemporary world.

This conciliar program of renewal leads me to add a particular act of entrustment of the contemporary world to the act of entrustment of the Church to the Mother of God and the Mother of the Church which I pronounced last year.

I desire to make reference in this way to the act which Pope Pius XII performed forty and thirty years ago and which was recalled also by Pope Paul VI, when he proclaimed Mary "Mother of the Church" on the occasion of the closure of the third session of the Council.

The contemporary world is threatened in various ways. It is perhaps threatened more than it has been at any other time in the course of history. So it is necessary for the Church to wake and watch at the feet of Him who is the Sole Lord of history and Prince of the age to come. I therefore desire *to watch and wake together with the whole Church,* raising a cry to the Heart of the Immaculate Mother.

I invite all to join with me in spirit.

May 12

Toward an Anniversary

The pilgrimage to Fatima, in Portugal, where ... the anniversary of the Virgin's first apparition, in distant 1917 ... is also the anniversary of a happening of particular meaning for me....

I am going to meet the generous sons and daughters of Portugal. I am moved by desire to give testimony of my esteem and my affection, and, at the same time, "to communicate some spiritual gift to them, that they may be strengthened." I go in particular as a pilgrim of fraternity and peace on earth to the land which the Virgin chose for launching her heartfelt appeal to the world for *prayer, conversion* and *penitence*.

Actually it is not only to express my gratitude to Our Lady that I am going on pilgrimage to Fatima. I go to that blessed place also to hear anew, in the name of the whole Church, the message which resounded 65 years ago on the lips of the Common Mother, concerned for the fate of her children. That message reveals itself to be more current and urgent today than ever. How can we not feel troubled by the spread of secularism and of permissiveness, which are such a grave menace to the fundamental values of Christian moral norms?

May 13

The Great Divine Test

Praised be Jesus Christ!

Dearest brothers and sisters. I know that you are united with me in these days and especially at the hour of recitation of the *"Regina Coeli."*

I thank you with emotion for your prayers and I bless you all. I feel particularly near the two persons wounded together with me. *I pray for the brother who struck me and whom I have sincerely pardoned.*

In union with Christ, Priest and Victim, I offer my sufferings up for the Church and for the world. To You, Mary, I repeat: *Totus tuus ego sum* — I am totally yours.

May 14

Fatima

I am in Portugal to realize a dream which I have long held dear, as a man of the Church and as one desiring to get to know Fatima directly. . . . I am here today thanks be to God "rich in mercy." This pilgrimage of mine has a dominant motive: Fatima. I will first follow a Marian itinerary, through Vila Vicosa, Sameiro, then the "City of the Virgin." On the way to Fatima and on the way back, I will bear Our Lady's canticle of thanksgiving in my heart, for having had my life saved by God. . . . I repeat, in an attitude of adoration: "My being proclaims the greatness of the Lord, my spirit finds you in God my savior. . . ."

But, since I cannot evangelize unless there are those to be evangelized, I here render homage to the lively, dynamic Church which is identified with the majority of the Portuguese population, and which has known how to maintain its option for Christ, over the centuries, *with fidelity to the Redeemer of mankind* — who is here venerated above all in the mysteries of His Passion and His Eucharist — with devotion to Our Lady, who will be proclaimed Queen and Patroness of Portugal, in adherence to the Apostolic See of Rome, and by giving the world Saints of the importance of St. Anthony of Lisbon. I also render homage to this universal Saint.

May 15

The Apparitions at Fatima

Praised be our Lord Jesus Christ! and his Mother, Mary Most Holy!

Yes, with Her and through Her the supplication, so often prayed and sung here breaks at this moment from out of my heart: "My God, I believe, I adore, I hope in and love You!"

This first thought of adoration of mine to be manifested in this blessed land of Fatima is addressed to the Most Holy Trinity: Blessed be *God,* rich in mercy, for the great love with which He has loved us! In fact, we were created in His Word, the *Son,* and reconciled by means of the blood of the same Son, we became a family, and were erected on the foundation of the apostles in the building (the Church), so as to become God's dwelling by means of the *Holy Spirit,* so we ought to repeat ceaselessly: "My God, I believe, I adore, I hope in and love you!"

Ave Maria! — Hail Mary!

Blessed are you and blessed is the fruit of your womb, Jesus! Hail, full of grace, Mother of God and Our Mother! In accomplishment of your prophecy, O Lady, here, as I enter this your dwelling of Fatima, and as I greet you, adored Mother, permit me to use the words which You taught us, to proclaim before the brethren: "My being proclaims the greatness of the Lord, my spirit finds you in God my savior. . . ."

May 16

The Holy Father's Thanks to Fatima

Gratitude, communion, life! These three words contain the explanation of my presence here on this day. And, if you will permit me, the explanation of your presence too.

Here I touch upon the culminating point of my journey in Portugal. I want to tell you something in confidence: I had already long had the intention to come to Fatima, as I had occasion to say on my arrival at Lisbon. But, ever since the well-known attempt on my life in St. Peter's Square, on regaining consciousness, my thought turned immediately to this Shrine, to put *my thanksgiving there, in the heart of the celestial Mother,* for having saved me from the peril.

In everything that was happening I saw — I do not weary of repeating this — a special maternal protection of the Madonna. And in the coincidence — there are no simple coincidences in the designs of Divine Providence — I saw an appeal as well, and, who knows, a recalling of attention to the message which began from here 65 years ago, through the means of three children, the son and daughters of humble country people, the little shepherds of Fatima, as they are universally known.

May 17

Gathered With Mary, The Mother of Jesus

It was "thanks to the Lord that I was not assassinated." I said that the first time on the occasion of the feast of the Virgin of the Rosary. I say it again now, at Fatima, which speaks to us so much of the Rosary — of recitation of the third part of the rosary — as the little shepherds were reciting. The Rosary, its third part — is and shall ever be a prayer of thanksgiving, of love and of confident entreaty, the prayer of the Mother of the Church!

I have come on pilgrimage to Fatima, like most of you, dear pilgrims, with the rosary beads in my hand, the name of Mary on my lips and the song of the mercy of God in my heart. "To me too He has done great things . . . His mercy is from age to age" (*Lk* 1:49-50).

Gratitude, communion, and life: these are sentiments which unite us, pilgrims "gathered here in the same place," we who form the present generation of the Church, for whom Pentecost has already occurred: gathered "with Mary, the Mother of Jesus," we wish to confirm our assiduity in respecting "the apostles' teaching, fraternal union, the breaking of bread and prayer. . . ."

May God will that tomorrow, on returning from our pilgrimage, after these hours of intimacy with Christ, with "the Father in heaven," and with Mary our Mother, and enlivened by the Holy Spirit, "poured out in our hearts" (*Rom* 5:5), we may set off with joy, "praising God and winning the approval of all the people" (*Acts* 2:47).

May 18

Bless Us, O Most Beloved Mother

You certainly know that I have cultivated the Christian practice of pilgrimage ever since my youth. On my apostolic journeys as Successor of Peter — from Mexico to Equatorial Guinea — visits to Marian shrines as a pilgrim have been some of the loftiest moments, from the personal point of view, of my encounters with the People of God spread over the earth, and with men and women, our brethren in the great human family. And it is always with emotion, the same emotion as on the first occasion, that I set in the hands of Mary Most Holy all the good that I may do and shall go on yet to do in service of Holy Church.

At this hour, here at the shrine of Fatima, I wish to repeat now, before you all, *totus tuus* — all yours, O Mother! I ask you to offer me and all these brethren up to the "Father of Mercies," in homage and gratitude, hiding and covering our poverty with your merits and those of your Divine Son. And may we be accepted, blessed and strengthened in our good resolves, which we wish to bind up, like a bunch of flowers, with a ribbon "woven and gilded" for you, O Mother: "Do whatever He tells you."

Give us your blessing, Lady, *our most beloved Mother!*

May 19

The Message of Fatima

"Be converted (do penance) and believe in the Gospel" are the first words of the Messiah addressed to mankind. The message of Fatima is, in its fundamental kernel, the call *to conversion and penitence,* as in the Gospel. This call was pronounced at the beginning of the twentieth century, so it was addressed to this century particularly. The Lady of the message seemed to read the "signs of the times" with special perspicacity, the signs of our time.

The call to penitence is a maternal appeal and, at the same time it is strong and decisive. That charity "which rejoices in the truth" knows how to be plain and decided. As always, the call to penance is linked with *the call to prayer.* In accordance with the tradition of many centuries, the Lady of the message of Fatima points to the Rosary. It may rightly be described as "the prayer of Mary," the prayer in which She feels particularly at one with us. With this prayer are embraced the problems of the Church, of the See of Peter, the problems of the whole world. Moreover, remembrance is made of sinners, for them to be converted and saved, and the souls in purgatory.

The words of the message were addressed to children aged from 7 to 10 years. Children, such as Bernadette of Lourdes, are particularly privileged in these apparitions of the Mother of God. Hence the fact that her language also is simple, to the measure of their powers of understanding. The children of Fatima became the interlocutors of the Lady of the message and her collaborators as well.

May 20

St. Bernardine of Siena

St. Bernardine was the inventor and propagator of the trigram IHS (Iesus). He had it painted on a tablet in gold, with rays all about it. He gave particular symbolic significance to those rays. By this means, Friar Bernardine spread devotion to the Most Holy Name of Jesus wherever he went. It had been practiced in monasteries and convents for centuries, but now it became a common good of the Christian people.

How I wish that celebration . . . of St. Bernardine may also, indeed above all, contribute to this aim: to bring back the name of Jesus to the doors and interiors of houses, as the sign of faith and Christian life of a family, in Italy and in other countries. I ask this of fathers and mothers of families, but also of young people, whom I esteem and love, young couples above all: Put the name of Jesus upon your houses. I repeat this request in the very words of St. Bernardine: "The name of Jesus, put it upon your houses, in your chambers and hold it in your hearts." In his time, St. Bernardine had the intuition that the mystery of Jesus, "the way, and the truth, and the life" (*Jn* 14:6), enclosed in his name, which means *salvation,* was the announcement which men needed, then as at all times. He therefore devoted himself to preaching the gospel under the holy sign: "refuge of the penitent, banner of the combatant, medicine of the languishing, comfort of the suffering, honor of believers, splendor of the evangelized, merit of the operators, aid of the inconstant, sigh of the meditative, satisfaction of the implorer, joy of the contemplative, glory of the triumphant."

May 21

The Meaning of Consecration to Mary

Consecrating oneself to Mary means helping Her to offer ourselves and mankind to Him Who is Holy, infinitely holy; it means letting oneself be aided by Her — by having recourse to Her Mother's Heart, opened beneath the cross to love for every person, for the whole world — to offer the world, and man, and mankind, and all nations, to Him Who is infinitely holy. God's holiness was manifested in the redemption of man, of the world, of the whole of mankind, of the nations: a redemption which occurred through the sacrifice of the Cross. "I consecrate myself for their sakes," Jesus said *(Jn* 17:19).

The world and man *were consecrated through the power of the redemption.* They were consecrated to Him who is infinitely holy. They were offered and confided to Love himself, to the merciful Love.

The Mother of Christ summons us and invites us to join with the Church of the living God *in this consecration of the world,* in this entrustment whereby the world, mankind, the nations, all individual people are offered to the Eternal Father through the power of the Redemption of Christ. They are offered up in the Heart of the Redeemer pierced on the Cross.

The Mother of the Redeemer calls us, asks us and aids us to join in this consecration, in entrustment of the world. Then indeed do we find ourselves as near as possible to the Heart of Christ pierced on the Cross.

May 22

St. Rita of Cascia

All know how the earthly journey of the saint of Cascia was articulated into various states of life, following one another chronologically, and — what is more important — arranged in ascending order, marking the various stages of development of her life of union with God.

Why is Rita a saint? Not so much by reason of the fame of the prodigies which popular devotion attributes to the effectiveness of her intercession with God almighty, as for the astonishing "normality" of her daily life, which she lived first as *wife* and *mother,* then as *widow* and finally as an *Augustinian nun.*

She was a spiritual daughter of St. Augustine. She put his teachings into practice without having read them in books. He had greatly recommended consecrated women "to follow the Lamb wherever he goes" and to "contemplate with interior sight the wounds of the Crucified, the scars of the Risen One, the blood of the Dying Man . . . weighing all on the balance of charity." He was obeyed *ad litteram* — to the letter — by Rita. Especially in her forty years of cloistered life, she showed the continuity and solidity of the contact which she had established with the divine victim of Golgotha.

Rita was indeed "the strong woman" and "the wise virgin" at the same time, those of whom Scripture tells us (*Prov* 31:IX; *Mt* 25:1-13). In all the states of her life she indicated, not only with words, the authentic path to sanctity, as a faithful follower of Christ even to the Cross. That is why I have willed to represent her sweet and suffering personality to all her devotees throughout the world, with the wish that, by taking inspiration from her, they will respond — each in his and her own state of life — to the Christian vocation, its demand for clarity, testimony and courage. *Sic luceat lux vestra coram hominibus* . . . — your light must shine before men . . . (*Mt* 5:16).

May 23

Mary, God's Humble Handmaid

As we give thanks to the Omnipotent, whose name is Holy, we too wish to raise up a hymn of our exultation together, because He has looked upon the lowliness of his servants.

The Blessed Virgin intoned the *Magnificat,* knowing that, to accomplish the plan of salvation for all mankind, the Lord willed to bring her, a humble maiden of His People, into association with it. We are here to intone our *Magnificat,* after the example of Mary, knowing that we have been summoned by God to a service of redemption and salvation, in spite of our inadequacy.

The grander the task to be achieved, the poorer the instruments called to collaborate with the divine plan. Because it is true that the power of God's arm is made evident by the weakness of the means employed, so it is also that, the smaller the human persons invited to serve, the greater the things which the Almighty is disposed to accomplish through our means. . . .

"The Almighty has done great things for me," Mary declared. She was fully aware of the greatness of her mission; but at the same time, she recognized herself to be and remained, "a lowly servant," attributing all the merit to God the Savior. The grandeur of the redemptive mission is accomplished in Mary through perfect accord between the divine omnipotence and humble human docility.

May 24

Mary, Mother of Mercy

Mary is also she who, in a particular and exceptional way — unlike any other — experienced mercy, and at the same time, always in an exceptional way, made her participation in the revelation of the divine mercy possible with sacrifice of heart. Such sacrifice is closely bound up with the cross of Her Son, at the foot of which she was to stand on Calvary. That sacrifice of hers was a singular participation in revelation of mercy, that is, of God's absolute fidelity to His own love, to the alliance which He had willed to make from all eternity and which He concluded in time with man, with the people, with mankind. It was participation in that revelation which was definitively accomplished through the cross.

No one has experienced the mystery of the cross as did the Mother of the Crucified — the astounding encounter between transcendent divine justice and love, that "kiss" which mercy gave to justice (*cf. Ps* 85:24). No one on the same level as you, Mary, has taken that mystery into the heart, that truly divine dimension of the redemption, which was actuated on Calvary through the death of the Son, together with sacrifice of your motherly heart, with your definitive *"fiat* — let it be done. . . ."

Mary is therefore she who knows the divine mercy most deeply. She knows the price, she knows how high it is. It is in this sense also that we also call her Mother of Mercy, Our Lady of Mercy, Mother of the Divine Mercy. Deep theological meaning lies in each of these titles, for they express her soul's particular preparation, that of all her personality, for knowing how to see that mercy in which one becomes a participant "from age to age" (*Lk* 1:50), according to the eternal design of the Most Holy Trinity.

May 25

In Honor of St. Gregory VII

Prayer to Mary for sacred vocations.
O Mary, Mother of God, Mother of the Church,
in this hour so meaningful for us,
we are one heart and one mind: as were Peter,
the Apostles, the brethren,
joined in prayer, with You, in the Cenacle.

We entrust to You our lives.
To You we all, one and all, repeat: *totus tuus ego sum.*
That You may take up our consecration,
and unite it with that of Jesus and Your own,
as oblation to God the Father, for the life of the world.

We pray You to look upon the needs of your
    children,
as you did at Cana, when You were touched to the
    heart
by that family's situation.
Today, the greatest need of this Your family

is for vocations — presbyteral, diaconal,
religious and missionary.

So, reach, with your "suppliant omnipotence"
the hearts of many of our brethren,
that they may listen, understand, respond to the voice
    of the Lord.
Repeat to them, in the depths of their consciences, the
    invitation
addressed to the servants at Cana: Do whatever Jesus
    tells you.

We shall be ministers of God and of the Church, vowed
to evangelize, sanctify, nourish our brethren: teach
us and give us the attitudes of the good shepherd;
feed and give increase to our apostolic dedication;
strengthen and ever regenerate our love for the
suffering; enlighten and enliven our resolves toward
virginity for the Kingdow of Heaven; infuse and
keep in us the sense of fraternity and communion.

May 26

St. Philip Neri

You know that, during the period of his life in Rome,
from 1534, when he came the first time as a poor and
unknown pilgrim, until 1595, the year of his blessed
death, Saint Philip Neri had a *most lively love for Rome!* He
lived, labored, studied, suffered, prayed, loved, died for
Rome! Rome he had in his mind and in his heart, in his
worries, in his projects, in his institutions, in his joy, and
also in his sorrows!

For Rome, St. Philip Neri was a man of culture and of charity, of study and of organization, of teaching and of prayer. For Rome, he was a holy priest, a tireless confessor, an igenious educator, and the friend of all. In a special way, he was an expert counsellor and delicate director of consciences. Popes, cardinals, bishops and priests, princes and politicians, religious and artists had recourse to him. Illustrious persons confided in his heart of a father and a friend, persons such as the historian Cesare Baronio, the celebrated composer Palestrina, St. Charles Borromeo, St. Ignatius Loyola, and Cardinal Federico Borromeo.

But that bare little room in his apartment was above all the goal of an immense multitude of persons belonging to the people, the suffering, the deprived, the marginal in society, boys and girls, who ran to him, to have a word of advice, pardon, peace, encouragement, material and spiritual aid.

He lived in a dramatic century, intoxicated by discoveries of human genius and classical and pagan art, but in radical crisis because of the change of mentality. St. Philip was a man of profound faith and a fervent priest, he was genial and farsighted, and was endowed with a special charisma: he was able to keep intact the deposit of truth received, and he transmitted it whole and pure, by living it entirely and announcing it without compromises.

This is why his message *is always topical* and we ought to hear it and follow his example.

May 27

Mary's Spiritual Motherhood

Jesus, dying on the cross, said to John, "There is your mother." From that moment, and from when "the disciple took her into his care," the mystery of *Mary's spiritual motherhood* has had its accomplishment in history with boundless amplitude. Motherhood means concern for the life of the child. Now, if Mary is the mother of all mankind, then her concern for the life of man *has universal extension.* A mother's concern embraces the whole man. Mary's maternity has its beginning in her maternal care for Christ. In Christ, she accepted John beneath the cross, and, in him, *she accepted every human and all humanity.* Mary embraces all with a particular solicitude in the Holy Spirit. In fact, as we profess in our Creed, it is He who "gives life. . . ."

Mary's spiritual motherhood is therefore *participation in the power of the Holy Spirit,* of Him who "gives life." It is likewise the humble handmaid of her who says of herself: "I am the servant of the Lord."

In the light of the mystery of the spiritual maternity of Mary, let us try to understand the extraordinary message which began to resound in the world from Fatima on May 13, 1917, and continued for five months until October 13 of the same year.

May 28

The Significance of Marian Shrines

"Took her into his care" can also mean, literally, "into his house."

A particular manifestation of the motherhood of Mary with regard to mankind is to be found in places where she meets with them — *houses which she inhabits;* houses where a particular presence of the Mother is felt.

Such places and such houses are very numerous. And they are very varied — alcoves in dwellings or wayside shrines where the image of the Mother of God shines out, chapels and churches erected in Her honor. But there are also some places where people *feel the presence of the Mother to be particularly alive.* Sometimes these places radiate their light fulsomely; they attract people from afar. Their brightness may cover a diocese, an entire nation, sometimes more nations and even continents. These are *Marian shrines.*

In all these places that singular testament left by the Crucified Lord is realized in a marvelous manner: man there feels consigned and entrusted to Mary. Man hastens there in order to be with her as with his own Mother, man opens his heart to Her and talks about everything. "He takes Her into his house," that is, into all his problems, which are sometimes difficult. His own and others' problems. Problems of families, of society, of nations, of the whole of mankind.

May 29

Usefulness of Marian Shrines

We are all journeying along the roads of the world, toward our last destination, which is the heavenly fatherland. We are only passing through here below. For this reason, nothing can give us a profound sense of the meaning of our earthly life and stimulate us to live it as a brief experimental stage — and one of enrichment as well — as can an inner *attitude of seeing ourselves as pilgrims.*

Marian shrines are scattered throughout the world. They are like so many milestones, set up to mark the stages of our itinerary on earth: they enable us to pause for a rest, to restore ourselves from the journey, to regain joy and security on the way, together with strength to go on. They are like oases in the desert, formed to provide water and shade.

Here, then, in direct contact with nature, the soul is spontaneously led to contemplation, to colloquy with God, to a deeper sense of our earthly pilgrimage, to rising above the level of everyday worries, so as to get nearer the realitiy of values which never pass away.

The Most Blessed Virgin is venerated as Our Lady of Grace, and the gospel of her feast is the song of the *Magnificat.*

"My being proclaims the greatness of the Lord, my spirit finds joy in God my savior, for he has looked upon his servant in her lowliness. . . . God who is mighty has done great things for me, holy is his name."

May 30

Bringing Mary into Our Homes

"From that hour onward, the disciple took her into his care."

May the same be said of us? *Do we welcome Mary into our homes?* We really should bring her with full rights into the home which is our life, our faith, our affections, our commitments, to recognize the maternal role which is proper to her, that is, a function of guidance, admonition, exhortation, or even of silent presence only, which is sometimes enough to inspire strength and courage on its own. . . . After Jesus' ascension, the first disciples gathered "with Mary, the mother of Jesus." So, she was also there, in their community. Indeed, perhaps it was she who gave it cohesion. And the fact that she is described as "the mother of Jesus" shows how much she was linked with the personality of her Son.

It shows, in other words, that Mary always reminds us of the salvific value of the work of Jesus, our only Savior. On the other hand, it shows that belief in Jesus Christ cannot dispense us from including the person of her who was His mother in our act of faith as well.

In the family of God, Mary safeguards each one's difference within the communion among all. At the same time, she can be a teacher to us of availability to the Holy Spirit, of trembling participation in Christ's total dedication to the will of the Father, of intimate sharing, above all, in the Son's Passion and in assured spiritual fecundity. "There is your mother." Let everyone feel these words as addressed to himself and herself, and so find confidence and drive for ever more decisive and serene progress upon the committed path of one's own life.

May 31

The Visitation of Mary Most Holy

Today's Feast of the Visitation presents us ... with an aspect of Mary's interior life: her attitude of *humble service and disinterested love* for those in need. ...

"Whoever loves God must also love his brother" *(1 Jn 4:21)*, St. John was to say.

But who put this message into practice better than Mary? And who, if not Jesus, whom she bore in Her womb, drove her, spurred her, inspired her to this continuous attitude of generous service and disinterested love for others?

"The Son of Man ... has come, not to be served by others, but to serve ..." *(Mt 20:28)*, Jesus told His disciples. But His mother had already perfectly practiced this attitude of her Son. ...

The mystery of the Visitation is *a mystery of joy.* John the Baptist exulted for joy in St. Elizabeth's womb. She, filled with joy at the gift of motherhood, broke forth in blessings upon the Lord. Mary uttered the *Magnificat,* a hymn overflowing with messianic joy.

But what is the mysterious, concealed source of such joy? It is Jesus. Mary had already conceived Him through the work of the Holy Spirit, and He is now beginning to defeat what is the root of fear, of anxiety, of sadness — sin, the most humiliating slavery for man.

Mother of beautiful love, pray for us! Teach us to love God and our brethren, as you have loved them. Cause our love for others to be ever patient, benign, respectful ... Cause of our joy, pray for us! Amen.

June

June 1

Awaiting Pentecost

Year after year, in her liturgy, the Church celebrates the Ascension of the Lord on the fortieth day after Easter. Year after year she passes the ten days from Ascension to Pentecost in prayer to the Holy Spirit. In a certain sense, year after year, the Church prepares herself for her birth anniversary. As the Fathers teach, she was born on the Cross on Good Friday; she revealed her birth to the world on the day of Pentecost, when the Apostles were "clothed with power from on high" (*Lk* 24:49), when they were "baptized with the Holy Spirit" (*Acts* 1:5).

Let us try to persevere in this rhythmn of the Church. In the course of these days she invites us to take part in the novena to the Holy Spirit. It may be said that this is the oldest of all novenas, that in a certain sense it takes its origin from *what Christ the Lord established.* He recommended that the Apostles pass these days in prayer, in expectation of the descent of the Holy Spirit. That recommendation was not valid then only. It is valid always. And the period of ten days after the Ascension of the Lord brings the same call of the Lord with it every year. It also conceals within itself that same *mystery of Grace, linked with the rhythm of the liturgical season.*

We must benefit by this time. Now, too, let us try to collect our thoughts, in a private way, and enter in a certain way into the Cenacle together with Mary and the Apostles, preparing our souls to accept the Holy Spirit and his action in us. All that has great importance for the internal maturity of our faith, of our Christian vocation.

It also has great importance for the Church as community — every community in the Church and the entire Church, as the community of all communities, should mature, year after year, through the Gift of Pentecost.

June 2

Pray for the Gifts of the Holy Spirit

This year as well, we must prepare for accepting this gift. Let us try to share in the Church's prayer. It is impossible to apprehend the Spirit without listening to what he says to the Church.

"The oxygen-rich breath of the Spirit came to arouse drousy energies in the Church, to awaken charisms which were asleep, to infuse that sense of vitality and joy which is at all times the mark of the Church being young and up to date, ready and happy to re-announce her eternal message to the new times" — Paul VI.

Let us also pray alone. There is a particular prayer which will resound with due force in the liturgy of Pentecost. But we can also repeat it often, above all in the present period of waiting: "Come, Holy Spirit, send the rays of your light to us from heaven. Come, Father of the poor, come, giver of gifts, come, light of hearts . . . sweet guest of the soul, sweetest relief. . . . In fatigue, repose, in heart, refreshment, in tears, comfort. . . . Wash what is stained, bathe what is dry, heal what is bloody. Bend what is stiff, warm what is cold, straighten what is crooked."

So let us turn our prayers to the Holy Spirit in this period. Let us pray for *His gifts.* Let us pray for transformation of our souls. Let us pray for fortitude in confession, for coherence between our lives and the faith.

Let us pray for the Church, that she may fulfill her mission in the Holy Spirit; that she be accompanied by the counsel and the Spirit of her Spouse and her God. Let us pray for union of all Christians. For union in performing the same mission.

June 3

St. Charles Lwvanga and Companions, Martyrs

The *Martyrs of Uganda* . . . a new rank of testifiers to Christ forms up in the *candidatus exercitus* — the white-robed host — to which the Church has often dedicated a special place of worship on the soil of Rome. From Uganda, in fact, a stupendous testimony of faith reached us in the last century; today, therefore, we may say that Christian Rome looks once more to Christian Africa, because of the page of modern heroism which Africa has added to the roll of her martyrs and her history.

Dear pilgrims from Uganda . . . you are the heirs of the martyrs. . . . They have handed down to you the treasure of the Christian faith. It is a treasure whose value is all the more evident because of their witness to it. They were prepared to die rather than be robbed of it. They knew that it is worth more than all earthly wealth, because it gives access to riches that are infinitely superior and that last forever, because it is the gateway to a life with which the life of the body cannot be compared.

Prove yourselves worthy of the heritage that you have received. Show that you value your Christian faith as highly as did Saint Charles Lwanga and his holy companions. Live in accordance with the program that Paul VI put before you when he visited your country: "First, have great love for Jesus Christ. Second, be faithful to the Church. Third, be strong and courageous; be happy and joyful always. Because, remember this always, the Christian life is a most beautiful thing."

June 4

The Servant of God, Pope John XXIII

John XXIII, Angelo Giuseppe Roncalli. Little more than four years of pontificate, but distinguished by his personality as Supreme Pontiff — meek, serene, longsighted, he left an indelible mark upon the history of the Church.

A few months after his election, he announced, at St. Paul's outside the Walls, on 25 January 1959, the Ecumenical Council, the Roman Synod and the revision of the code of canon law for the Latin Church. He was able to see the conclusion of the Roman Synod; he began and followed only the initial stages of the Council and of juridical reform. But these two ecclesial events undoubtedly bear his prophetic mark and will remain linked with his name and his intuition.

His intuition let him see the need for interior renewal and *aggiornamento* (updating) of certain of the pilgrim Church's structures, for the Church must go forward and dialogue with the people of her time.

From the fecund magisterium of John XXIII came two documents which aroused profound echoes and emotion throughout the world on their publication: the encyclical *Mater et Magistra* of 15 May 1961 and *Pacem in terris* of 11 April 1963. I cannot but emphasize the intense drive which John XXIII gave to *ecumenicism,* through his personality, his works, and his magisterium. In his solemn announcement of the Council he laid down Christian unity as one of the great purposes of that ecumenical session. Non-Catholic communities were invited to follow it in "this search after unity and grace."

"I offer my life," he said, "for the Church, continuation of the Ecumenical Council, peace in the world, union of Christians. . . . My earthly day is ending; but Christ lives and the Church goes on with her task; souls, souls, *ut unum sint, ut unum sint* [that they may be one]. . . ." Those were his last words uttered on this earth.

June 5

Oh Holy Spirit, Fill Our Hearts

Pentecost. The Cenacle in Jerusalem opens before the eyes of our faith, the upper room from which the Church came and in which the Church ever remains. It was exactly there that the Church was born as the living community of the People of God, as a community conscious of its mission in the history of man.

During these days the Church prays: "*Come, Holy Spirit,* fill the hearts of your faithful and enkindle in them the fire of your love!" These words are very often repeated, but today they sound with particular ardor.

Fill the hearts! Reflect what is the measure of the human heart, if only God can fill it through the Holy Spirit! The marvelous world of human science opens up before us with its manifold branches. Your self-consciousness certainly develops side by side with this science of the world. You certainly have often put the question to yourself, "Who am I?" I would say that this is the most interesting question. The fundamental question. With what measure is man to be measured? Shall we measure him by the physical powers at his disposal? With the senses which enable him to make contact with the outer world? Or measure him by the gauge of the intelligence, ascertained through various tests and exams?

The answer given today, the answer given by the liturgy of Pentecost indicates two gauges: *the need to measure man with the measure of the heart*. . . . In the language of the Bible, the heart signifies man's *spiritual inner part,* it particularly means the *conscience*. . . . So we must measure man according to the gauge of the conscience, with the measure of the spirit open to God. Only the Holy Spirit can fill up this heart, that is, lead it to self-realization through love and wisdom.

June 6

Who Is the Holy Spirit?

Who is this Holy Spirit? He is God himself. The third Person of the Blessed Trinity. He is sent to each of us by the Father and the Son. He is their greatest gift and he remains constantly with us. He abides in us.

The clearest description of the work of the Holy Spirit has been given by Saint Paul, who said that the Spirit produces "love, joy, peace, patient endurance, kindness, generosity, faith, mildness and chastity" *(Gal* 5:22). *Qualities such as these are ideal in every walk of life and in all circumstances*: at home, with your teachers and friends; in the factory or at the university; with all the people you meet.

The Prophet Isaiah also attributed special gifts to the Holy Spirit: "a spirit of wisdom and understanding, a spirit of counsel and of strength, a spirit of knowledge and fear the Lord" *(Is* 11:2). Saint Paul is right in saying: "Since we live by the Spirit, let us follow the Spirit's lead" *(Gal* 5:25).

With gifts and qualities such as these we are equal to any task and capable of overcoming any difficulties. Yet our lives remain our own, and the Spirit acts on each of us differently, in harmony with our individual personality and the characteristics we have inherited from our parents and from the upbringing received in our homes.

Because he is so near to us, yet so unobtrusive, we should turn to the Holy Spirit instinctively in all our needs and ask him for his guidance and help. The Spirit comes to help us in our weakness. What more could be done for us? What more can we expect of God than that?

June 7

The Guiding Influence of the Holy Spirit

A correct understanding of the teaching of Jesus makes us react in a creative and co-operative fashion to the challenges that face us in life, without fear of acting mistakenly and alone, but under the guiding influence of his own Holy Spirit at every moment and in every circumstance, be it great or small.

This extraordinary divine assistance is guaranteed to all who offer their lives to Jesus. God the Father's plan of salvation embraces all mankind; his one same Holy Spirit is sent as gift to all who are open to receive him in faith. We each form a part of God's overall plan. *An exclusively personal and private attitude to salvation is not Christian* and is born of a fundamentally mistaken mentality. Consequently, *your lives cannot be lived in isolation,* and even *in deciding your future you must always keep in mind your responsibility* as a Christian towards others. There is no place in your lives for apathy or indifference to the world around you. There is no place in the Church for selfishness. You must show a conscientious concern that the standards of society fit the plan of God. Christ counts on you, so that the effects of his Holy Spirit may radiate from you to others and in that way permeate every aspect of the public and the private sector of national life. "To each person the manifestation of the Spirit is given for the common good" (*1 Cor* 12:7).

Do not let the sight of the world in turmoil shake your confidence in Jesus. Not even the threat of nuclear war. *Follow the example of Our Blessed Lady,* the perfect model of trust in God and wholehearted cooperation in his divine plan for the salvation of mankind. Keep in mind the advice she gave the servants at Cana: "Do whatever he (Jesus) tells you" (*Jn* 2:5). Jesus changed the water into wine for his Mother on that occasion. Through her intercession he will transform your lives.

June 8

Pentecost Goes On

"The day of Pentecost" . . . a day of particular solemnity which stands side by side with Easter Day itself, by reason of the dignity of the celebration and the spiritual riches contained in it.

Is it possible to establish a comparison between the Pentecost of which the Acts of the Apostles speak, that which occurred fifty days after the Lord's resurrection, and the Pentecost of today? Yes. It is not only possible, it is also certain, undoubted and corroborating to recognize that link *in the life* and *for the life* of the Church, both at the level of her two thousand years of history and of that of the events of the time in which we are living, as men and women of this generation.

We have the right, the duty and the joy to say that Pentecost goes on. We rightfully speak of the "perpetuity" of Pentecost. Gathered in that same Cenacle, which had been the place of the first Eucharist, then of the first meeting with the Risen One, the Apostles *discovered the power of the Holy Spirit.* Made strong by that power, they began to act, that is, to carry through their service. The apostolic Church was born. And we are gathered here to *renew the mystery of that great day.*

That mystery ought to be manifested in a particular way through the Sacrament of Confirmation. . . . Having made suitable preparation, numerous Christian boys and girls . . . in the diocese of Rome are about to receive it. . . . My first greeting . . . goes to these children. It is intended to show the predilection and confidence that I nourish in their regard. My greetings then extend to their godfathers and godmothers, their parents and relatives, and those participating in this meaningful and stirring celebration.

June 9

The Holy Spirit, the Gift of Holiness

We must now reflect on the fact that Pentecost began *on the very evening of the Resurrection,* when the Risen Lord breathed on those in the Cenacle and said, "Receive the Holy Spirit. If you forgive men's sins, they are forgiven them." So, this is the Easter gift, because we are at *the first day,* as it were, at the generating element, of that numerical series of days in which the day of Pentecost is precisely the 50th — the element, the reality, of the Resurrection, whereby, according to a relationship of causality even before that of chronology, *Christ gave the Holy Spirit to the Church* as the divine gift, and as the incessant and inexhaustible *fount of sanctification.*

"Receive the Holy Spirit. . . ." And this gift of holiness begins to act: sanctification starts off with remission of sins. First there is *Baptism,* the sacrament of total cancellation of sins; then there is *Penance,* the sacrament of reconciliation with God and the Church; then again there is the *Anointing of the Sick.* But this work of sanctification always attains its culmination in the *Eucharist,* the sacrament of the fullness of holiness and grace. And, in this marvellous flow of supernatural life, what place is due to *Confirmation?* It must be said that the same sanctification is expressed in reinforcement of it as well, that is, in *Confirmation.* In it, too, is the superabundant fullness of the Holy, sanctifying Spirit, operating in a special direction: the dynamic direction, the efficacy of inner-inspired and directed action.

The nature of the Sacrament of Confirmation flows out in this *conferring of strength,* communicated to each of the baptized, to make him or her a perfect Christian and soldier of Christ, ready to testify courageously to his resurrection and its redemptive power: "Then you are to be my witnesses. . . "

June 10

Confirmation Creates Witnesses to Christ

The Sacrament [of Confirmation] . . . confirms and seals
what was already mysteriously effected in you in
Baptism, when you became adoptive children of God by
full right, that is, you were beneficially brought within
the range of his love's action — not only the love which
he has for every creature as the creator, but above all, the
range of that most special love which he showed for man
in Jesus Christ, as Redeemer.

With this chrism, you acquire a quite particular relationship directly with the Lord Jesus. You are officially
consecrated to him as witnesses to the Church and the
world. He has need of you, and he wants to employ you,
as strong, happy, generous boys and girls. In a certain
way, you lend him your countenances, your hearts, your
whole persons, so that his behavior towards others will be
as you behave yourselves. If you are good, responsive,
dedicated to the well-being of others, loyal servants of
the Gospel, then Jesus himself will be giving that good
impression; but if you should be weak and unspirited,
then you will be casting a shadow over his real identity,
and you will not be honoring him.

So you see that you are called to a very lofty task,
which turns you into true, complete Christians. Confirmation actually brings you to the Christian's adulthood.
That is, it trusts you and acknowledges a sense of responsibility in you which is not to be expected of young
children. The child is not yet master of himself, of his
acts, of his life. But the adult has the courage of his own
choices, he knows how to bear the consequences, he is
capable of paying in person, because he has gained such
an inner maturity that he can decide on his own, employ
his existence as he thinks best, and above all give love,
instead of only receiving it.

June 11

The Holy Spirit, the Secret Force
in Confirmation

No one succeeds in being an authentic disciple of Christ, if he wishes to be so alone, on his own initiative and with his own energies. That is impossible. The result would be only a caricature of the true Christian. Just as one cannot become a human adult unless there be a new and decisive contribution from nature, so it is with the Christian on another level. But with the chrism you receive a pouring out and a particular endowment of the Holy Spirit. He, just like the wind, from which the word "spirit" comes, enlivens, urges, refreshes.

He is *our secret strength,* I would say, the inexhaustible reserve and propellent energy of all our thinking and doing as Christians. He gives you courage, as he gave it to the Apostles in the Cenacle at Pentecost. He makes you understand the truth and beauty of Jesus' words. He gives you life. He is actually the Spirit of God and the Spirit of Christ. That means that when he comes to you, he does not come alone but also brings the seal of the Father and his Son Jesus with him. At the same time, he introduces you into that trinitarian mystery. It is not easy to discuss this, but that does not mean that it thereby ceases to be the foundation of and unmistakeable stamp upon our Christian identity.

These are big things, but just think that from now on you cannot and must not be without them, because you now become adults in the faith.

Dearest, I wish with all my heart that your lungs will always be full of this air of the Holy Spirit, whom you receive in abundance today, and who enables you and the whole Church to breathe according to the rhythm of Christ himself.

June 12

Confirmation and the Struggle against Evil

On the first Pentecost our Savior gave the Apostles the power to forgive sins when he poured into their hearts the gift of the Holy Spirit. The same Holy Spirit comes to you today in the Sacrament of Confirmation, to involve you more completely in the Church's fight against sin and in her mission of fostering holiness. He comes to dwell more fully in your hearts and *to strengthen you for the struggle with evil.*

My dear young people, the world of today needs you, for it needs men and women who are filled with the Holy Spirit. It needs your courage and hopefulness, your faith and your perseverance. The world of tomorrow will be built by you. Today you receive the gift of the Holy Spirit so that you may work with deep faith and with abiding charity, so that you may help to bring to the world the fruits of reconciliation and peace.

Strengthened by the Holy Spirit and his manifold gifts, commit yourselves wholeheartedly to the Church's struggle against sin. Strive to be unselfish; try not to be obsessed with material things. Be active members of the People of God; be reconciled with each other and devoted to the work of justice, which will bring peace on earth.

On the first day of Pentecost the Holy Spirit came upon the Apostles and upon Mary and filled them with his power. Today we remember that moment and *we open ourselves again to the gift of that same Holy Spirit.* In that Spirit we were confirmed. In that Spirit we are called to share in the mission of Christ, to become the People of Pentecost, the apostles of our time.

June 13

St. Anthony, an Evangelical Man

During the whole course of his existence Anthony was an *evangelical man*. And if we honor him as such, it is because we believe that the Holy Spirit of the Lord dwelled in him with particular effusion, enriching him with his marvelous gifts and moving him "from within," to undertake an activity which was most remarkable in the forty years of his life, but is still far from being exhausted in time — it goes on, vigorously and providentially, in our day as well.

I would ask you first of all to meditate exactly on the mark of evangelicality. It is also the reason why Anthony is proclaimed "the Saint."

Without making exclusions or preferences, this is a sign that sanctity had reached summits of exceptional heights in him. It imposed itself on all through the power of example and gave to devotion to him utmost expansion in the world. It is really difficult to find a city or town or country in the Catholic sphere where there is not at least an altar or image of the Saint. His serene features enlighten with a gentle smile millions of Christian homes, where, through him, faith nourishes hope in the providence of the heavenly Father. Believers, the lowliest and most defenseless above all, consider and feel him to be their Saint, an ever ready and potent intercessor for them.

Exsulta, Lusitania felix; O felix Padua, gaude. Exult, happy Portugal; O happy Padua, rejoice. I repeat these words with my predecessor Pius XII. Rejoice, Padua, in the glories of your Roman, indeed your pre-Roman origins; to the grand events of your history you add the most noble title of custodian of the living, throbbing memory of St. Anthony, in his glorious tomb. From you, in fact, his name has spread and resounds throughout the world still, because of this special characteristic: the genuiness of his evangelical outlines.

June 14

St. Anthony, Preacher of Penance

Preaching and *Penance:* this is a great binomen of pure evangelical origin. It is put to you again through the luminous example of Anthony, because it is completely valid and urgent in our days, even though they are so different from his. Times change. Methods and forms of pastoral action do change according to the Church's sage directives. But the fundamental principles, the sacramental order above all, remain unchanged. Likewise unchanged are the nature and problems of man, that creature who is the apex of the divine creation, yet seems to be always exposed to the dramatic possibility of sin. That means that there is urgent need to announce the kerygma of salvation, unchanged in its content, *to man of today as well;* that is, there is need to preach salvation. There is urgent need as well today to offer the instrument *to sinful man* — the Sacrament of Reconciliation (that is, Penance). To sum up, the *activity of evangelization* remains necessary, in the twofold direction of announcement and of offering of salvation.

Celebrations of St. Anthony will not have been only celebrations if conscience develops in ... priests ... of these two unrenounceable and precious ministries; if desire, indeed need, to benefit for your spiritual progress, grows in you laity. Is it not true that a good confession very often enters into this same process as a departure point and as an arrival point? All that is always in the evangelical line of penance-conversion. . . .

Penance and reconciliation. After the great themes of evangelization, of catechesis and family, it has seemed fitting to examine this grave matter under all its aspects, not least the pastoral-sacramental aspect. It is a subject which engages a great part of the Church's life and activity in the world.

June 15

The Communal Dimension of Confirmation

If this is the particular significance of Confirmation for strengthening in us the "inner man," along the threefold line of faith, hope and charity, it is easy to see how, by direct consequence, this also has great significance for *building up the community of the Church, as the Body of Christ.* Due attention must be given to this second significance as well, because it enables us to grasp the communitarian dimension, properly, the ecclesial dimension, going beyond the individual dimension, of the reinforcing action of the Spirit.

We have heard Paul talking of this action, and of distribution on the Spirit's part of his charisma "for the common good." Is it not true that the vast, and today also very relevant, theme of the apostolate, and in a special way of the apostolate of the laity, must be set in that elevated perspective? If "to each is given a particular manifestation of the Spirit for the common benefit," how could a Christian feel a stranger, or be indifferent to, or be relieved of the task of building up the Church? The requirement of the lay apostolate derives from that and is defined as a dutiful response to the gifts received. I think in this regard — but I will only make a simple reference here — that it would be good to take up that Council text which presents the ministry incumbent on each member of the Church as a "noble pledge to labor," on the biblical and theological foundations of our engrafting into the mystical Body of Christ through Baptism, and the strength received from the Spirit *through Confirmation*. "For exercise of this apostolate the Holy Spirit also imparts particular gifts to the faithful," whence the obligation correlatively derives to *operate* and *cooperate* in "edification of the whole body in charity."

June 16

The Lasting Mark of Confirmation

Confirmation is received only once in a lifetime. Nonetheless, it must leave *a lasting trace*. Precisely because it indelibly marks the soul, it can never be reduced to a distant memory of worn-out, evanescent religious practices. We must therefore ask ourselves how the sacramental, vital encounter with the Holy Spirit, which we have received from the hands of the Apostles through the chrism, can and ought to *endure and be more profoundly rooted* in the life of each of us.

This is splendidly demonstrated by the sequence sung at Pentecost, *"Veni, Sancte Spiritus"* — "Come, Holy Spirit." It reminds us, above all, that we have to invoke that marvelous gift with faith and insistence. It also teaches us how and when we ought to ask for it. O, come, Holy Spirit, send us the radiance of your light. . . . Perfect consoler, give us your sweet relief, repose in fatigue and comfort in tears. Give us your strength, because without it nothing is in us, nothing is without fault!

Pentecost is the day of joy, and I am glad to express, once again, such a sentiment by reason of the fact that we can in this way renew the mystery of Pentecost in St. Peter's Basilica. But the Spirit of God is not circumscribed — he blows where he will, he penetrates everywhere, with sovereign and universal liberty. It is for this reason that, from the depths of this Basilica, as the humble successor of Peter, he who inaugurated the ministry of the Word, with intrepidly apostolic courage, just on this day of Pentecost, I find the strength to cry *Urbi et Orbi*, to the City and the World: "Come, Holy Spirit, fill the hearts of your faithful, and kindle in them the fire of your love." So may it be for the whole Church, for the whole of mankind!

June 17

Interior Conversion, Essential for Ecumenism

As Christians today strive to be sources of reconciliation in the world, they feel the need, perhaps more urgently than ever before, to be fully reconciled among themselves. For *the sin of disunity among Christians,* which has been with us for centuries, *weighs heavily upon the Church.* The seriousness of this sin was clearly shown at the Second Vatican Council, which stated: "Without doubt, this discord openly contradicts the will of Christ, provides a stumbling block to the world, and inflicts damage on the most holy cause of proclaiming the good news to every creature."

Restoration of unity among Christians is one of the main concerns of the Church in the last part of the twentieth century. And this task is for all of us. No one can claim exemption from this responsibility. Indeed everyone can make some contribution, however small it may seem, and all are called to that interior conversion which is the essential condition for ecumenism. As the Second Vatican Co··· :il taught: "This change of heart and holiness of life. long with public and private prayer for the unity of Christians, should be regarded as the soul of the whole ecumenical movement, and can rightly be called spiritual ecumenism."

June 18

The Holy Spirit, Source of All Unity

The Holy Spirit, who is the source of all unity, provides the Body of Christ with a "different gift" *(1 Cor* 12:4) so that it may be built up and strengthened. As the Holy Spirit granted the Apostles the gift of tongues so that all gathered in Jerusalem on that first Pentecost might hear and understand the one Gospel of Christ, should we not expect the same Holy Spirit to grant us the gifts we need in order to continue the work of salvation and to be reunited as one body in Christ? In this we trust and for this we pray, confident in the power which the Spirit gave to the Church at Pentecost.

"Send forth your Spirit . . . and . . . renew the face of the earth" *(Ps.* 104:30). These words of the psalmist are our heartfelt prayer today, as we ask Almighty God to renew the face of the earth through the life-giving power of the Spirit. Send forth your Spirit, O Lord, renew our hearts and minds with the gifts of light and truth. Renew our homes and families with the gifts of unity and joy. Renew your Church on earth with the gifts of penance and reconciliation, with unity in faith and love.

Send forth your Spirit, O Lord, and renew the face of the earth!

June 19

The Most Holy Eucharist

The Church was born on the day of Pentecost from the power of the Holy Spirit. *It is being born constantly in the Eucharist,* where bread and wine become the Body and Blood of the Redeemer. And this too occurs through the power of the Holy Spirit.

When the apostles had believed and confessed with their hearts that "Jesus is the Lord," *the power of the Holy Spirit consigned the Eucharist to their hands* — the Body and Blood of the Lord, that Eucharist which Christ had entrusted to them in that same Cenacle, during the last supper, before his Passion.

He said then, as he gave them the bread: "All of you, take it and eat of it, *this is my body,* offered up in sacrifice for you." On giving them the cup of wine, he said, "Take and drink of it, all of you: this is the cup of my blood for the new and eternal alliance, poured out for you and for all in remission of sins." And after having said this, he added, *"Do this in memory of me."*

When the day of Good Friday arrived, and then the Sabbath, the mysterious words of the last supper were accomplished through Christ's sufferings. You see, his Body had been given over. His Blood had been shed. And when the risen Christ stood in the middle of the apostles on the evening of Easter, their hearts were to beat a new rate, that of faith, under the breath of the Holy Spirit.

See, the Risen One stands before them! *He gives them the Eucharist.* And see how he now says, "As the Father sent me, I also send you." He sent them out in the power of the Holy Spirit *with the word of the Eucharist* and *with the sign of the Eucharist,* as he truly said, "Do this in memory of me."

"Jesus is Lord."

June 20

Born from the Holy Eucharist

The Church is born on Pentecost Day. It is born under the potent breath of the Most Holy Spirit, who orders the apostles to quit the Cenacle and undertake their mission.

On the evening of the Resurrection, Christ said to them: "As the Father sent me, so do I send you." On the morning of Pentecost the Holy Spirit caused them to undertake that mission. So they went out among people and set off along the roads of the world.

Before that happened, the world — the human world

— had entered the cenacle. "All were filled with the Holy Spirit. They began to express themselves in foreign tongues and make bold proclamation, as the Spirit prompted them" *(Acts* 2:4). With *that gift of tongues* the world of mankind also entered into that Cenacle — those who speak various languages and to whom it is necessary to speak in various languages for them to be included in the announcement of the marvels God has accomplished *(Acts* 2:11).

So, the Church was born on the day of Pentecost, under the potent breath of the Holy Spirit. In a certain sense, she was born into the whole world inhabited by man, where people speak different languages. She was born to go out to the whole world, teaching all nations in their diverse languages.

She was born so that, as she teaches men and nations, she may always be born anew through the word of the Gospel; that she may be always being born anew in them from the Holy Spirit, *from the sacramental power of the Eucharist.*

All those who receive the word of the Gospel, all those who nourish themselves on the Body and Blood of Christ in the Eucharist under the breath of the Spirit, profess: "Jesus is Lord" *(1 Cor* 12:3).

June 21

The Church Grows by the Eucharist

And so, under the breath of the Holy Spirit, beginning from the Pentecost at Jerusalem, *the Church grows.* In her is a diversity "of charisms," and diversity "of ministries," and diversities "of operations," but *"the same Spirit,"* but *"the same Lord,"* but *"the same God who accomplishes all of them in everyone"* *(1 Cor* 12:4-6).

In every man, in every human community, in every country, in every language and nation, in every generation, the Church is conceived anew and grows anew.

It grows as a body, because, as the body unites many members in itself, many organs, many cells, so the Church unites many people *in one with Christ.*

Multiplicity is manifested in unity, through the work of the Holy Spirit, and unity contains multiplicity in itself: *"It was in one Spirit* that all of us . . . were baptized into one body. All of us have been given to drink of the one Spirit"* *(1 Cor* 12:13).

It is on the basis of this spiritual unity that the Church is born and manifests herself every day as ever new; *she is the Sacrament of the Body and Blood,* the great memorial of the Cross and of the Resurrection, the Sign of his new and eternal Alliance, which Christ himself put into the hands of the apostles and laid down as the foundation of their mission.

In the power of the Holy Spirit, the Church is built up *as body through the Sacrament of the Body.* In the power of the Holy Spirit, the Church is built up *as people* of the new Alliance, through the Blood of the new and everlasting Alliance.

The vivifying power of this Sacrament is inexhaustible, in the Holy Spirit. The Church lives from it, in the Holy Spirit, with the very life of her Lord: "Jesus is Lord."

June 22

Saints John Fisher and
Thomas More, Martyrs

I would like to recall another aspect of Baptism which is perhaps the most universally familiar. In baptism we are given a name; we call it our Christian name. In the tradition of the Church it is a saint's name, a name of one of the heroes among Christ's followers, an apostle, a martyr, a religious founder, like Saint Benedict, whose monks founded Westminster Abbey. . . . Taking such names reminds us again that we are being drawn into *the Communion of Saints,* and at the same time that great models of Christian living are set before us. London is particularly proud of two outstanding saints, great men also by the world's standards, contributors to your national heritage, John Fisher and Thomas More.

John Fisher, the Cambridge Scholar of Renaissance learning, bishop in his loyalty to the faith and in his devoted attention to the people of his diocese, especially the poor and the sick. Thomas More was a model layman living the Gospel to the full. He was a fine scholar and an ornament to his profession, a loving husband and father, humble in prosperity, courageous in adversity, humorous and godly. Together, they served God and their country — bishop and layman. Together they died, victims of an unhappy age. Today we have the grace, all of us, to proclaim their greatness and to thank God for giving such men to England. In this England of fair and generous minds, no one will begrudge the Catholic community pride in its own history.

June 23

The Most Holy Eucharist, Christ's Redemptive Sacrifice

Dearest brothers and sisters! In the Eucharist the Redemption is seen again in today's actions — Christ's sacrifice, by becoming the Church's sacrifice, produces its fruits of reconciliation and salvation in the whole of mankind.

When, in the name and in the person of Christ, the priest utters the words, "This is my body offered in sacrifice for you," he not only affirms Christ's presence; he also expresses the sacrifice with which Jesus gave his life for the salvation of all. In his discourse at Capernaum after the multiplication of the loaves, to induce understanding of the worth of the Bread which he wished to provide for the hungry crowds, he had already declared: "The bread I will give is my flesh, for the life of the world" (*Jn* 6:51). The gift of the eucharistic bread was to cost Jesus the sacrifice of his own flesh. Thanks to the sacrifice, this flesh would be able to communicate life.

The words of consecration over the wine are even more explicit: "This is the chalice of my blood for the new and eternal Alliance, shed for you and for all in remission of sins." The blood given as drink is the blood shed on Calvary for the constitution of the New Alliance. The first Alliance had been broken by sin; Christ established a new Alliance, which shall never be broken, because it is realized in his very person, whereby mankind has been reconciled definitively with God. So, in consecration of the bread and the wine, the redeeming sacrifice is made present.

In the Eucharist there is not only a remembrance of the sacrifice offered once for all on Calvary. *That sacrifice becomes present to us* by being sacramentally renewed in every community which offers it up by the hand of the consecrated priest.

June 24

The Birth of St. John the Baptist

"And you, O child, shall be called prophet of the Most High." These words are about the saint of today. With these words the priest Zachariah greeted his own son, after having regained his power of speech. With these words he greeted the son to whom, through his will and to the surprise of the whole family, he gave the name of John. Today the Church recalls those events to us by celebrating the solemnity of the birth of Saint John the Baptist.

It might also be called *the day of the calling of John,* son of Zachariah and of Elizabeth of Ain-Karim, to be the last prophet of the Old Alliance, to be the messenger and immediate Forerunner of the Messiah — Jesus Christ. For he, who came into the world in such unusual circumstances, bore the Divine Call with him. This call derived from the design of God himself, from his salvific love, and was written in the history of man from the very moment of his conception in the womb of his mother. All the circumstances of that conception, together with the birth itself of John at Ain-Karim, indicate an unusual call: "Prepare the way of the Lord, and make straight his paths."

We know that John the Baptist responded to that call with the whole of his life. We know that he remained faithful to it until his last breath. And that breath was breathed in prison, by order of Herod, at the desire of Salome, acting at the instigation of her vengeful mother Herodias. But the liturgy does not mention all that now; it keeps it for another day. Today the liturgy tells us *to rejoice at the birth* of the Precursor of the Lord. It tells us to give thanks to God for the call given to John the Baptist.

June 25

The Most Holy Eucharist, the Church's Sacrifice

It is true that the sacrifice of Calvary was enough to obtain all the graces of salvation for mankind: the eucharistic sacrifice but gathers the fruits. But Christ willed that his oblation should become continually present to join the Christian community together. The Eucharist is at one and the same time *Christ's sacrifice and the Church's sacrifice,* because in it Christ unites the Church with his redemptive work and lets the Church share in his oblation.

How important it is, then, for the faithful, as they take part in the Eucharist, to assume a personal attitude of offering. It is not sufficient that they listen to the word of God, nor that they pray in common. It is necessary for them to make Christ's oblation their own, offering up their pains, their difficulties, their trials, and, even more, themselves, together with Him and in Him so as to make this gift rise even to the Father, with the gift which Christ makes of himself.

By entering into the Savior's sacrificial offering, they share in the victory won by him over the evil of the world. When we are shaken by the sight of evil spreading in the universe, with all the devastation which it produces, we should not forget that such unleashing of the forces of sin is overcome by the saving power of Christ. Whenever the words of consecration are uttered in the Mass and the body and blood of Christ become present in the act of the sacrifice, the triumph of love over hatred, of holiness over sin, is also present. Every Eucharistic celebration is stronger than all the evil in the universe; it means real, concrete accomplishment of the Redemption, and ever deeper reconciliation of sinful man with God, in prospect of a better world.

June 26

The Most Holy Eucharist, the Sacrifice of Humanity

By extending the application of the work of redemption to humanity, the Eucharistic sacrifice contributes to the building *of the Church.* On Calvary, Christ merited salvation not only for every single man but also for the whole community. His oblation obtained the grace of reunification of mankind in the Body of the Church. The Eucharist tends to realize this objective concretely by building up the ecclesial community every day. The sacrifice of the altar has the effect of reinforcing the Church's holiness and favoring her expansion in the world. We may say that in this sense the Eucharistic celebration is always a missionary act. It invisibly obtains a greater force of penetration for the Church into all human environments.

Building up the Church means, in addition, consolidating unity more and more. It was no accident that, at the Last Supper Jesus prayed for his disciples to be united. So we can understand how, in every Eucharistic celebration, the Church follows the example of the Master by praying that unity may be evermore real and ever more perfect.

In this way, the Eucharist causes ecumenical rapprochement among all Christians to make progress and, within the Catholic Church, tends to tighten the bonds uniting the faithful, above and beyond legitimate differences existing among them. By cooperating in a responsible manner in such a unifying dynamic, Christians will show the world that their Master did not suffer for the unity of mankind in vain.

June 27

Transmission of the Most Holy Eucharist

"I received from the Lord what I handed on to you" *(1 Cor* 11:23).

Paul's testimony, which we have just heard, is the testimony of the other Apostles: they handed on what they had received. And, like them, their successors went on faithfully transmitting what they had received. The Successor of Peter, who is speaking to you, makes himself a faithful echo of that same testimony: "I received from the Lord what I handed on to you."

And what the Apostles conveyed to us is Christ himself and his commandment to repeat and transmit to all peoples what He, the Divine Master, said and did at the Last Supper: "This is my body, which is for you" (*1 Cor* 11:24).

This tradition has lasted almost two thousand years. We too, as we enter into it, repeat the gesture of "the breaking of the bread" today. We repeat it on the . . . anniversary of that breathless moment when God came so very close to man and, through total giving of himself, testified to the "incredible" dimension of a boundless love.

"This is my body, which is for you." How not feel a profound vibration in the soul as the thought that when pronouncing that "you," Christ meant to refer *to each of us as well* and offered himself up to death for each of us? And how not feel deeply moved by the thought that that "offering of his own body" for us is no distant act, belonging to the cold pages of historical chronicles, but is an event which is living now as well — *but in a bloodless way* — in the Sacrament of the Body and of the Blood, set upon the table which is the altar? The seed of *deathless life* is set in our frail *mortal flesh*.

June 28

Taking the Most Holy Eucharist into the World

As we reflect on the mystery, how much we comprehend the jealous love with which the Church guards this treasure of inestimable value! And how logical and natural it seems that, in the course of their history, Christians have felt the need to give expression *in the external world as well* to their joy and gratitude at the reality of such a great gift. They grew aware of the fact that celebration of this divine mystery could not be reduced to being kept within the walls of a church, however large and artistic that church might be, but that it was necessary to take it out *along the streets of the world,* for He whom the frail species of the host conceal came to earth so as really to be "the life of the world" *(Jn* 6:51).

That is how the Corpus Christi procession came about. The Church has celebrated it for many centuries now with quite particular solemnity and joy. We too shall set off shortly in procession through the streets of our city. We shall go forward with hymns and prayers, bearing the sacrament of the Body and Blood of the Lord with us. We shall go among houses, schools, workshops, offices and shops. We shall go where the life of mankind is bubbling, where its passions are boiling, where its conflicts explode, where its sufferings are consumed and its hopes flower. We shall go to give testimony with humble joy that in that little white Host is the answer to the most pressing queries, comfort for every pain and sorrow of the most lacerating kind; there is a pledge of satisfaction for that burning thirst for happiness and love which everyone bears in himself and herself, in the secret of the heart.

Let us go out across the city, out to meet our brothers and sisters and we shall show the sacrament of the presence of Christ to all.

June 29

Blest Are You, Simon

"Blest are you, Simon son of Jonah!" (*Mt* 16:17). That blessing was never withdrawn. Just as that confession which Peter made at that time in the vicinity of Caesarea Philippi was never thereafter darkened in his soul.

He spent the rest of his life with it, down to his last breath. He had it with him as he passed that terrible night of the capture of Christ in the garden at Gethsemane, the night of his own weakness, of his great weakness, which showed itself in his denial that he knew the man . . . but that did not destroy his faith in the Son of God. The trial of the cross was recompensed by the testimony of the Resurrection. It brought a final argument to the confession made in the neighborhood of Caesarea Philippi.

Now Peter went, with this faith in the Son of God, to face his mission, that which the Lord has assigned to him. When, by Herod's order, he was in prison at Jerusalem, in chains and condemned to death, it seemed that his mission was not to go on for long. But Peter was liberated by the same power by which he was called. An even longer path was destined for him. He found the end of that path on 29 June of the year 68 of the present era, which is conventionally numbered from the birth of Christ. That end is indicated by a tradition which is confirmed by the results of many rigorously conducted researches.

"The flesh and the blood" were destroyed to the very end: they were subjected to death. But that which had once been *revealed to him by the Father* (*cf. Matt* 16:17) *survived the death of the flesh*. It became the beginning of

the eternal meeting with the Master, of whom he testified to the very end. It was *the beginning of the blessed
vision* of the Son of the Father. And it became *the unshakeable foundation of the Church's faith.* Its stone, its rock.

"Blessed are you . . . son of Jonah."

June 30

St. Paul, Apostle of All the Gentiles

"The Lord stood by my side." Do we remember well
where and how that occurred; do we recall what happened by the walls of Damascus? "But the Lord stood by
my side and gave me strength, so that through me the
preaching task might be completed and all the nations
might hear the gospel" (*2 Tim* 4:17).

In a grandiose passage, Paul outlines the labor of his
whole life. He is writing from here, from Rome, to his
beloved disciple, Timothy, as he approaches the end of
his life entirely devoted to the Gospel.

In this passage, too, there is penetrating consciousness of sin and grace; of grace which overcomes sin and
opens the way to glory: "The Lord will continue to rescue me from all attempts to do me harm and will bring
me safe to his heavenly kingdom" (*2 Tim* 4:18).

Today the Roman Church recalls in a particular fashion and in memory of him, two last sights in the same
direction: *the direction of Christ crucified and arisen again* —
the sight of Peter in his last agony on the cross and that
of Paul dying under the sword.

Those were two sights of faith, that faith which filled

their lives till the end and laid the basis of divine light in the story of man on earth. Thus they remain in our memory. And we freshen our faith in Christ with particular force.

July

July 1

Hail, True Body, Born of the Virgin Mary

Today, on this feast . . . we manifest special devotion for the Eucharist, for the Most Sacred Body of Christ. As we do so, our thoughts turn to Her from whom God, the Son of God, took this Body. We turn to the Virgin whose name is Mary.

In particular, we turn to her as we gather . . . to recite the Angelus . . . the prayer which reminds us three times a day of the mystery of the Incarnation: "The Word was made flesh and came to dwell amongst us."

Let us therefore greet with veneration and love that Body of the Eternal Word and her who, as Mother, gave His Body to the Eternal Word.

This body is the Sacrament of the Redemption of man and of the word: "He truly suffered, and was immolated on the Cross for mankind."

This Body, suffering unto death on the Cross, together with the Blood shed as the sign of the New and Eternal Alliance, became the Church's greatest Sacrament, to which today we desire to render particular adoration and show particular love and gratitude. In fact, this Body is really Food, just as the Blood is really Drink; for our souls, under the species of bread and wine. It restores man's inner strength and fortifies him on the path to eternity. It enables us already here on earth to have a foretaste of that union with God in truth and love to which the Father calls us, in Christ His Son. Hence our final invocation: "*May we taste you in the hour of death.*"

May all of us be able to receive you, Body of God, at the last hour of our life on earth, before we appear in God's sight!

July 2

The Sacrament of the Sick

We acknowledge that the Anointing of the Sick is for the benefit of the whole person. We find this point demonstrated in the liturgical texts of the sacramental celebration: "Make this oil a remedy for all who are anointed with it; heal them in body, in soul and spirit, and deliver them from every affliction."

The anointing is therefore a source of strength for both the soul and the body. In her teaching on this sacrament, the Church passes on the truth contained in our first reading from Saint James: "Is there anyone sick among you? He should ask for the presbyters of the church. They in turn are to pray over him, anointing him with oil in the Name of the Lord. This prayer uttered in faith will reclaim the one who is ill, and the Lord will restore him to health. If he has committed any sins, forgiveness will be his" (*James* 5:14–15).

This sacrament should be approached in a spirit of great confidence; we too must believe in Christ's healing love and reaffirm that nothing will separate us from that love.

My dear brothers and sisters, you will find the crucified Lord in the midst of your sickness and suffering. As Veronica ministered to Christ on his way to Calvary, so Christians have accepted the care of those in pain and sorrow as privileged opportunities to minister to Christ himself. I commend and bless all those who work for the sick in hospitals, residential homes and centers of care for the dying. I would like to say to you, doctors, nurses, chaplains and all other hospital staff: Yours is a noble vocation. Remember it is Christ to whom you minister in the sufferings of your brothers and sisters.

July 3

St. Thomas, Apostle

All this presupposes faith being in us, a living faith, at once humble and joyous. The Gospel . . . reminded us of the episode of Thomas's unbelief. Certainly, that apostle's hesitant attitude comes in some way as an aid in our own indecision, because it occurred on the occasion of a new and convincing manifestation of himself on the part of Jesus. In the end, he too fell on his knees before Jesus, and openly confessed: "My Lord and my God."

Yet Jesus did not praise his early attitude but went on to formulate a beatitude, addressed to all those who would come after him, and to each of us: "Blest are they who have not seen and who believe." This is the kind of faith which we ought to renew, in the wake of those innumerable generations of Christians who have confessed Christ for two thousand years, as the invisible Lord, and have done so even unto martyrdom. For us, as for innumerable others, the ancient words of St. Peter's First Epistle must hold good: "You love him without having seen him; now, without having seen him, believe in him." This is genuine faith; it is absolute dedication to things which are not seen, but which are capable of filling and ennobling a whole life. The ideals which you profess and serve are also invisible. But if, instead of abstract ideals of duty, law, service, you think of Jesus Christ, then those very same ideals take on a name, and you have one more reason for giving yourselves generously for the good of mankind, your brethren.

Dearly beloved, may your . . . meeting with Christ be a stimulus and viaticum for all of you on your path, may it be an incessant source of strength and courage in your commitment to fulfilling the functions inherent in your state in life and also for an incisive Christian testimony.

July 4

Independence Day

Dear friends in New York, my visit to your city would not have been complete without coming to Battery Park, without seeing Ellis Island and the Statue of Liberty in the distance. Every nation has its historical symbols. They may be shrines or statues or documents; but their significance lies in the truths they represent to the citizens of a nation and in the image they convey to other nations."

Such a symbol in the United States is the Statue of Liberty. This is an impressive symbol of what the United States has stood for from the very beginning of its history; this is *a symbol of freedom*. It reflects the immigrant history of the United States, for it was freedom that millions of human beings were looking for on these shores. And it was freedom that the young Republic offered in compassion. . . .

I wish to pay homage to this noble trait of America and its people, its desire to be free, its determination to preserve freedom and its willingness to share this freedom with others. May the ideal of liberty, of freedom, remain a moving force for your nation and for all the nations in the world today!

It greatly honors your country and its citizens that on this foundation of liberty you have built a nation where the dignity of every human person is to be respected, where a religious sense and a strong family structure are fostered, where duty and honest work are held in high esteem, where generosity and hospitality are not idle words and where the right to religious liberty is deeply rooted in your history.

July 5

The World Created by God for Man

If therefore our time, the time of our generation, the time that is approaching the end of the second millennium of the Christian era, shows itself a time of great progress, it is also seen as a time of threat in many forms for man. The Church must speak of this threat to all people of good will and must always carry on a dialogue with them about it. Man's situation in the modern world seems indeed to be far removed from the objective demands of the moral order, from the requirements of justice, and even more of social love. We are dealing here only with that which found expression in the Creator's first message to man at the moment in which he was giving him the earth, to "subdue" it. This first message was confirmed by Christ the Lord in the mystery of the Redemption. This is expressed by the Second Vatican Council in those beautiful chapters of its teaching that concern man's "kingship," that is to say his call to share in the kingly function — the *munus regale* — of Christ himself. The essential meaning of this "kingship" and "dominion" of man over the visible world, which the Creator himself gave man for his task, consists in the priority of ethics over technology, in the primacy of the person over things, and in the superiority of spirit over matter.

This is why all phases of present-day progress must be followed attentively. Each stage of that progress must, so to speak, be x-rayed from this point of view. What is in question is the advancement of persons, not just the multiplying of things that people can use. It is a matter — as a contemporary philosopher has said and as the Council has stated — not so much of "having more" as of "being more."

July 6

St. Maria Goretti, Virgin and Martyr

Maria Goretti was a martyr of chastity, that is, of a specific virtuous moral behavior, which has always been highly honored in the history of Christianity, even though in our age — as in others — many efforts have been made to depreciate its value. The message which comes from the story of Maria Goretti is certainly not a Manichean one, of devaluation of the body and of sexuality, because a whole deep and sound theology of the body belongs properly to biblical revelation. Rather is it a message concerning personal dignity at the simple human level, which must be defended against every ruse and every violence, and it is one which also concerns consecration of one's energies, including physical energies, to the Lord and to the Church, in radical obedience to God's law.

The Christian does not cultivate chastity or any other virtue only for itself, by making an isolated end or absolute ideal of it. "If I hand over my body to be burnt, but have not love, I gain nothing." Chastity is a most noble value, if it be turned toward Christ the Lord and made part of the whole context of typical Christian living. The Holy Spirit confers his particular fundamental and unmistakeable stamp on this; it has "self-mastery" as one of its fruits, preceded and surrounded by many others.

Therefore, the call coming from Maria Goretti and addressed to all of us, to the young of both sexes particularly, is to take deep care of our baptismal identity and make part of the framework of such formation, as one of its components, well-nourished and jealous cultivation of one's integral dignity — not only Christian but also human. Chastity is an expression of first importance.

July 7

In Christ the Visible World is Created Again

To this question, dear brothers, sons and daughters, a fundamental and essential response must be given. Our response must be: Our spirit is set in one direction, the only direction for our intellect, will and heart is — towards Christ our Redeemer, towards Christ, the Redeemer of man. We wish to look towards him — because there is salvation in no one else but him, the Son of God — repeating what Peter said: "Lord, to whom shall we go? You have the words of eternal life."

Through the Church's consciousness, which the Council considerably developed, through all levels of this self-awareness, and through all the fields of activity in which the Church expresses, finds and confirms herself, we must constantly aim at him "who is the head," "through whom are all things and through whom we exist," who is both "the way, and the truth" and "the resurrection and the life," seeing whom, we see the Father, and who had to go away from us — that is, by his death on the Cross and then by his Ascension into heaven — in order that the Counsellor should come to us and should keep coming to us as the Spirit of truth. In him are "all the treasures of wisdom and knowledge," and the Church is his Body. "By her relationship with Christ, the Church is a kind of sacrament or sign and means of intimate union with God, and of the unity of all mankind," and the source of this is he, he himself, he the Redeemer. . . .

In Jesus Christ, the visible world which God created for man — the world that, when sin entered, was "subject to futility" — recovers again its original link with the divine source of wisdom and love.

July 8

The Church Never Ceases

The Church does not cease to listen to his words. She rereads them continually. With the greatest devotion she reconstructs every detail of his life. These words are listened to also by non-Christians. The life of Christ speaks, also, to many who are not capable of repeating with Peter: "You are the Christ, the Son of the living God." He, the Son of the living God, speaks to people also as Man: it is his life that speaks, his humanity, his fidelity to the truth, his all-embracing love. Furthermore, his death on the Cross speaks — that is to say the inscrutable depth of his suffering and abandonment. The Church never ceases to relive his death on the Cross and his Resurrection, which constitute the content of the Church's daily life.

Indeed, it is by the command of Christ himself, her Master, that the Church unceasingly celebrates the Eucharist, finding in it the "fountain of life and holiness," the efficacious sign of grace and reconciliation with God, and the pledge of eternal life. The Church lives his mystery, draws without wearying from it and continually seeks ways of bringing this mystery of her Master and Lord to humanity — to the peoples, the nations, the succeeding generations, and every individual human being — as if she were ever repeating, as the Apostle did: "For I decided to know nothing among you except Jesus Christ and him crucified." The Church stays within the sphere of the mystery of the Redemption, which has become the fundamental principle of her life and mission.

July 9

Christ Is Everyone's Life

Jesus Christ is the Chief way for the Church. He himself is our way "to the Father's house" and is the way to each man. On this way leading from Christ to man, on this way on which Christ unites himself with each man, nobody can halt the Church. This is an exigency of man's temporal welfare and of his eternal welfare. Out of regard for Christ and in view of the mystery that constitutes the Church's own life, the Church cannot remain insensible to whatever serves man's true welfare any more than she can remain indifferent to what threatens it. In various passages in its documents the Second Vatican Council has expressed the Church's fundamental solicitude that life in "the world should conform more to man's surpassing dignity" in all its aspects so as to make that life "ever more human." This is the solicitude of Christ himself, the good Shepherd of all men. In the name of this solicitude, as we read in the Council's Pastoral Constitution, "the Church must in no way be confused with the political community, nor bound to any political system. She is at once a sign and a safeguard of the transcendence of the human person."

Accordingly, what is in question here is man in all his truth, in his full magnitude. We are not dealing with the "abstract" man but the real, "concrete," "historical" man. We are dealing with "each" man, for each one is included in the mystery of the Redemption and with each one Christ has united himself for ever through this mystery.

July 10

The Christian Vocation

What does our divine Master wish to teach us, each and every one of us, today? With words simple and clear, *Jesus* outlined the requirements for admission to his heavenly Kingdom. *He offered reflections on every aspect of daily life. Jesus proposed a new concept of living.* In the short introductory phrases to his Sermon on the Mount, Jesus sounded the keynote of the new era he had come to proclaim.

The new spirit is to be gentle, generous, simple and above all sincere. To avoid being arrogant, censorious or self-seeking. The disciples of the new Kingdom must seek happiness even amidst poverty, deprivation, tears and oppression. To aim for the kingdom requires *a radical change* in outlook, in mentality, in behavior, in relations with others. Just as the law was revealed to Moses on Mount Sinai, so, in this Sermon on the Mount, *Jesus, the new Lawgiver, offers to all mankind a new way of life, a charter of Christian life.*

It is this loving Fatherhood of God which pervades every word of Jesus. Throughout this discourse he appeals to his listeners to respond to the Father, with a response of filial love. *Everyone who will be animated by this new spirit is a child of God.* It is the spirit of sons, and it makes us cry out, "Abba, Father" (*Rom* 8:14-15). Love will be the mainspring of the new era. Jesus affirmed this on a later occasion, saying: "Anyone who loves me will be true to my word, and my Father will love him; we will come to him and make our dwelling place with him" (*Jn* 14:23)

July 11

St. Benedict of Nursia

St. Benedict was endowed with profound human sensibility. In his project for reform of society, he looked to man above all, following three guidelines: the value of the single man as person; the dignity of work, understood as service to God and the brethren; the necessity for contemplation, that is, of prayer.

Having understood that God is the Absolute and that we live in the Absolute, he understood that the soul of everything ought to be prayer: *"Ut in omnibus glorificetur Deus"* — *"That God be glorified in all things."* We may therefore sum up by saying that St. Benedict's message is a call to inner knowledge. Man must first of all enter into himself, he ought to know himself deeply, he should discover yearning for God and traces of the Absolute in himself.

The theocentric and liturgical character of the social reform propounded by St. Benedict seems to follow the celebrated exhortations of St. Augustine: *"Noli foras ire, teipsum redi; in interiore homine habitat veritas"* — "Do not go out, go back to yourself; truth dwells in the inner man."

St. Gregory tells of the life of St. Benedict in his celebrated *Dialogues.* He writes that he "dwelled alone with himself under the eyes of Him who watches us from above; *solus superni spectatoris oculis habitavit secum."*

Let us listen to St. Benedict's voice: from interior solitude, from contemplative silence, from victory over the noise of the outer world, from this "dwelling with oneself" is born dialogue with oneself and with God, leading even to the peaks of asceticism and mysticism.

July 12

St. Benedict, Father of Europe

The voice of our times, in which we live with anxiety and trepidation, tells us that mankind is tending more and more toward unity. Need is felt for greater knowledge of one another, among individuals and among peoples.

Europe is accomplishing her unity, especially today; not only economic unity, but social and political unity as well, with respect for the individual nationalities. The problems having to be faced and resolved are many and complicated; they range from the cultural field and the field of education to those of law and economics. St. Benedict was declared by Pius XII to be "Father of Europe," and Paul VI decreed him to be Europe's heavenly patron. Listening to St. Benedict, we know that the times are moving us toward an ever more intense understanding of one another, such as may overcome social inequalities, egotistical indifference, undue use of force, intolerance.

And is not this the message of the Christian faith? This Christian faith which is the soul and spirit of Europe and which calls upon us to be mild, patient, merciful, peacemaking, pure of heart, poor in spirit, hungry and thirsty for justice. St. Benedict's voice thus joins with the voice of the times. May the Beatitudes be the living program for all Europe!

We would here pray for the peace of Christ. And if we look at all the present seeking after greater unity among the peoples of Europe, let us also hope that it will lead as well to profound awareness of the roots — spiritual roots, Christian roots. Why? Because, if you have to build a house in common, there is need to build the foundations deeper. A superficial foundation is not enough. And that deeper foundation is always called "spiritual."

May Mary assist us all to be in agreement for uniting Europe and the whole world under the one sun who is Christ.

July 13

The Pope at Castel Gandolfo

It seems you are glad to see me. That means that Castel Gandolfo is not overpopulated — for there is always room for one more citizen of it. *Deo gratias.* I too am very happy to be once more among you, and to remain a little longer this time. I came upon other occasions during the year, yet almost as a guest. This time, however, I will really be your fellow townsman and therefore, as it were, one of the faithful of the diocese of Albano as well. The Bishop is here near us. And I shall be a member of your parish, too. It is in this atmosphere that I would like to spend the weeks of my vacation among you.

Let us hope that other guests will come, above all for recital of the Angelus on Sundays, as last year. . . . So I will have to reeducate myself in the Italian language and I hope that you will be a help to me in that. I think Castel Gandolfo is the right place for such reeducation.

For my part, I promise you a certain internationalization of Castel Gandolfo during the vacation. I think that all the faithful who come up here ought to be able to feel at home. I therefore think that, with the permission of the local authorities, of Mr. Mayor, we shall be able to proclaim Castel Gandolfo an open city. So the Irish, who are here today, will be able to think that they are in

Galway; these Spanish sisters in Spain; and all the others, too, the French for example, who are from Chartres or Paris, should feel quite at home here, as if they were there.

This means that we shall try to get on well together under the protection of the Virgin who is venerated here. I wish you well, and I commend myself to your kindness and prayers.

July 14

Blessed Kateri Tekakwitha

The North American Indians of Canada and the United States . . . have come to rejoice in the beatification of Kateri Tekakwitha. It is a time to pause and to give thanks to God for the unique culture and rich human tradition which you have inherited and for the greatest gift anyone can receive, the gift of faith. Indeed, Blessed Kateri stands before us as symbol of the best of the heritage that is yours as North American Indians.

But today is also a day of great happiness for the Church throughout the world. We are all edified by her complete trust in the providence of God, and we are encouraged by her joyful fidelity to the Gospel of our Lord Jesus Christ. The Church has declared to the world that Kateri Tekakwitha lived a life on earth of exemplary holiness.

Her beatification should remind us that we are all called to a life of holiness, for in Baptism God has chosen each one of us "to be holy and spotless and to live through love in his presence." Holiness of life, union with Christ through prayer and works of charity, is not something reserved to a select few among the members of the Church. It is the vocation of everyone.

My brothers and sisters, may God bless you as he blessed her. May God bless all the North American Indians of Canada and the United States.

July 15

The Repose of the Summer Vacation

"Open O Lord, our hearts, that we may carefully hear the words of your Son."

This prayer is always relevant, just as what Mary and Martha said, and what Christ said to them and of them, always make us think. Today, however, I would utter this prayer in a particular manner. As I say it, I will think of all those who are benefitting from taking a rest in various parts of Italy and other countries as well, during this summer and in the course of the vacations. Taking a rest means leaving one's daily occupations behind, breaking away from the normal tasks of the day, the week and the year. It means leaving and separating from everything that could be meant by the symbol "Martha."

It is important for such rest not to be wasted, not to be just a vacuum (in which case it would not be real rest). It is important for the period of rest to be filled with meetings. Yes, I think so, certainly! Meetings with nature, with the mountains, with the sea and with the forests. Man in wise contact with nature recovers inner quiet and calm. But that is still not all that can be said of rest. There is need for it to be filled with a new content, with that content which is expressed by means of the symbol of "Mary." Mary means meeting with Christ, meeting with

God. She means opening one's inner sight to the word of His truth. She has this meaning for boys and girls especially. They are free of school or university obligations, and they take trips in this period, they get to know the world and people, they go to holiday camps and summer resorts. I know that among them there is no lack of some for whom the summer holidays are also the time for a special meeting with the Lord, in a fraternal community of young people of their own age. Such encounters are as precious as are the vacations themselves.

July 16

The Special Christian Vocation

It is essential for us to understand that Jesus has a *specific task in life for each and every one of us.* Each one of us is handpicked, called by name — by Jesus! There is no one among us who does not have a divine vocation! Now this is what Saint Paul wrote in his letter to the Ephesians: "Each one of us has received God's favor in the measure in which Christ bestows it.... It was he who gave apostles, prophets, evangelists, pastors, and teachers in roles of service for the faithful to build up the body of Christ" *(Eph* 4:11–12).

First and foremost, God has called us into existence. He has called us to be! He has called us, through his Son Jesus Christ, to a knowledge of himself as our Loving Father. He has called us to be his children! He has called us to fulfill his eternal plan in our individual lives, with Jesus as our guide. He has called us to be co-heirs with Jesus of his heavenly Kingdom! What God our Father is offering us through his Son is a *new life as his real children, with Jesus for our brother;* a pressing call to live, to love, to labor for the coming of his Kingdom. And, lest, bewildered at what we must do, we hesitate, Jesus offers to be himself our guide and says: "Come after me." (*Lk* 9:59).

July 17

Solitude and Silence Nourish Spiritual Life

You know how, before beginning his public life, Jesus retired in prayer for forty days in the desert. You too try to bring *a little silence* into your lives, so as to be able to think, to reflect, to pray with greater fervor and make resolutions with greater decision.

It is difficult to create "zones of desert and silence" these days, because you are continually being overcome by the complications of your work, the uproar of events, the attraction of the communications media, so much so that inner peace is compromised and the supreme thoughts which ought to characterize man's existence are hindered. It is difficult, but it is possible and important to know how to succeed in it.

You too, can put aside a little time, in the evening especially, for praying, for meditating, for reading a page of the Gospel or an episode in the life of some saint. Create a zone of desert and silence for yourself in that way, take part also in retreats and courses of spiritual exercises, organized in your dioceses and parishes.

Together with the importance of recollection, Jesus also inculcated the necessity for *commitment to overcome evil.* We know from what the Evangelists tell us that Jesus himself willed to suffer temptation. He did so in order to lay emphasis on its reality and to teach the strategy for fighting it and winning victory. Being Christian means accepting the reality of life and undertaking the necessary struggle against evil, according to the method taught by the Divine Master. I exhort you to be courageous now and always, without becoming bewildered by difficulties, and always trusting in Him who is your Friend and your Redeemer, and watching and praying to keep your faith sound and your grace lively.

July 18

Prayer Detects God's Presence in Our Souls

Prayer is so important that Jesus himself tells us: *"Pray constantly" (Lk* 21:36). He wants us to pray to his Father, as he himself did. The Gospel tells us that Jesus prayed all night before choosing his Apostles *(cf. Lk* 6:12). And later on, in his passion, at the height of his suffering, Christ "prayed with all the greater intensity" *(Lk* 22:44).

Jesus not only gave us the example of prayer, he actually *taught us how to pray.* One of the most beautiful scenes of the Gospel shows Jesus gathered with his disciples, teaching them to pray: "Our Father in heaven, hallowed be your name, your kingdom come, your will be done on earth as it is in heaven." Jesus was showing his disciples the value of praising God: the importance of God's name, his Kingdom and his Holy will. At the same time Jesus was telling them to ask for bread, for pardon and for help in trials. "Give us this day our daily bread, and forgive the wrong we have done as we forgive those who wrong us. Subject us not to the trial but deliver us from the evil one" *(cf. Mt* 6:9-13; *Lk* 11:2-4).

My dear young people, it is through prayer that Jesus leads us to his Father. It is in prayer that the Holy Spirit transforms our lives. It is in prayer that we come to know God: to detect his presence in our souls, to hear his voice speaking through our consciences, and to treasure his gift to us of personal responsibility for our lives and for our world.

It is through prayer that we can *clearly focus our attention on the person of Jesus Christ* and see the total relevance of his teaching for our lives. We begin to see things his way.

July 19

Prayer Transforms Our Lives

Prayer transforms our individual lives and the life of the world. Young men and women, when you meet Christ in prayer, when you get to know his Gospel and reflect on it in relation to your hopes and your plan for the future, then everything is new. Everything is different when you begin to examine in prayer the circumstances of every day, according to the set of values that Jesus taught. These values are so clearly stated in the Beatitudes: "Blest are they who show mercy; mercy shall be theirs. . . . Blest too the peacemakers, they shall be called sons of God" (*Mt* 5:7-9).

In prayer, united with Jesus — your brother, your friend, your Savior, your God — you begin to breathe a new atmosphere, you form new goals and new ideals. Yes, in Christ you begin to understand yourselves more fully. This is what the Second Vatican Council wanted to emphasize when it stated: "The truth is that only in the mystery of the Incarnate Word does the mystery of man take on light." In other words, Christ not only reveals

God to man but also reveals man to himself. In Christ we grasp the secret of our own humanity.

But there is more. Through prayer you come *to experience the truth that Jesus taught:* "The words that I spoke to you are spirit and life" (*Jn* 6:63). In Jesus, whom you get to know in prayer, your dreams for justice and your dreams for peace become definite and look for practical applications. When you are in contact with the Prince of Peace, you understand how totally opposed to his message are violence and terrorism, hatred and war. In him you experience the full meaning of an interpersonal relationship that is based on generous love. Christ offers you a friendship that does not disappoint, a fidelity beyond compare.

July 20

Prayer Helps Read "the Signs of the Times"

Through prayer, especially to Jesus at Communion, you will understand so many things about the world and its relationship to him, and you will be in a position to read accurately what are referred as the "signs of the times." Above all, you will have something to offer those who come to you in need.

Through prayer you will possess Christ and be able to communicate him to others. And this is the greatest contribution you can make in your lives: *to communicate Christ to the world.*

Through prayer you will receive the strength to resist the spirit of the world. You will receive the power to show compassion to every human being — just as Jesus did. Through prayer you will have *a part in salvation history* as it unfolds in your generation. In prayer you will be able to enter into the heart of Jesus and understand his feelings towards his Church. By using the Psalms, the prayerbook that Jesus used, you will be able to repeat, under the action of the Holy Spirit, the praise and thanksgiving that have been offered to God for centuries by his people. In all the circumstances of your lives, you will find that Jesus is with you — he is close to you in prayer. It is prayer that will bring joy into your lives and help you to overcome the obstacles to Christian living. . . .

When you go to Jesus in prayer — and through him to the Father — you will always find inspiration in Mary his Mother. With every generation of disciples you will learn to pray with her, and with her to await the action of the Holy Spirit in your lives (*cf. Acts* 1:14).

July 21

Purity Is Life According to the Spirit

"Know you not that your body is a temple of the Holy Spirit, who is within — the Spirit you have received from God. You are not your own. You have been purchased, and at a price" (*1 Cor* 6:19-20). "Do you not see that your bodies are members of Christ?" (*1 Cor* 6:15).

The Apostle indicates the mystery of the redemption of the body accomplished by Christ as the source of a particular moral duty, which commits Christians to purity, to that which Paul himself describes elsewhere as need to guard his body "in sanctity and honor" (*1 Thes* 4:4). Maintaining one's own body "in sanctity and honor" means *forming it through abstension from immodesty,* and this is the indispensable way. However, it always bears fruit in the deepest experience of that love which was written "in the beginning" according to the image and likeness of God himself, in every human being, hence also in our bodies. St. Paul therefore exhorts us, "Glorify God in your body" (*1 Cor* 6:20).

Purity is the virtue, that is, capacity, to "keep one's body in sanctity and honor." It is allied with the gift of piety, as fruit of the dwelling of the Holy Spirit in the "temple" of the body. It actuates such a fullness of dignity in the body in interpersonal relations, that *God himself is glorified.* Purity is the glory of the human body in the sight of God. It is God's glory in the human body, through which masculinity and femininity are manifested. From purity arises that singular beauty which permeates every sphere of the lives of people together and permits expression of the simplicity and the profundity, the cordiality and the unrepeatable authenticity, of personal entrustment.

July 22

Promulgation of the New Code of Canon Law

The Code of Canon Law is really extremely necessary for the Church to be visible. She has need of norms both so that her hierarchic and organic structure may be visible and that the exercise of the functions divinely entrusted to her, especially that of the sacred power and administration of the Sacraments, may be adequately organized. Also so that reciprocal relationships among the faithful may be regulated according to justice, based on charity, and that the rights of individuals may be well guaranteed and well defined. Finally, so that common undertakings, adopted for the sake of ever more perfect Christian life, may be sustained, reinforced and promoted through the canonical norms.

In conclusion, by their very nature, the canon laws have to be observed. So the utmost diligence was adopted during the long period of preparation of the Code, so that the norms should be accurately expressed and be seen to be based on a solid juridical, canonical, theological foundation.

Trusting, therefore, in the aid of divine grace; borne up by the authority of the Holy Apostles Peter and Paul; well aware of what I am doing, accepting the prayers of bishops throughout the world, who have collaborated with me in collegial spirit; with that supreme authority with which I am invested, by means of this Constitution, which is to be valid for all future time, I promulgate this present Code, as it has been ordered and revised. And I command that it shall have force of law for the future in the whole of the Latin Church, and I confide it to the vigilant custody of those whose duty it is to see that it be observed.

July 23

From the Cross of Christ:

The Example of Obedience

"He humbled himself, obediently accepting even death, death on a cross!" (*Phil* 2:8). He humbled himself; he made himself obedient. These are words which seem out of date today, when there is a whole systematic opposition to obedience, which is presented as a humiliation of one's personality, a defeat of the intelligence and of the will, abdication of one's human dignity. Autonomy, revolt, rebellion, are preached instead.

But it is certainly Jesus who gave us *the example of obedience* even unto death on the cross. All saints have passed through a test, sometimes even a heroic test, of obedience. As did Mary Most Holy, as did St. Joseph, who but obeyed the voice of God calling them to a sublime mission indeed but also to a disconcerting and mysterious one!

Why must you obey? First of all, because obedience is necessary in the general framework of Providence — God did not create us by chance but for a quite clear and distinct purpose: his everlasting glory and our happiness. All those who have responsibility over us ought, in God's name, to help us to reach the goal willed by the Creator. Moreover, exterior obedience teaches us to obey the inner law of conscience, that is, God's will expressed in the moral law.

And how should we obey? With love, also with holy courage, well knowing that obedience is almost always difficult. It costs sacrifice, it demands commitment and sometimes even entails heroic effort. We must look at Jesus Crucified! We must also obey with confidence, convinced that God's grace is never lacking, and then the soul is flooded with immense inner joy. The effort of obedience is repaid with continual inner gladness.

July 24

The Fruit of the Redemption
Is the New Creature

The fruit of the Redemption is the "new creature"; the Redemption is a "new creation." Why "new"? Because, by reason of sin, man fell from his "original justice." He broke the Alliance with God. In consequence, he suffered interior disintegration, on the one hand, and, on the other, incapacity to build communion with others in the truth of self-giving. We shall never reflect enough on this destruction worked by sin. We are celebrating . . . to deepen our consciousness of sin, the indispensable starting point for participating in the mystery of the Redemption personally.

The Redemption worked by Christ brought man back to "the dignity of his first origins," as the liturgy says. In Christ, God re-created man, so that Christ became the second and true Adam, whence the new humanity takes its origin. "If anyone is in Christ, he is a new creation. The old order has passed away; now all is new!" (2 Cor 5:17). It is a matter of change in the very essence of the human person who has been redeemed.

What you have done is put aside your old self with its past deeds and put on a new man, one who grows in knowledge in the image of his Creator (Col 3:9). As will have been noted, these latter words of St. Paul's recall that text of Genesis according to which man was created in God's image. The new creation, which the Redemption is, renews man by bringing him back to the fullness of his deepest being, by reintegrating him in his truth: which is that *he is God's image.*

July 25

St. James the Apostle

A friend of Jesus, one of the Lord's predilect disciples, the first of the Apostles to bear testimony to the Gospel with his blood: St. James the Greater, the son of Zebedee. . . .

St. James was the brother of John the Evangelist. They were the two disciples to whom — in one of the most important of the dialogues recorded by the Gospel — Jesus put that famous query: Can you drink the cup that I must drink? And they answered, "We can." Theirs was the word of readiness, of valiance, an attitude which is very fitting to the young, and not only to them, but to all Christians as well, particularly those who agree to be apostles of the Gospel. Those disciples' generous response was accepted by Jesus. He told them, "You shall drink of my cup."

Those words were accomplished in St. James, the son of Zebedee. He gave testimony to Christ's resurrection with his blood, at Jerusalem. . . . St. James the Greater accomplished his *vocation of service* in the kingdom established by the Lord. Like the Divine Master, "he gave his life in ransom for many." We have testimony of that . . . at Compostella. A testimony of faith, which entire generations of pilgrims have sought over the centuries "to touch" with their own hands and "kiss" with their lips, coming for this purpose from the countries of Europe and from the East.

So it is that the apostolic testimony endures at Compostella and that dialogue of the generations is realized. This is the means through which faith, the Church's authentic faith, grows, faith in Jesus Christ, Son of God made man, who died and was raised again so as to offer us salvation. He who is rich in mercy is Redeemer of man. A faith which is translated into lifestyle according

269

to the Gospel, that is to say, a way of living which reflects the Beatitudes, shows itself in love, as the key to human existence, and adds power to the values of the person, to commit the person to solving the human problems of our time.

July 26

St. Ann, Mother of Mary Most Holy

The personage that is St. Ann reminds us of Mary's early home, where she, Christ's Mother, came into the world, bringing that extraordinary mystery of the Immaculate Conception with her. She was there surrounded by the love and care of her parents, Joachim and Ann. There she learned from her mother, St. Ann, how to be a mother. And although she had given up the idea of motherhood, from the human point of view, the Heavenly Father nonetheless gratified her with the most perfect and most holy maternity, while still accepting her total donation. From the height of the Cross, Christ, in a certain sense, transferred His own Mother's motherhood to his favorite disciple; he extended it to the whole Church at the same time, to all mankind. So when we, as heirs of the divine promise, find ourselves within the range of this motherhood, and when we feel its profundity and fullness, we can think that it was certainly St. Ann who first taught Mary, her daughter, to be a mother.

In Hebrew, "Anna" means "God has given a grace." When meditating on this significance of St. Ann's name, St. John Damascene exclaimed: "Since it had to be that the virgin Mother of God should be born of Ann, nature did not dare precede the seed of grace; but it remained without its own fruit so that grace might produce its own. In fact, that firstborn had to be born, from whom the firstborn of every creature would be born."

Let us turn our hearts to her, and, through her, to Mary, Daughter and Mother. Let us repeat:

Monstra te esse Matrem
Sumat per te preces,
Qui pro nobis natus,
Tulit esse Tuus.

Show yourself a Mother,
Prayers through you
May He receive, who chose
To be your son.

July 27

A Holy Husband and Wife

St. Ann and St. Joachim were, in their time, members of the people which rose from the faith of Abraham, of that people formed by Moses, which Exodus describes as thirsting to know God's face. This is indeed the mark of prayer, of contemplation, that for which your Center seeks to train you. I imagine — and you will too — that this passage often fed the meditations of Teresa of Jesus and of John of the Cross, who are especially dear to your hearts, and to mine! As for today's Gospel, it reminds us realistically that mankind is always and again marked by traces of holiness and by areas of sin. It is always in need of redemption.

Dear Christians, young and old, the essential is certainly that, in the world as it is, the Lord's disciples should be channels of God's salvific action, by being ceaselessly purified, enlightened and comforted by frequently approaching the God of tenderness and piety. In their time and place, Ann and Joachim were a very precious link in the divine plan for salvation of humanity. May we — and you young people particularly — become more and more humble and courageous, poor servants, available for the Church of Christ, which is precisely the Sacrament of Salvation. And may your service be moreover marked by trusting and regular bonds with the pastors of the particular churches!

The life, the death and the resurrection of Christ are made present through celebration of each Eucharist. May He himself accord you the grace to cooperate generously in applying his grand work of redemption! Amen.

July 28

Christ Came to Bring Joy

I come to you as a servant of Jesus Christ, and I want to speak about him. Christ came to bring joy: joy to children, joy to parents, joy to families and to friends, joy to workers and to scholars, joy to the sick and to the elderly, joy to all humanity. In a true sense, joy is the keynote of the Christmas message and the recurring motif of the Gospels. Recall the first words of the Angel to Mary: "Rejoice, O highly favored daughter, the Lord is with you" (Lk 1:28). And at the birth of Jesus, the angel announced to the shepherds: "I come to proclaim good news to you, tidings of great joy to be shared by the whole people" (*Lk* 2:10). Years later as Jesus entered Jerusalem riding on a colt, "the entire crowd of disciples began to rejoice and praise God loudly." "Blessed is He who comes as King in the name of the Lord!" (*Lk* 19:37–38). We are told that some Pharisees in the crowd complained, saying: "Teacher, rebuke your disciples." But Jesus answered: "If they were to keep silence, I tell you the very stones would cry out" (*Lk* 19:39–40).

Are not those words of Jesus still true today? If we are silent about the joy that comes from knowing Jesus, the very stones of our cities will cry out! For we are an Easter people and "Alleluia" is our song. With Saint Paul I exhort you: "Rejoice in the Lord always! I say it again. Rejoice!" (*Phil* 4:4).

And rejoice because he is the master of our life!

July 29

St. Martha

Martha and Mary! In the history of Christian spirituality, these two sisters have been understood as personages dedicated respectively to action and to contemplation. Martha is taken up with housework, whereas Mary sits at Jesus' feet to listen to his words. We can derive two lessons from the Gospel text.

First of all, Jesus' final remark is to be noted: "Mary has chosen the better portion and she shall not be deprived of it." He forcefully emphasized the fundamental and irreplaceable value which hearing the word of God has for our existence. That word ought to be our constant reference point, our light and our strength. But we must listen to it. We must learn how to be quiet, create room for solitude, or, better, for private meeting and intimate colloquy with the Lord. We must know how to contemplate. Unfortunately, our daily lives are in danger of experiencing — actually do experience — cases of inner pollution. But contact in faith with the word of the Lord purifies us, elevates us and gives us back energy.

But there is a second lesson to be learned; it is that we must never see any contrast between action and contemplation. We actually read in the Gospel that it was Martha (and not Mary) who received Jesus "to her home." There is harmony between these things.

The hospitality which Abraham gave to three mysterious personages sent by the Lord teaches us that we can serve the Lord also through our slightest daily tasks, and be in contact with Him. According to an ancient interpretation, Abraham's three guests were images of the Holy Trinity, no less. Pray and work — *Ora et labora!* These words contain a whole program: not of opposition, but of synthesis, not of contrast but of fusion between equally important elements.

July 30

St. Leopold Mandic, "the Confessor"

Leopold Mandic was in his time a heroic servant of reconciliation and penitence.

St. Leopold left no theological or literary works; he did not fascinate through his culture, he did not found social works. To all who knew him he was but a poor friar, small, and subject to ill health.

His greatness lay elsewhere: *in his immolating of himself*, day after day, for the whole period of his priestly life, that is, for fifty-two years, in silence, in discretion, in *the humility of a little cell, a confessional.* "The good shepherd gives up his life for his sheep." Friar Leopold was always there, ready, smiling, prudent, modest, confident, discreet, a faithful father of souls, respectful master and comprehensive and patient spiritual counsellor.

If we wished to define him by means of one single word, in the way his penitents and fellow friars did during his lifetime, then he was "the Confessor." He knew only how to hear confessions. But it was there that his greatness resided — in this way he had of fading away, so as to make room for the true Shepherd of Souls.

Father Leopold was a priest for whom preaching was impossible, because of a pronunciation defect. He was a priest who ardently desired to dedicate himself to the missions and to the very end he was waiting for the day when he could set off. But he never went because his health was too frail. He was a priest with ecumenical spirit. It was so big that he offered himself as a victim to the Lord, in daily donation, for the sake of restoration of full unity between the Latin and the Oriental Churches which were still separated, for the sake of their once again being "one sole flock under one sole shepherd." But he lived his ecumenical vocation in a wholly hidden way: "I will be a missionary here, in obedience and in exercise of my ministry." And again: "Every soul which asks for my ministry shall be my Orient for the present."

July 31

St. Ignatius Loyola

A son of the Church who may well be regarded with delight and rightful pride. . . . When speaking of St. Ignatius at Loyola, the crib and site of his conversion, the spiritual exercises spontaneously come to mind. They are a well-tried method for effectively approaching God. The Company of Jesus, which is spread throughout the world, has reaped much fruit through them; and goes on reaping so much, in the cause of the Gospel.

He knew how to obey when, as he recovered from his wound, the voice of God forcefully struck his heart. He was responsive to the inspirations of the Holy Spirit and thereby understood what solutions were required for the evils of his time. He was obedient to the see of Peter at every moment and desired to put a ready instrument into the hands of Peter for evangelization. To that end, he bequeathed such obedience as one of the characteristic marks of his Company's charism. . . .

Listen to St. Paul: "Be imitators of me, as I am of Christ . . . as I seek to please all men in all things, not seeking my own convenience, but that of all, that they may be saved." We may put these words of the Apostle in the mouth of St. Ignatius today also, after so many centuries. The charisma of founders ought to continue in the communities which they originated. It must at all times constitute the life principle of each religious family. "Let the spirit and the purposes proper to the founders, as well as sound traditions, be recognized and faithfully maintained, all that constitutes the patrimony of each institution." Loyola is a call to fidelity. Not only for the Company of Jesus but also indirectly for other institutions.

August

August 1

St. Alphonsus Liguori

St. Alphonsus established the purpose [of the Redemptorist order] as announcement of the word of God "to the more abandoned souls." The [Vatican] Council wisely recalled that authentic renewal of religious life is not to be had without a "return to the sources." You are aware of the norms which the Council fathers laid down in this respect: "Let there be faithful interpretation and observation of the spirit and purposes of the founders, and of sound traditions, for all that constitutes the patrimony of each institution."

In the awareness of this . . . to bring the precise meaning of evangelization in the world today into focus . . . who are to be regarded as "poor" and "abandoned" in our social context, so as to establish "commitment priorities," toward which to direct the . . . missionary effort, always with respect for legitimate pluralism? This is necessary for avoiding useless waste of energy and for keeping the character which St. Alphonsus gave to the order — that which the people of God has so clearly appreciated over the centuries.

In this respect, I would particularly draw your attention to the opportunity of giving a new impulse to the traditional missions. . . . If conducted according to criteria in keeping with the modern mentality, those missions can be an indispensable instrument for the periodical and vigorous renewal of Christian life. As you well know, St. Alphonsus had very great confidence in them.

August 2

Ever Rejoice

How many people have never known . . . joy? They feed on emptiness and tread the paths of despair. "They sit in darkness and in the shadow of death" (*Lk* 1:79).

And we need not look to the far ends of the earth for them. They live in our neighborhoods, they walk down our streets, they may even be members of our own families. They live without true joy because they live without hope.

They live without hope because they have never heard, really heard the Good News of Jesus Christ, because they have never met a brother or a sister who touched their lives with the love of Jesus and lifted them up from their misery.

We must go to them therefore as messengers of hope. We must bring to them the witness of true joy. We must pledge to them our commitment to work for a just society and city where they feel respected and loved.

And so I encourage you, be men and women of deep and abiding faith. Be heralds of hope. Be messengers of joy. Be true workers for justice. Let the Good News of Christ radiate from your hearts, and the peace he alone gives remain forever in your souls. My dear brothers and sisters in the black community: "Rejoice in the Lord always, again I say rejoice."

August 3

True Christian Liberation

The Church has the duty to announce the liberation of millions of human beings . . . but she also has the corresponding duty to proclaim liberation in its integral, profound meaning, as Jesus announced it and realized it: "Liberation from everything oppressing mankind, liberation which is, above all, salvation from sin and the evil one, in the joy of knowing God and being known by him." Liberation made of reconciliation and pardon. Liberation gushing from the reality of being children of God, whom we may call "Abba, Father" *(Rom* 8:15), by virtue of which we recognize our brother in every man, whose love may be transformed by God's mercy. Liberation as overcoming various servitudes and idols which man shapes for himself, and as growth of the new man. Liberation which is not diminished in the mission proper to the church . . . to the economic, political, social and cultural dimension. . . .

It is necessary to avoid reductions and ambiguities at all costs. There are many signs which help to distinguish whether it is a question of Christian liberation: . . . fidelity to the word of God, to the Church's living tradition, to her *magisterium*; the sense of communion with the bishops, first of all, and with the other sectors of the People of God.

It is a question of the form of love with which we direct our concern for the poor, for the sick, the deprived, the defenseless, the oppressed, and how we discover the image in them of Jesus, "poor and suffering, seeking to liberate us. and how we seek to serve Christ in them." Let us make no mistake — the humble and simple faithful, almost by evangelical instinct, grasp spontaneously when the Gospel is being served in the Church and when it is being emptied out and stifled, in other interests.

August 4

Evangelization

There is no true evangelization unless the teaching, the life, the promises, the kingdom, the mystery of Jesus of Nazareth, Son of God, be proclaimed. The vigor of the faith of millions of people will depend on living consciousness of this truth.

So we should confess Christ in the face of the history of the world, with profound, strongly felt, lively conviction, as Peter confessed him: "You are the Messiah, the Son of the living God" (*Mt* 16:16). This is the Good News which is unique in a certain sense. This is the sole Gospel and "even if we, or an angel from heaven, should preach to you a gospel not in accord with the one we delivered to you, let a curse be upon him" (*Gal* 1:8).

Evangelization in the present and in the future may not cease from affirming the Church's faith: Jesus Christ, the Word and Son of God, became man to dwell among mankind and, through the power of his ministry, offer it salvation, God's great gift.

It is from this faith in Christ, from the bosom of the Church, that we draw our capacity to serve man, our peoples, to imbue their cultures with the Gospel, to transform hearts, to humanize systems and structures. Any silences, omissions, mutilations, or inadequate stressing of the integrity of the mystery of Jesus Christ, which causes movement away from the faith of the Church, cannot constitute the valid content of evangelization.

In accomplishing my task of evangelizing all mankind, I will not grow tired of repeating: "Have no fear!" Open up even more, open the doors completely to Christ! Open the gates of states, economic and political systems, the vast fields of culture, civilization, and development, to this saving power.

August 5

Remembering Pope Paul VI

The faith which lets man pass from things visible to the invisible reality of God and eternal life resembles that path to which Abraham was called by God, who is described as "the father of all who believe." Hence the attitude of spirit befitting the believer is an attitude of vigilance, the expression of spiritual aspiration to God through faith. When we accept these words and meditate on them, our thoughts turn to the event which occurred . . . at Castel Gandolfo. . . . Pope Paul VI died. Just in these August days, on the feast of the Transfiguration of the Lord. The entire life of this "Servant of the Servants of God" was a pilgrimage, an aspiration in faith, toward what is infinite and invisible: to God who is invisible and who revealed himself to us in Jesus Christ, his Son. It was an aspiration to eternity.

Paul VI followed Christ's call. He walked the way of faith pointed out to him and guided others upon it, first as a priest, then as Archbishop of Milan, finally as Pope, in the Roman See of Peter. And in that spiritual aspiration, he watched with the watchfulness of a faithful servant. The whole of his life gave testimony of this aspiration and this vigilance, toward himself and toward others.

I commend the soul of that great Pope to God. Let us learn from him that simple, downright, childlike faith which was aware, mature and tested at the same time. That faith which this epoch of ours requires from us Christians, "Faith plain to see and courageous. Faith full of hope, faith living through love."

August 6

The Transfiguration of the Lord

"His face became as dazzling as the sun, his clothes as radiant as light. Suddenly Moses and Elijah appeared to them conversing with him" (*Mt* 17:2-3). But at the center of the event are the divine words, which endow it with its true significance: "This is my beloved Son on whom my favor rests. Listen to him" (*Mt* 17:5). We thus understand that this is a christophany: that is, the transfiguration represents the revelation of the Son of God, about whom the account brings several things to light — his glory, by reason of the splendor acquired; his centrality, almost the summary of the history of salvation, signified by the presence of Moses and Elijah; his prophetic authority, legitimately stated by means of the peremptory invitation, "Listen to him"; and, above all, the qualification of "Son," which emphasizes the close and unique relations existing between Jesus and the Heavenly Father.

The words of the transfiguration, moreover, repeat those already present in the story of the baptism in the

Jordan, as if it were to signify that, also after having covered an exact portion of the way of his public life, Jesus remained the same "beloved Son" which he was proclaimed at the beginning.

The apostles showed their delight: "Lord, how good that we are here!" (*Mt* 17:4). But Christ let them know that the event on Mount Tabor is only *on the path toward the revelation of the paschal mystery*: "Do not tell anyone of the vision until the Son of Man rises from the dead" (*Mt* 17:9).

There is need to seek ... nearness to Christ. It is necessary to live in intimacy with him, to open one's heart to him, one's conscience.

August 7

Catechesis

Catechesis has always been considered by the Church as one of her fundamental duties, arising from the risen Lord's last command: to make disciples of all peoples, to teach them to observe everything which he had prescribed. In catechesis, it is Christ, the Incarnate Word and Son of God, who is taught to catechumens, and everything else is in reference to him. Christ alone is our master, our teacher. Every other teacher is so to the degree that he is Christ's spokesman, consenting to Christ teaching through his mouth.

Catechesis is first of all a way ... it must render a vital encounter possible with the Person of Christ, through faith. Being Christian means saying "Yes" to Christ. This "Yes" ... consists in abandoning oneself to the Words of God by resting on them. But even more it means trying to know better the profound sense of this Word.

Catechesis is necessary. *All have need to be catechized.* Catechesis ought to be a permanent school of faith and accompany the great stages of life, a beacon lighting the way. We live in a difficult world, where anguish springs up from seeing man's best accomplishments get out of hand and turn against him. Such anguish sets up an atmosphere of uncertainty. It is in this world that catechesis ought to help Christians to be "light" and "soul," for their joy and for service to all.

Catechesis ought to teach the young and the adults to be lucid and coherent in their faith, to affirm their Christian and Catholic identity with serenity, to adhere strongly in this way to the absolute of God, and be able to give testimony of him everywhere and in all circumstances.

August 8

St. Dominic

The first of the principles of faith affirms *the absolute primacy* of God in the intelligence, in the heart, in the life of man. You know well how St. Dominic responded to this requirement of faith in his religious life: "He spoke only with God or of God." If one does not accept this subordination, if one exalts the greatness of man to the detriment of the primacy of God, one arrives at the failure of the ideologies that postulate the self-sufficiency of man and give rise to the proliferation of errors of which the modern world bears the weight and of which it does not succeed in breaking the cultural and psychological yoke.

I will now repeat a few words of that "Prayer to St. Dominic," which was written by his successor, Master Jordan, and which must be very familiar to you:

"You, having once begun the way of perfection, left all in order to follow naked the naked Christ, preferring to pile up treasures in heaven. But, with even greater strength did you renounce yourself, and manfully bearing the cross, you strove to follow, the footsteps of the sole true guide: the Redeemer.

"You, inflamed with zeal for God and supernatural ardor, through the superabundance of your charity, spent all in an immense outpouring of generosity, for perpetual poverty, for the apostolic life and preaching of the Gospel. And, for the sake of this great work, and not without inspiration from on high, you established the Order of Preaching Friars. . . .

"You, who sought salvation of the human race with so much zeal, come to the aid of the clergy, of the Christian people. . .

"Be for us verily a 'Dominicanus,' that is, a careful watchdog for the Lord's flock. . . ."

August 9

Missionary Activity

"Some do not become Christians simply because there is a dearth of those who make them Christians" (St. Francis Xavier). In the face of this objective dearth, the Church may not be silent or remain peaceful, ignoring the needs of so many millions of our brothers who await the announcement of the message of salvation: God, recalls

St. Paul, "wants all men to be saved and come to know the truth" (*1 Tim* 2:4).

The command addressed by the risen Christ to his disciples, "Go, preach" (*Mt* 28:19), efficaciously establishing the image and the function of the Pilgrim Church, expresses the missionary dynamism that is intrinsic to her nature. Incessantly moved by the Spirit, she is perennially "sent" to the nations to transmit to them the inexhaustible source of that living water, that flows from the word and the work of the Lord. Evangelization, or rather missionary activity, therefore, corresponds to the specific vocation of the Church which, always respecting liberty, encounters men of today who still *"in umbra mortis sedent"* (*Lk* 1:79); one can in fact say that the *Church* is *mission incarnate.* Not in vain did the Council explicitly affirm: "The Pilgrim Church is missionary by her every nature. For it is from the mission of the Son and the mission of the Holy Spirit that she takes origin, in accordance with the decree of the Father." As the Church, the depositary of the Good News, cannot help speaking, so she must of necessity continue sending today, no less than in other times, apostles and missionaries who know how to speak to men of the transcendent and liberating salvation, leading them to the knowledge of truth in full fidelity to the Spirit.

August 10

The Importance of the College of Cardinals

It was an act of confidence and at the same time one of great courage, when the decision was taken to call a "non-Italian" to be Bishop of Rome. Nothing further can be said, we can only bow our heads before such a decision on the part of the Sacred College. The latest events involving the Church had deprived her twice in two months of her universal Pastor. Perhaps never so much as in these events had the Christian people experienced the importance, the delicacy, the responsibility of the tasks which the Sacred College of Cardinals has to perform. Never so much as in this period had the faithful demonstrated such affectionate esteem and such benevolent comprehension for the most eminent fathers of the College.

I would emphasize another element . . . the *sense of fraternity* which has been more and more made manifest and cemented within the Sacred College. "*O quam bonum et quam iucundum habitare fratres in unum!* — Oh, how good and how pleasant it is for brethren to dwell in unison." The Sacred College had to face one of the most delicate problems of the Church, twice, and at a very short interval: the problem of electing the Roman Pontiff. And the Church's authentic universality shone forth on those occasions. One could really witness what St. Augustine affirmed, "The Church speaks the language of all peoples."

Experiences, needs, complex church problems varied, and sometimes diverse. But such variety has been and certainly will be always in concord with one sole faith, since St. Augustine himself emphasizes the beauty and variety of the Church as Queen: "These languages compose the variety in the garments of the Queen. As the variety of the garments preserves a unity, so all tongues fuse in one sole faith."

August 11

The Bishop's Role in the Church

Among the papers that were left to me by Paul VI there is a letter written to him by a bishop, on the occasion of the latter's appointment to the episcopate. It is a beautiful letter; and in the form of a resolution it includes a clear affirmation of the bishop's role of guarding and teaching the deposit of Christian doctrine, of proclaiming the whole mystery of Christ.

Because of the splendid insights that this letter offers I would like to share part of it with you. As he pledged himself to be loyal in obedience to Paul VI and to his successors, the bishop wrote: "I am resolved to be faithful and constant in proclaiming the Gospel of Christ; to maintain the content of faith, entire and uncorrupted, as handed down by the Apostles and professed by the Church at all times and places; and, with the help of Almighty God, I am determined to build up the Church as the Body of Christ and to remain united to it by your link, with the Order of Bishops, under the authority of the Successor of Saint Peter the Apostle; to show kindness and compassion in the name of the Lord to the poor and to strangers and to all who are in need; to seek out the sheep who stray and to gather them into the fold of the Lord; to pray without ceasing for the people of God; to carry out the highest duties of the priesthood in such a way as to afford no grounds for reproof."

This, then, is the edifying witness of a bishop, an American bishop, to the episcopal ministry of holiness and truth.

August 12

The Bishop, Living Sign of Jesus Christ

Basic to the whole identity of a bishop is the fact that he is meant to be *the living sign of Jesus Christ.* "In the bishops," states the Second Vatican Council, "our Lord Jesus Christ, the supreme High Priest, is present in the midst of those who believe."

This basic truth gives us a deep insight into ourselves and *our need for holiness of life.* The supernatural effectiveness of our ministry is linked in so many ways to our degree of holiness — to the degree in which we are configured to Christ by charity and grace. For this reason we should accept Saint Paul's invitation as being directed mainly to ourselves: "Put on that new man created in God's image, whose justice and holiness are born of truth" (*Eph* 4:24).

Holiness therefore becomes for us the first priority in our lives and in our ministry. There is no doubt about it: our fidelity to the love of Jesus and our friendship with him are essential for all the apostolic works that are part of our daily lives. Only union with Christ makes it possible for us to be effective ministers of the Gospel.

Let us remember the words of Jesus: "He who lives in me, and I in him, will produce abundantly" (*Jn* 15:5). As bishops we are asked to meditate on the holiness of Christ. Indeed our people ask us for more than this: they want, and they need, the witness of a prophetic anticipation of the *holiness* to which we invite them. They ask us to be their leaders in holiness, to trace out clearly for them the path for following Christ.

August 13

The Bishop Is Not Alone

Bishops ... know how much ... priests depend on [them] ... and how much [they] depend on ... priests. Together and not alone ... commissioned to proclaim the Gospel and build up the Body of Christ ... brothers and ... co-workers. ...

The Second Vatican Council and its implementing documents have done much to show the genuine place of the religious in the apostolate of the local churches ... for the co-ordinating of pastoral activity but also for ensuring that the splendid contribution of men and women religious is adequately utilized in the spirit of shared responsibility of the Gospel, "that the word of the Lord may make progress" (2 Thes 3:1). ... And what of the laity? I am deeply convinced also that the increased scope of the lay apostolate is a source of special strength for ... pastors of God's people. The Second Vatican Council was emphatic in stating how much the laity contribute to the welfare of the entire Church.

In all of this, the task of the bishops remains a formidable one: a ministry of heavy responsibility, but the presence of Christ and the right measure of shared responsibility assumed by the community are more than enough to convince us all as bishops that we are not alone.

August 14

St. Maximilian Kolbe

Saint Maximilian Maria Kolbe gave his life in the concentration camp of Oswiecim (Auschwitz) to save a married man who was the father of two children. A certain link exists between the Martyrs of Nagasaki and Father Kolbe. It is their readiness to give testimony of the Gospel message.

Permit me to indicate another link which I have discovered . . . that between St. Maximilian's sublime sacrifice and his work as a missionary at Nagasaki. Was it not the same conviction in faith, the same commitment for Christ and the Gospel which set him on the way to Japan and, later, on the way to the bunker of starvation? There was no division in his life, no uncertainty, no change of direction, but only the expression of the same love in differing circumstances.

When he arrived in Japan in 1930, he immediately resolved to accomplish, in a Japanese environment, what he had discovered as his special mission: promoting devotion to the Virgin and being an instrument of evangelization by means of the printed word. Founding the "City of the Immaculate" and publishing the "Seibo No kishi" were two sides of the one same great design for him — to bring Christ, the Son of God, born of the Virgin Mary, to all peoples. You know how his efforts were not marked or restricted by human calculation but were borne forward by his tireless trust in Divine Providence. God did not make that trust vain. The project which he launched . . . in an old printing works . . . acquired a fresh, unexpected dimension — the inspiring force flowing from his sacrifice.

There is yet another element regarding evangelization in St. Maximilian's life — it is devotion to Mary.

August 15

The Assumption of Mary Most Holy into Heaven

Today we find ourselves on the threshold of eternity. The life of the Mother of Christ has now been concluded on earth. And behold, at the moment when the law of death is accomplished in her — death which has been defeated by the resurrection of her Son — the canticle of salvation and of grace once more arises from the heart of Mary. It is the canticle of the assumption into heaven, the *Magnificat*: "God who is mighty has done great things for me" *(Lk* 1:49). He had done them from the beginning. . . .

When . . . he liberated her from the yoke of the heritage of original sin. When he called her totally to Himself, to His service. And then through the Annunciation, at Nazareth, the night of Bethlehem, and the thirty years of hidden life. Subsequently, through the experiences of the years of the teaching life of Her Son Christ, the horrible sufferings of his cross and the dawn of the resurrection.

Indeed, "God . . . has done great things in me. . . ." Our Mother's whole heart is manifested in the words of the *Magnificat. They are her spiritual testament.*

Each of us has to look at his and her own life with the eyes of Mary — what He did in her, He did for us, and therefore did it as in us.

Mary's words give us *a new outlook of life.* The outlook of an excellent and persevering faith. A faith which is the light of daily life. Of days sometimes tranquil but often stormy and difficult. A faith which, finally, lightens up the darkness of the death of each one of us.

Let this outlook on life and death be the fruit of the feast of the Assumption.

August 16

The Glory of Mary Assumed into Heaven

On the solemnity of the Assumption of Mary into heaven
. . . the Church proclaims the *glory of her final assumption
in heaven.* At the same time, we wish, through the glory
of her birth into heaven, to venerate the blessed moment
. . . of her birth on earth. . . .

But, before all, the birth into heaven, the Assumption
into heaven.

The first aspect of this is the Visitation, in the house
of Zachary. On the threshold of the hospitable home of
Zachary and Elizabeth, Mary uttered a sentence which
concerned the beginning of the mystery of the Redemption. She said: "God who is mighty has done great things
for me, holy is his name." Through today's liturgy, this
statement enters into the context of the Assumption. In
today's liturgy, the whole of the *Magnificat* uttered on the
occasion of the Visitation, becomes the hymn of Mary's
assumption into heaven.

The second aspect: The Assumption of the Mother of
Christ into heaven forms part of the victory over death,
of that victory, the beginning of which is found in the
Resurrection of Christ. At very heart of the Redemption
achieved by the Cross of Calvary, in *the very power of the
Redemption* revealed in the Resurrection, the source is
found of that victory over death experienced by the
Mother of the Redeemer, that is to say, her assumption
into heaven.

The third aspect: the daughter of the king, garbed in
precious fabrics, enters to take her place by the throne of
the king. Mary, Mother of the Redeemer, is the first to
participate in this reign of glory and of union with God
in eternity. This is what is expressed by the mystery of
her assumption into heaven, with her soul and her body.

August 17

Toward the Second Millennium
since the Birth of Mary Most Holy

Through the assumption of the Mother of God into heaven, her birth into heaven, we desire to honor *the blessed moment of her birth on earth.* Many ask themselves: When was she born? Many are putting that question to themselves especially now that the second millenium of the birth of Christ is approaching. The birth of the Mother obviously has to precede the birth of her Son in time. Would it not be opportune to celebrate the second millennium of the birth of Mary beforehand?

The Church makes reference to history and historical dates when she celebrates anniversaries and jubilees (with respect for the precision which science contributes). However, the right rhythm of anniversaries and jubilees is determined by the history of salvation. It is in this sense that we agree that the jubilee of the Redemption . . . refers to the death and resurrection of Christ. We constantly emphasize at the same time that this . . . extraordinary jubilee is *to prepare the Church for the grand jubilee of the second millennium (the year 2,000).* In this regard, our Year of the Redemption also takes on the character of an Advent: it introduces us to the expectation of the jubilee of the coming of the Lord.

But Advent is quite especially Mary's time. We desire to enter into this Advent through this . . . Jubilee of the Redemption. We desire that her coming, her own birth on earth, shall also be present in this jubliee of this salvific event, which has an Advent character . . . to honor Mary's birth into heaven, through the solemnity of the Assumption, but also to honor the blessed moment of her birth on earth.

August 18

The Priest Must Be Close to Christ
and to the People

You [priests] must be *men of God, his close friends.* You must develop daily patterns of prayer, and penance must be a regular part of your life. Prayer and penance will help you to appreciate more deeply that the strength of your ministry is found in the Lord and not in human resources. You must try to deepen every day your friendship with Christ.

You must also learn to share the hopes and the joys, the sorrows and the frustrations of the people entrusted to your care. Bring to them Christ's saving message of reconciliation. Visit your parishioners in their homes. It is a pastoral practice that should not be neglected. Teach your people boldly about the faithful love of God. And do not forget all those with special needs, to whom Jesus Christ wants to offer peace of conscience and the forgiveness of all sins.

Through you, Jesus Christ wants to enkindle hope anew. . . . Through you in your heart, Jesus Christ wants to love those of whom he died. Teach all your people that you believe in that faithful love by the fidelity with which you live your own life. You must proclaim the Gospel with your life.

When you celebrate the Sacraments at the decisive moments of their lives, help them to trust in Christ's promised mercy and compassion. When you offer the redeeming Sacrifice of the Eucharist, help them to understand the need for transforming this great love into works of charity.

My brothers, be aware of *the effect on others of the witness of lives.*

August 19

The Priest, A Gift of God to His Church

My greeting goes in the first place to the priests, both diocesan and religious, sharers in the one priesthood of Christ the High Priest, "taken from among men and made their representative before God, to offer gifts and sacrifices for sins" *(Heb* 5:1). Your presence gives me great joy and fraternal support.

In you I recognize the good shepherd; the faithful servant, the sower who goes out to sow the good seed, the laborer in the vineyard, the fisherman who launches his net for a catch. *You are Christ's close friends:* "You are my friends . . . *(Jn* 15:15).

As priests we must recognize the mystery of grace in our lives. It is a gift. It is an act of trust on Christ's part, calling us to be "administrators of the mysteries of God" *(1 Cor* 4:1). It is a sacramental configuration with Christ the High Priest. The priesthood is not ours to do with as we please. We cannot re-invent its meaning according to our personal views. Ours is to be true to the One who has called us.

The priesthood is a gift to us. But in us and through us the priesthood is *a gift to the Church.* Let us never separate our priestly life and ministry from full and wholehearted communion with the whole Church. Brothers in the priestly ministry, what does the Church expect from you? The Church expects that you and your brothers and sisters, the religious, will be the first to love her, to hear her voice and follow her inspiration, so that the people of our time may be served effectively.

August 20

The Priest Must Love His Priesthood
and Not Alter God's

As priests you are at the service of Christ the Teacher. A very important part of your ministry is to preach and teach the Christian message.

Saint Paul describes his own attitude to this ministry: "We do not resort to trickery or falsify the word of God. We proclaim the truth openly and commend ourselves to every man's conscience before God" (2 Cor 4:2). *We must not tamper with God's word.* We must strive to apply the Good News to the ever-changing conditions of the world but, courageously and at all costs, we must resist the temptation to alter its content or reinterpret it in order to make it fit the spirit of the present age.

The message we preach is not the wisdom of this world but *the words of life* that seem like foolishness to the unspiritual man. We should not be surprised then if our message of conversion and life is not always well received. Do everything in your power to present the word as effectively as possible, believe in the power of the word itself, and never become discouraged.

How careful we must be about our preaching! It should be the continuation of our prayer. To spend your lives, in the service of the People of God, through word and sacrament — this is your great task, your glory, your treasure. We must love our vocation and mission. But we must also *be seen* to love our priesthood. Let your people see that you are men of prayer. Let them see that you treat the sacred mysteries with love and respect. Let them see that your commitment to peace, justice and truth is sincere, unconditional and brave.

August 21

To Teachers of Sacred Theology

Theology is called to concentrate its reflection upon its radical, decisive themes: *the mystery of God,* of the Trinitarian God, who revealed himself in Christ as the God-Love. *The mystery of Christ,* the Son of God made man, illuminated the profoundest aspects of human existence, definitively, with his Death and his Resurrection. *The mystery of man* — in the insuperable tension between his finiteness and his yearning for the infinite, man bears within himself an unrenounceable question of the ultimate meaning of life.

The Christian faith is ecclesial; it arises and remains bound up with the community of those who believe in Christ, what we call the Church. As a reflection born of this faith, "theology is ecclesiastical science, because it grows in the Church and works in the Church; therefore, it is never practiced by specialists isolated in a sort of ivory tower. It is at the service of the Church, so it ought to feel itself dynamically integrated into the Church's mission, especially her prophetic mission." The theologian's task therefore includes the character of being an ecclesiastical mission, as participation in the Church's evangelizing mission and as illustrious service to the ecclesiastical community. Hence the theologian's grave responsibility.

The essential connection between theology and faith, founded and centered on Christ, fully lights up the link that theology has with the Church and her magisterium. One cannot believe in Christ, one cannot believe with Catholic faith in the Church, without believing in her unrenounceable magisterium. . . . So, be true to your faith, without separating Christ from his Church, nor the Church from her magisterium.

August 22

Christ Awaits the Seminarians Whom He Called

You [seminarians] are those whom the Church and society await, with anxiety, in view of the extreme need for ministers of God, who should be enlightened and upright, balanced and sage, convinced, courageous priests. In this troubled and anguished epoch of ours, the Church goes on announcing and testifying to Jesus Christ, the light and salvation of mankind. And the Lord calls you as well to this grand and unending mission.

To you as well may therefore be applied those words of the Lord's reported by the Prophet Isaiah: "I, the Lord, have called you for the victory of justice, I have grasped you by the hand; I formed you and set you as a covenant of the people, a light for the nations, to open the eyes of the blind, to bring out prisoners from confinement, and from the dungeon, those who live in darkness" (*Is* 42:6-7).

Let yourselves be led by the hand of the Lord, because he wishes to accomplish Redemption today through your means. The Redemption is always of today, because the parable of the good seed and the weeds is always of today. The Beatitudes are always of today. Mankind always has need of Revelation and of the Redemption of Christ, so he is waiting for you!

There are always souls to enlighten, sinners to pardon, tears to dry, disappointments to console, sick to encourage, children and youngsters to guide. There is, there ever shall be, man to love and to save, in Christ's name! This is your vocation; it ought to make you happy and courageous.

But you must prepare yourselves with a sense of great responsibility and profound and convinced seriousness:

seriousness in your cultural education, especially your philosophical, biblical, theological learning, and in ascetics and discipline, so as to consecrate yourselves totally and joyously alone to Jesus and to souls.

August 23

The Seminary Must Provide a
Sound Discipline

The seminary must provide a sound discipline to prepare for a life of consecrated service in the image of Christ. Its purpose was well-defined by the Second Vatican Council: The discipline required by seminary life should not be regarded merely as a strong support of community life and of charity. For it is a necessary part of the whole training program designed to provide self-mastery, to foster solid maturity of personality and to develop other traits of character which are extremely servicable for the ordered and productive activity of the Church.

When discipline is properly exercised, it can create an atmosphere of recollection which enables the seminarian to develop interiorly those attitudes which are so desirable in a priest, such as joyful obedience, generosity and self-sacrifice. In the different forms of community life that are appropriate for the seminary, you will learn the art of dialogue: the capacity to listen to others and to discover the richness of their personality, and the ability to give of yourself. Seminary discipline will reinforce rather than diminish your freedom, for it will help develop in you those traits and attitudes of mind and heart which God has given you . . . and help you to serve more effectively his people. Discipline will also assist you in ratifying day after day in your hearts the obedience you owe to Christ and his Church.

August 24

The Memory of Pope John Paul I

I am the way, the truth, and the life; no one comes to the Father but through me.

These words help us to direct our memories toward Pope John Paul I, who was called to the Chair of Peter. We desire once again to meditate on the inscrutable decrees of Divine Providence. You see, after scarcely thirty-three days of pastoral labor in the Roman See, it was given to him to "go to the Father," by the way which is Christ himself: way, truth, life. So, through Christ, that unusual servant of the servants of God, to whom Christ entrusted his Church, his fold on earth, came to the Father. Christ had entrusted his Church and his fold to him so that that goodness and that pastoral solicitude with which his heart was filled, should be manifested, at least for a short while. The heart of a Good Samaritan.

When, during the Council, he, Albino Luciani, preached spiritual exercises to priests, he was accustomed to base them completely on the evangelical parable of the merciful Samaritan. And it was certainly in this spirit that he desired to serve the whole Church. That was his spirit. All those who met Cardinal Albino Luciani and then Pope John Paul I, could see this, without any mistake. And although his pontifical service lasted so short a time, yet the spirit of the Good Samaritan was manifested once again through him and has remained in the Church. The way of the Good Samaritan orders us *to bend* to suffering mankind. And as we do this, our heart is raised toward God; love which is directed to man actually always finds its ultimate source in God, who is Love.

August 25

The Seminary Must Teach God's Word

I would like to communicate to all seminarians how much you mean to me, and how much you mean for the future of the Church, for the future of the mission given to us by Christ.

This personal conviction about the importance of seminaries prompted me to write these words in my Holy Thursday Letter to the Bishops of the Church: "The full reconstitution of the life of the seminaries throughout the Church will be the best proof of the achievement of the renewal to which the Council directed the Church."

If seminaries are to fulfill their mission in the Church, two activities in the overall program of the seminary are crucially important: *the teaching of God's word* and *discipline*. The intellectual formation of the priest, which is so vital for the times in which we live, embraces a number of the human sciences as well as the various sacred sciences. These all have an important place in your preparation for the priesthood. But the first priority for seminaries today is the teaching of God's word in all its purity and integrity, with all its demands and in all its power. This was clearly affirmed by my beloved predecessor Paul VI when he stated that scripture is a "perpetual source of spiritual life, the chief instrument for handing down Christian Doctrine, and the center of all theological study." Therefore, if you, the seminarians of this generation, are to be adequately prepared to take on the heritage and challenge of the Second Vatican Council, you will need to be well-trained in the word of God.

August 26

Feast of Our Lady of Częstochowa

Today, 26 August 1982, I find myself by the altar in the chapel of the recent Popes at Castel Gandolfo. Pius XI was apostolic nuncio in Poland in the early years after regaining independence. He brought the image of the Mother of God of Jasna Gora into this chapel and set it over the main altar. It had been presented to him by the Polish episcopate. The remembrance of Jasna Gora had certainly gone deep into the heart of that successor of St. Peter, since he willed to have this image on the main altar of his chapel.

So, here, before this altar, today, I feel a *profound link with Jasna Gora,* which is celebrating the Jubilee of the six hundred years of presence of the Mother of God, Queen of Poland, in her most venerated image.

My dear compatriots! However difficult the lives of Poles may be this year, may consciousness win in you that this life is embraced by the Heart of the Mother. As she won in Maximilian Kolbe, Knight of the Immaculate, so may she win in you.

May the Mother's heart win! May the Lady of Jasna Gora win in us and through us! May she win even through our afflictions and defeats. May she ensure that we shall not desist from trying and struggling for truth and justice, for liberty and dignity in our lives. Do not Mary's words, "Do as he [my Son] tells you," means this too? May power be fully manifested in weakness, according to the words of the Apostle of the Gentiles and according to the example of our compatriot, Father Maximilian Kolbe. Mary, Queen of Poland, I am near You, I remember You, I watch!

August 27

The Seminary, School of Fidelity

I want to remind you [seminarians] of the importance of *fidelity*. Before you can be ordained, you are called by Christ to make a free and irrevocable commitment to be faithful to him and to his Church. Human dignity requires that you maintain this commitment, that you keep your promise to Christ no matter what difficulties you may encounter, and no matter what temptations you may be exposed to.

It is important that one's commitment be made with full awareness and personal freedom. And so during these years in the seminary, take time to reflect on the serious obligations and the difficulties which are part of the priest's life. Consider whether Christ is calling you to the celibate life. You can make a responsible decision for celibacy only after you have reached the firm conviction that Christ is indeed offering you this gift, which is intended for the good of the Church and for the service of others.

To understand what it means to be faithful we must look to Christ, the "faithful witness," the son who "learned obedience from what he suffered" *(Heb* 5:8); to Jesus who said: "I am not seeking my own will but the will of him who sent me" *(Jn* 5:30).

We look to Jesus, not only to see and contemplate his fidelity to the Father despite all opposition but also to learn from him the means he employed in order to be faithful: especially prayer and abandonment to God's will. Remember that in the final analysis perseverance in fidelity is a proof not of human strength and courage but of the efficacy of Christ's grace.

August 28

St. Augustine, Doctor of the Church

St. Augustine! He, who had been elevated so high in contemplation of divine truth and had also gone so deeply into the abysses of the mysteries of God and man, understood the absolute necessity for humble and totally trusting prayer. For, however acute man's intelligence may appear to be, the mystery always infinitely surpasses that intelligence and prayer becomes a need of the soul: "in prayer the heart alters and in this conversion the inner eye becomes pure." Pray in hope, pray with faith and love. Prayer is as necessary as the grace it obtains for us.

"Late have I love thee, O beauty so ancient and so new, late have I loved thee!" St. Augustine exclaimed with peaceful regret. But, once he had arrived at the truth, he consecrated himself to it radically, and thenceforth lived only for it, testifying to it, preaching it, defending it, sacrificing himself totally for it: "O truth eternal and truthful love and beloved eternity! Thou art my God, I long for thee night and day" (*Confessions* VII, 10,16). And in his *Soliloquies:* "Now I love Thee only, Thee alone I follow, Thee solely I seek. Thee alone am I disposed to follow, for Thou alone justly rulest, and so I desire to be Thy property."

Love the truth before all, while feeling lively comprehension of the contemporary society in which we live.

Love, then, the truth above all, with the scrupulousness of orthodoxy, avidly listening to the teacher who speaks inwardly, and remaining humbly attached to the Church, mother of Salvation.

Love, finally, the truth, by dedicating yourselves carefully to the work of your perfection.

August 29

The Religious State, a Prophetical Sign of God's Kingdom

Brothers and sisters, members of religious communities! I would greet every one of you personally. Hear from each of you the *"magnalia Dei* — the wonderful works of God," how the Holy Spirit operates in your lives! In the entrails of your hearts, in the struggle between grace and sin, in the various moments and circumstances of your pilgrimage of faith — in how many ways Christ has spoken to you and said, "Come to me!"

In your religious consecration, you have brought your baptismal grace to a degree of "total donation to God supremely loved," you have become a sign of higher life, a "life more important than food and the body, more than clothing" *(Lk* 12:23). Through profession of the evangelical counsels, you have become a *prophetical sign in the eternal kingdom of the Father.* In this world you look to "the only thing necessary," to the "inexhaustible treasure"; you possess the source of inspiration and strength for the various forms of apostolate which your institutions are called upon to accomplish.

Those of you who belong to contemplative communities serve the people of God "in the heart of Christ." You prophetically remind those engaged in building the earthly city that unless the Lord lay the foundations, it is built in vain. Yours is a singular testimony to the gospel message, and it is very necessary, because persons of our time often succumb to a false understanding of independence with respect to the Creator.

And you, brothers and sisters, whose vocation is that of active labor in ecclesiastical service, you have to bring contemplation into it. Adhere to God with your minds and hearts. With love and apostolic ardor, collaborate in the work of redemption and of spreading the kingdom of God.

August 30

The Contemplative Life

The contemplative life has occupied and will go on occupying a place of honor in the Church. . . . Lives are dedicated to prayer and silence, to adoration and penitence in the cloister, "it is hidden with Christ in God." This consecrated life is the development of and has its foundation in the gift received in baptism. Through this sacrament, God chose us in Christ "before the foundation of the world that we might be holy and immaculate before him in charity"; through it he actually delivered us from sin and incorporated us in Christ and His Church that we might "live a new life."

This new life has borne fruit . . . in the radical following of Jesus Christ through virginity, obedience and poverty, which is the foundation of the contemplative life. It is the center of your life, the reason for your existence: "Good of all goods and Jesus mine," as St. Teresa summed it up.

However, the experience of the cloister makes this following more absolute, to the point of identifying the religious life with Christ: "Our life is Christ," St. Teresa said, so making St. Paul's exhortations her own. This identification of the religious with Christ constitutes the center of the consecrated life and the seal identifying . . . a contemplative. In silence, in the framework of humble and obedient living, watchful waiting for the Spouse turns into pure and true friendship: "I can deal with him as with a friend, even though he is the Lord."

The Church well knows that . . . quiet and separated life, in the exterior solitude of the cloister, is the leaven of renewal and the presence of the Spirit of Christ in the world.

August 31

Secular Institutes:
A Leaven in and for the World

I feel the need to draw your attention to *three conditions of fundamental importance* for your mission to be effective: Above all, you ought to be *true disciples of Christ.* In as much as you are members of a secular Institute, you will to be so through the radical quality of your commitment to follow the evangelical counsels in such a manner that not only shall your state in life not be thereby altered—you are and remain laity — but also in order that it shall be reinforced, in the sense that *your lay state* may be consecrated, may be more exigent, and that commitment in the world and for the world, which this lay state implies, may be permanent and faithful.

The second condition is that, at the level of knowledge and experience, you shall be *truly competent in your specific field,* so as to exercise, through your presence, this apostolate of testimony and engagement toward others which your consecration and your life in the Church impose on you.

The third condition on which I would ask you to reflect consists of this resolve which is proper to you: that is, determination *to change the world from inside.* You are actually wholly entered into the world, and not only through your sociological circumstances; you are required to be so inserted above all by reason of a required interior attitude. You must therefore consider yourselves as "part" of the world, as engaged in sanctifying it, in totally accepting the demands therefrom deriving, and the legitimate autonomy of the realities of the world, of its values and of its laws.

Dear Sons and Daughters, your field of action is very vast, as you see. The Church expects much of you. She has need of your testimony for bringing the world the "glad news" whereby every authentically human aspiration can find its achievement in Christ.

September

September 1

The Laity Profess Their Faith

"In the same way, your light must shine before men, so that they may see goodness in your acts and give praise to your heavenly Father" *(Mt* 5:16).

You are the salt of the earth! You are the light of the world!

"The Christian vocation is by its very nature a vocation to the apostolate."

Here is the root of the kernel of announcement and testimony of the Christian faith. Hence, the first attitude assumed by the testifier to the faith is that of *professing this same faith which he practices,* becoming gently converted by the Spirit of God and conforming one's life to this Divine Wisdom. Inasmuch as we are witnesses to God, we are not proprietors who can do what we like with the announcement received. We are responsible for a gift which must be faithfully transmitted. With fear and trembling because of his own frailty, the Apostle trusts in the manifestation of the Spirit, in the persuasive force of "the power of God" *(1 Cor* 2:4-5).

It is not a question of adapting the Gospel to the wisdom of the world. In words which might interpret Paul's experience, we can affirm today: it is not analyses of reality, use of the social sciences, or employment of statistics — though these are useful and sometimes valuable instruments — which will determine the content of the Gospel received and professed. Even less will connivance with secularized ideologies open our hearts to the announcement of salvation. The apostle must not let himself be led away by the pretended sagacity of the "princes of this world," founded on power, on riches and on pleasures, which, while it propounds the mirage of a human happiness, actually leads to total destruction of those who succumb to its cult.

Only Christ! Let us proclaim him, in thanksgiving and wonder. In him is already the fullness of "what God has prepared for those who love him" *(1 Cor* 2:9). It is the announcement which the Church entrusts to all who are called to proclaim, celebrate, communicate and live the infinite Love of the Divine Wisdom.

September 2

The Laity Spread Their Faith

The Divine Wisdom is that *sublime science* which preserves the savor of salt, so that it will not become tasteless, which feeds the light of the lamp, so that it may light up the depths of the human heart, guide its secret yearnings, its seeking and its hopes.

The Pope exhorts all laity to assume their dignity and responsibility with coherence and vigor. . . . The Christian vocation is essentially apostolic. Only in this dimension of service to the Gospel will the Christian find the fullness of his dignity and responsibility. In fact, the laity are "incorporated in Christ through baptism, and constituted People of God; to their measure, they are made partakers of the sacerdotal, prophetic, and kingly office of Christ"; they are called to holiness and are invited to announce and realize Christ's Kingdom until He returns.

If you wish to be faithful to this dignity, it is not enough to accept passively those riches of the faith which are handed down in your tradition and by your culture. A treasure is entrusted, talents are offered, which ought to be accepted with responsibility, so that they may bear fruit in abundance. The grace of Baptism and of Confirmation is renewed by the Eucharist and restored by Penance. It possesses vital energies for vitalizing faith and, with the creative dynamism of the Holy Spirit, for directing the activities of the members of the Mystical Body. The laity too are called to this interior spiritual growth, which makes them *fellow workers of the Holy Spirit.* With his gifts, he renews, rejuvenates and perfects the work of Christ.

September 3

The Apostolate of the Believing Laity

It will be necessary to confirm once again that growth of affirmation of the laity's Christian identity does not diminish or limit its possibilities. Rather does it define, nourish and add power to this presence and to this specific and original task entrusted by the Church to her sons and daughters in the various fields of personal, professional and social activity.

The Gospel itself urges us *to share every one of man's situations and conditions,* with a passionate love for everything to do with his condition of being a creature of God's, "made in the divine image" *(Gen* 1:27) and sharing in the divine descent through the grace of Christ. The Second Vatican Council rightly emphasized that the principal task of the Catholic laity is to impregnate and transform the entire texture of human society with the values of the Gospel, with the announcement of a Christian anthropology, deriving from these values.

Paul VI specified the fields of the apostolate of the laity as follows: "Their own field of evangelizing activity is the vast and complicated world of politics, of society, and of economics, but also of culture, of the sciences, of the arts, of international life, of the mass media. It also includes other realities which are open to evangelization, such as human love, the family, the education of children and young people, professional work, suffering."

No human activity is extraneous to the responsible evangelizing task of the laity: life testimony and evangelizing effort for Christian families; the vast field of the world of work shaken by potent crises; the field of politics, with its more sensitive decisions; the world of culture, of intellectuals, scientists, educators and artists.

September 4

No Apostolate without Interior Life

A special recommendation, which I entrust to the Christian hearts of all laity. No apostolate exists, no apostolate can exist (either for priests or for laity) without interior life, without prayer, without a persevering striving toward holiness. . . . Such holiness is the gift of Wisdom, which for the Christian, is a particular actuation of the Holy Spirit received in baptism and in confirmation: "Now God grant I speak suitably and value these endowments at their worth: for he is the guide of Wisdom and the director of the wise. For both we and our words are in his hand, as well as all prudence and knowledge of crafts" (Wis 7:15-16).

May you all be called to sanctity! You have need of the abundance of the Holy Spirit for accomplishing the new and original task of the lay apostolate with his Wisdom! Hence you have to be united to Christ, for sharing in his sacerdotal, prophetic and royal office, in the difficult and marvelous circumstances of the Church and the world of today.

Yes. We have to be in his hands so as to be able to accomplish our Christian vocation! In his hands for bringing all things to God. In the hands of the eternal Wisdom, for participating fruitfully in Christ's own mission! In God's hands for building his kingdom in the temporal realities of this world!

Dear brothers and sisters, I ask the Lord today for a holiness that may flourish in an original and creative apostolate, impregnated with divine Wisdom, I so pray for all of you, for all laity.

I implore this through the Virgin's intercession.

September 5

God's Plan for Marriage and the Family

God created man in his image and likeness by calling him into existence *for love's sake;* at the same time He called him *to love.* God is love and lives a mystery of personal communion of love in himself. In creating mankind in his image and continually conserving it in love, God inscribes the vocation, consequently the capacity and responsibility of love and communion, in the humanity of man and woman. So, love is the fundamental and native

315

vocation of every human being. Inasmuch as he is an incarnate spirit, that is, a soul expressing itself in the body, a body informed by an immortal spirit, man is called to love in this his unified totality. Love also embraces the human body and the body is made a partaker of spiritual love.

Christian revelation knows two specific ways of realizing the human person's vocation, as a whole, to love. These ways are matrimony and virginity. In the forms proper to them, both one and the other are a rendering of the deepest truth on man, that of his "being in God's likeness."

Consequently, sexuality — through which the man and the woman give themselves to each other by means of acts proper and exclusive to spouses — is actually not something purely biological but concerns the intimate core of the human person as such. Sexuality is realized in a truly human way only if it is an integral part of the love with which the man and the woman commit themselves to each other until death.

This totality is required by conjugal love. It also corresponds to the demands of responsible fecundity. Because this is directed toward engendering a human being, it surpasses the sheerly biological order by its very nature.

September 6

Family, Become What You Are

In God the Creator and Redeemer's plan, the family not only discovers its "identity," that which it "is," but it also discovers its "mission," that which it can and ought "do." The tasks which the family is called upon by God to accomplish in history derive from its very essence and represent its dynamic and existential development. Every family discovers and finds an irrepressible call in itself. This call defines at once its dignity and its reponsibility: Family, "become" what you "are"!

Getting back to the "principle," the beginning, of God's creative gesture is therefore a necessity for the family, if it will know itself and realize itself according to the inner truth, not only that of its being but is also that of its historical action. Since it is constituted in the divine plan as "the intimate community of life and love," the family has the mission of becoming ever more what it is, that is, a community of life and love. So the family receives the mission *to safeguard, reveal, and communicate love,* as living reflection and real participation in God's love for humanity, and Christ the Lord's love for the Church his Spouse.

Every particular task of the family's is the expression and concrete actuation of that fundamental mission. It is therefore necessary to penetrate more thoroughly into the singular richness of the family's mission, and examine each of its manifold and unitary contents. It was in this sense, beginning from love, and in constant reference to it, that the recent Synod brought out the four general tasks of the family: 1) formation of a community of persons; 2) service to life; 3) participation in developing society; 4) participation in the Church's life and mission.

September 7

Reminisence of Pius IX

My predecessor of happy memory, Pius IX . . . inaugurated the railway line between Rome and Velletri.

That pontifical visit to the city of Velletri was really due to that event of notable technological and social importance. I am pleased to be able to recall that great Pope's presence in this place in those circumstances as a meaningful act of testimony of the favor with which the Church follows every discovery of the human mind and skill and every achievement of authentic progress.

The Church really takes care to sustain and encourage man's commitment to conquering the world, and she does so by virtue of the mission which is proper to her, that of illuminating every reality in the temporal order with the light of the Gospel.

So it was in the past, in spite of momentary misunderstandings. So it is also today.

September 8

The Most Holy Child Mary

While we get ready to raise our prayer to the Immaculate Mother of God, we cannot fail to recall that yesterday, September 7, the church celebrated the liturgical festivity of the birth of the Blessed Virgin Mary, "hope and dawn of salvation for the entire world."

This Marian feast is profoundly rooted in the devotion and in the hearts of the faithful. They look to Mary with ardent trust and stirring hopes, conscious how, in God's plan, that birth gave a concrete beginning to those salvific events in which Mary was to be closely associated with her Son.

We should therefore be filled with exultation as we commemorate Our Redeemer's Mother. "Indeed," St. Peter Damian said, "if Solomon, and the whole people of Israel with him, celebrated such a plentiful and magnificent sacrifice for the dedication of the material temple, what and how much joy will the birth of the Virgin Mary bring to the Christian people? For into her womb, as into a most holy temple, God descended in person to receive human nature and deigned to dwell among men visibly."

To the Child Mary let us offer our humble prayer today for the world and for the Church.

September 9

The Sacrament of Matrimony

By virtue of the sacramental character of matrimony, the spouses' reciprocal belonging to each other is, through the agency of the sacramental sign, the real representation of Christ's own relationship with the Church.

The spouses testify, before each other and before their children, to the salvation of which the sacrament makes them partakers. As is every sacrament, matrimony is the memorial, actualization, and prophecy of that event of salvation: "In this memorial, the sacrament gives them the grace and the duty to retain remembrance of the mighty works of God and to give testimony of them to their children. As actualization, it gives them

319

the grace and the duty to put into practice the demands of a pardoning and redeeming love, in the present, toward each other and the children. As prophecy, it gives them the grace and the duty to live and give testimony of the hope of future meetings with Christ. "The spouses partake of the event of salvation as two, as a couple, to the point that the prime and immediate effect of matrimony is the Christian conjugal bond, the typically Christian union of two, because it represents the mystery of the Incarnation of Christ and his mystery as Alliance. And the content of the participation in Christ's life is also specific: conjugal love entails a totality where all components of the person, the claims of the body and of the instincts, the power of feeling and affection, the aspirations of the spirit and of the will, all enter in. It aims at a profoundly personal unity, that which goes beyond union in one flesh and leads to making but one heart and one soul. It demands the indissolubility and the fidelity of the reciprocal and definitive giving and opens to fecundity."

September 10

To Confraternities and Ecclesiastical Movements

Dearest brothers and sisters, confraternities, associations, groups and movements are the field where laity may best apply their Christian talents. Grave difficulties exist, often linked with a social context which has lasted for centuries. They are more than ever the object of your pastors' zealous attention. In view of them, everyone has to commit himself and herself, and always keep an honest, just, delicate, responsible conscience.

The following declaration of the [Second Vatican] Council seems more than ever appropriate in this regard: "The most flourishing associations will be of very little use unless they are directed to educating people in Christian maturity. . . ." For an effective place within present society to be gained, therefore, solid spiritual formation and great moral strength are necessary, so as never to be resigned to evil, not to yield passively to a fatalistic sense of the inevitable, which humiliates and depresses. Sociological analyses are certainly interesting, useful and even necessary to be able to gain knowledge of the various situations. But what is above all indispensable is analysis of one's own conscience. Everyone must carry out such an analysis every day before God, oneself, and the community in which one lives. Dearly beloved, lift up your hearts. Keep this psychological and spiritual mobilization of the conscience ever lively and effective, and vivify it particularly with the power of prayer.

A great personality of the Church's history, Cardinal John Henry Newman, before his conversion to Catholicism, wrote a poem which became famous: "Lead, kindly Light, amid the encircling gloom, lead thou me on. The night is dark, and I am far from home — Lead thou me on."

September 11

The Progress of Our Generation

We have every right to believe that our generation too was included in the Mother of God's words, when she glorified that mercy in which those who let themselves be guided by fear of God partake "from generation to generation."

All of us at present living on earth are the generation which is conscious of the approach of the third millennium and deeply feels the turn taking place in history.

The present generation knows that it is privileged, because progress offers it many possibilities which were unsuspected only a few decades ago. Man's creative activity, his intelligence, his labor, have caused profound changes in the field of science and technology, as in social and cultural life. Man has extended his power over nature, and has acquired deeper knowledge of his own social behavior. He has seen obstacles and distances fall away, no longer separating men and nations, thanks to an increased internationalism, to a clearer awareness of the unity of the human race and the acceptance of reciprocal dependence in authentic solidarity; and thanks, finally, to the desire — and the possibility — to make contact with brothers and sisters away and beyond divisions artificially created by geography or national or racial frontiers.

Above all, the youth of today know that the progress of science and technology cannot only procure new material goods, but a vaster participation in a common consciousness as well. For example, the development of information technologies will multiply man's creative capacities and enable him to gain access to the intellectual and cultural riches of other peoples. New communications techniques will help greater sharing in events and an increased exchange of ideas. The gains of biological, psychological and social science will aid man to penetrate the wealth of his own being better.

September 12

Shadows and Imbalances of Our Generation

Certain difficulties exist, which indeed are seen to be on the increase. There is disquiet and impotence which force a radical response, which man feels he has to give. The picture of the contemporary world also presents shadows and imbalances not always merely superficial.

In truth, the imbalances from which the contemporary world suffers are bound up with that *deeper imbalance* which is *rooted in man's heart.* It is actually within man that many elements are in contrast. On the one hand, as a creature, he experiences his limitations in a thousand ways; on the other hand, he becomes aware that he is without limitations on his aspirations and is called to a higher life. He is drawn by many attractions, but he is always constrained to choose one and give up the others. Moreover, weak and sinful as he is, he not rarely does what he would not, and does not do what he would. He therefore suffers from a division in himself, and from that arise many and very grave discords in society. . . .

In view of the present evolution of the world, those who put the prime questions to themselves or feel them with renewed acuity, are becoming more and more numerous. *What is the meaning of pain, of evil, of death,* which, in spite of all progress, continue to subsist? What is the worth of these new conquests which have been won at such a high price? Has that picture of tensions and threats characteristic of our age perhaps become less disquieting? It seems not. On the contrary, the tensions and the threats seemed only to exist in outline . . . and did not reveal all the peril they concealed but, over these few years, they have revealed themselves more, have confirmed that peril in a different way, and do not permit the illusions of another time to be nourished.

September 13

The Church Lives with the People of Our Time

The Church shares with the people of our time the profound and ardent desire for a just life from every point of view, and does not fail to subject the various aspects of such justice to reflective thought, which the lives of man and society demand. Catholic social doctrine confirms this, amply developed over the last century. It is in the wake of such teaching that the education and the training of the conscience in the spirit of justice proceed, together with individual initiatives especially within the apostolate of the laity continuing to develop in that spirit.

However, it would be difficult not to see that programs very often undergo deformation in practice when they begin from the idea of justice and have to apply it among individuals, groups and human societies. Although such programs go on referring to the same idea of justice, experience nevertheless demonstrates that other, negative forces such as rancor, hatred, even cruelty, have got the upper hand over justice. In such a case, yearning to annihilate the enemy, to restrict his liberty, or even impose total dependence on him becomes the fundamental motive of action. This contrasts with the essence of justice, which, by its nature, tends to establish equality and equity among parties in conflict. This kind of abuse of the idea of justice and the practical alterations of it attest how much human action may *depart from justice* itself, even though undertaken in its name.

It is obvious that one's neighbor can sometimes be annihilated in the name of a presumed justice (historical or class, for example); he can be slain, deprived of liberty, stripped of the elementary human rights.

September 14

The Exaltation of the Holy Cross

"We adore thee, O Christ, and we praise thee, because by thy Holy Cross thou hast redeemed the world."

Those who died for the faith, embracing the Cross of Christ with love, repeating, "We praise thee, O Christ, because by thy Holy Cross thou hast redeemed the world. . . ."

We adore you, Jesus Christ! We adore you. We get down on our knees. We do not find words enough or gestures to express the veneration with which your Cross fills us, with which the gift of the Redemption penetrates us, offered to all mankind, to one and all, through the total and unconditional subjection of your will to the Will of the Father.

He revealed the Father's love in his love. From the height of the cross he has the right to speak to people of all times and say, "Whoever has seen me has seen the Father" (*Jn* 14:9). Through his death, he revealed to us that there is Love in the world: *Love stronger than death....* He opened the way of hope to us.

We desire, O Christ, to *cry out today to this merciful power,* the greatest power and force upon which man can rely. Have pity.

Let the power of your love show itself once again to be greater than the evil threatening us. Let it be shown to be greater than the manifold sins which arrogate to themselves in ever more absolute ways public rights of citizenship in the life of men and society. May the power of your Cross, O Christ, be seen to be greater than the author of sin, who is called "this world's prince" (*Jn* 12:32). Because through your Blood and your Suffering you redeemed the world. Amen.

September 15

Mary, Mother of Sorrows, Consoles

Mary Most Holy goes on being the loving consoler of those touched by the many physical and moral sorrows which afflict and torment humanity. She knows our sorrows and our pains, because *she too suffered, from Bethlehem to Calvary.* "And thy soul too a sword shall pierce." Mary is our Spiritual Mother, and the mother always understands her children and consoles them in their troubles.

Then, she has that specific mission to love us, received from Jesus on the Cross, to love us only and always, so as to save us! Mary consoles us above all by pointing out the Crucified One and Paradise to us!

O Virgin Most Holy, be the sole and perennial consolation of the Church which you love and protect! Console your bishops and priests, missionaries and religious who have to enlighten and save modern society, which is difficult and sometimes hostile! Console Christian communities by giving them the gift of numerous and solid priestly and religious vocations!

Console all those who are invested with authority and responsibility, civil and religious, social and political, so that they may always and only have the common good and integral development of man as their goal, in spite of difficulties and defeats!

Console . . . the so many families of those who have emigrated, the unemployed, the suffering, those who bear wounds in their bodies and souls caused by dramatic emergency situations; the young, especially those who find themselves abandoned and deprived of confidence for so many sad reasons; all those who feel ardent need in their souls for love, for altruism, for charity, for giving, who cultivate high ideals of spiritual and social gains!

O Mother of Consolation, console us all, and let all understand that the secret of happiness lies in goodness, in always faithfully following your Son, Jesus!

September 16

The Church Shares the Anxiety of Our Time

The experience of the past and of our own time shows that justice alone is not enough indeed it can lead to negation and annihilation of itself, unless *that deeper force which is love* be allowed to shape human living in its various dimensions. It was precisely historical experience which led, among other things, to formulation of the idea: *summum ius, summa iniuria* [the more law, the less justice].

This assertion does not depreciate justice and does not weaken the significance of order established upon it. It only indicates, under another aspect, how necessary it is to reach to the forces of the spirit, those even deeper forces conditioning the very order of justice.

Having a picture before her eyes of the generation to which we belong, the Church shares the anxiety of so many people of today. On the other hand, she must be concerned at the decline of many fundamental values. These constitute an undeniable treasure, not only of Christian morality but also simply of human morality, of moral culture, values such as respect for human life from the moment of conception, respect for matrimony as an indissoluble unity, respect for the stability of the family. Moral permissiveness strikes above all at this most sensitive area of human life and society. Side by side with it go the crisis of truth in human relationships, the lack of responsibility in speech, purely utilitarian relationships between one man and the other man, the decline of feeling for the true common good and the ease with which this latter is excluded. Finally, there is that desacralization which often turns into "dehuman-ization": the individual and the society, for whom and for which nothing is "sacred," decline morally, in spite of all appearances.

September 17

The Church Appeals to the Divine Mercy

The Church proclaims the truth of God's mercy, re-vealed in Christ crucified and risen again, and professes it in various ways. She furthermore seeks to put mercy into practice toward mankind through the means of men and women, since she sees that as an indispensable con-dition of concern for a better and "more humane" world, today and tomorrow. However, at no moment, and in no historical period, especially in an age so critical as ours, can the Church forget *prayer. It is a cry to the mercy of God* in the face of the manifold forms of evil which weigh upon mankind, and threaten it. . . .

Let us raise our supplications, let us be guided by the faith, the hope, the charity, which Christ has engrafted in our hearts. This attitude is at the same time love for God. Contemporary man has sometimes estranged God from himself very much, made him an outsider, proclaimed in various ways that God is "superfluous." So this is *love for that God,* the offense against whom and rejection of whom by man today we feel profoundly and are ready to cry with Christ on the cross: "Father, forgive them; they do not know what they are doing." At the same time it is *love for mankind,* for all mankind, without any exception or division at all: without difference of race, of culture, of language, of concept of the world, without distinction between friends and enemies. This is love for mankind and it desires every true good for each member of mankind, for every community, for every family, every nation, every social group, for the young, the adults, the parents, the old, the sick, for all, without exception. This is love, that is, careful concern to guarantee everyone every authentic good and to keep away and repel every evil.

September 18

Harmonize Technology with Conscience

The Church well maintains the *specific distinction* between scientific and religious knowledge and their methods. She is likewise certain of their complementarity and their profound harmony around one same God, Creator and Redeemer of man. She seeks to remove every misunderstanding from this subject. She respects natural science in its order. For her, that science is no menace, rather, it is a deeper manifestation of God the Creator. She rejoices at its progress, and therefore . . . encourages . . . research. . . . She admits as well that scientific culture today requires Christians to have a mature faith, an openness toward the language and to the questions of the learned, a sense of the orders of knowledge and of differing approaches to truth. In brief, she desires that the dialogue between science and faith shall enter into an ever more positive stage, even though it has known tensions historically, and be intensified at all levels.

Love for truth, sought after in humility, is one of the great values capable of uniting men and women of today across the various cultures. Scientific culture is not opposed to human culture or the culture of faith. *All authentic culture is open to the essential,* and there is no truth which cannot become universal.

I trust that the man of science will, at the level of his culture, preserve the sense of man's transcendence over the world, also of God's transcendence over man, and that, at the level of his action, he will link that universal sense of culture which is his characteristic, with a universal sense of fraternal love, which Christ particularly gave the taste to the world.

September 19

Faith and Culture:
An Organic and Constituent Link

Following in the footsteps of the [Second Vatican] Council, the session of the Synod of Bishops which was held in the autumn of 1974 enunciated its clear consciousness of the role of the various cultures in the evangelization of peoples. My predecessor, Paul VI, gathered the fruits of its labors in his apostolic exhortation, *"Evangeli Nuntiandi."* He there stated: "The Gospel, hence evangelization, certainly does not identify itself with culture and is independent of all cultures. However, the Kingdom which the Gospel announces is lived by people profoundly bound up with a culture, and the construction of the Kingdom cannot but be strengthened by the elements of culture and of the cultures of humanity. The Gospel and evangelization are independent of cultures but are not necessarily incompatible with them. They are capable of impregnating all of them, without subjecting themselves to any."

Drawing on the rich heritage of the Ecumenical Council, the Synod of Bishops and my venerated predecessor Paul VI, I too . . . proclaimed the existence of an organic and constituent link between Christianity and culture, with man, therefore, in his humanity. I said . . . this link of the Gospel with man "is actually creative of culture in its very foundations." And if culture is that which man, as man, becomes more man, then the very destiny of man is at stake in it.

September 20

Faith and Culture, a Constructive Dialogue

Where agnostic ideologies, hostile to the Christian tradition, or even explicitly atheist ideologies inspire certain leaders of thought, there is a greater urgency for the Church to interlace a dialogue with cultures, so that man of today may discover that, far from being's man's rival, God gives him the means to realize himself fully, in God's image and likeness. Man actually knows how to surpass himself infinitely. Evident proof of this is to be seen in the efforts which so many creative geniuses make in order to incarnate transcendental values of beauty and truth lastingly in works of art and thought, values which are more or less momentarily perceived as expressions of the absolute. So, encounters with cultures today are a terrain for privileged dialogue among people committed to the search for a new humanism for our time, beyond the divergencies separating them. . . .

On the other hand, it is urgent for our contemporaries, particularly Catholics, to interrogate themselves seriously on the conditions which are the basis of the development of the peoples. It is ever more evident that cultural progress is closely bound up with building a more just and more fraternal world. . . .

Consequently, by virtue of my apostolic mission, I feel the responsibility incumbent on me, at the heart of the collegiality of the Universal Church, and in contact and accord with local churches, to intensify the Holy See's relationships with all achievements of culture, also by maintaining a fresh relationship in fruitful international collaboration, within the family of nations, that is of the great "community of men united by diverse bonds, but above all, essentially by that of culture."

September 21

St. Matthew, Apostle and Evangelist

Dearest Brothers and Sisters! I first of all desire to give you my heartfelt greetings. . . . On this feast of St. Matthew, Apostle and Evangelist, the sacred liturgy has presented for our meditation the figure of this "sage scribe" who was so marvellously able to live and teach the Lord's words. Drawn by the Master's call to follow him, Matthew made no delay, but "got up and followed him" (*Matt* 9:9).

From then on there was a radical alteration of his life, of his way of thinking and working. He made himself a disciple of Jesus and announced that Gospel which he had written, in which the Christian is presented above all as a *follower* of Christ, one conscious of the duties coming

333

to him from his acceptance of the Gospel. And he performs them with courage, even to heroism, because following after Jesus prevails over every other duty.

You will recall Jesus' words: "None of those who cry out, 'Lord, Lord,' shall enter the kingdom of God but only those who do the will of my Father . . ." (*Mt* 7:21).

At this moment of taking on spiritual and social commitments, may the Lord help us to put the teachings of the Gospel into practice and courageously give testimony of our faith in the midst of the contemporary society to which we belong, through the intercession of his Mother and of St. Matthew, who consecrated the whole of his life to the cause of the Christian faith.

September 22

To Men of Culture

Through your scientific, philosophic, literary, and historical professional capacities, you can offer a service of authentic intellectual charity to your colleagues, to students, to society and all its institutions. You can also offer a service to the Church herself, as a cultural contribution, for catechesis, for evangelization and for human advancement.

Dearly beloved, you are not only intellectuals who reflect, evaluate and contemplate truth, closed as it were in an individualistic ivory tower. Do not let it be that only isolated voices launch messages to consciences and to the world. You too are solidly involved in a prophetical task of forming sensitive consciences capable of saying "No" to death, to hatred, to violence, to terror, to error, to evil, to degradation, but saying "Yes" to the good, to the beautiful, to truth, to justice, to responsibility, to life, to peace, to Love. You, too, must take on your responsibility, consciously.

Your contribution in this field is a conspicuous one. The young who have an educational contact with you, politicians who turn an ear to what you have to say, technicians who cannot do without you — let all these be aided by you to enter sagely and rationally into a vision of life and human society which promotes the common good of all mankind. When carried out with deep human and Christian conscientiousness, your task will be appreciated by the people. But, even more, it will be blessed by God, who is the God of Truth and Love. We will pray to Him together that He may always give us the courage of truth and charity.

September 23

The Believer and the World of Culture

There is a need to accomplish a continual effort of analysis and synthesis of what the believer's patient, sometimes painful, contribution ought to be in the world of culture. It obviously begins from history, measures itself by it, and interprets its process of becoming, by means of that reading of the signs of the times which belongs to the people of God, moved by the Faith, and "led by the Spirit of the Lord, who fills the universe."

That means that the man of faith is conscious of covering a path together with the rest of mankind within a history in which God achieves his plan of love. And, in the daily effort of his commitment, enlightened by God's Word, he seeks to gather up the scattered threads of this history, which may in the end be no less than a history of salvation. This vision of man and of history links with one's own adherence to Christ and His Church, because it is from Christ and His sacrament that the grace of a correct reading of the times is received.

Faith therefore, in its relation with culture, presents itself as a clarification of God's project, as an aid and complement to rationality. But rationality is not impoverished by having recourse to the Faith. The Sacred Council, recalling what the First Vatican Council taught, declares that "two orders of knowledge exist and are distinct. They are that of the Faith and that of reason, and the Church does not forbid human arts and disciplines . . . to make use of their own principles and own methods in the fields proper to each." She therefore "recognizes that just liberty," and so affirms "the rightful autonomy of culture, especially of the sciences."

September 24

St. Gellert of Esstergom, Bishop and Martyr

The personality of St. Gerhardt or Gellert appears before us in three successive forms typical of the Christian life: that of a monk, that of an apostle, that of a martyr. The monk is a man of God who dedicates his life completely to God in prayer and labor. The apostle is the announcer of the saving good news of the Gospel, who educates the Christian to holiness of life and leads the pagan to Christianity. The martyr is he who gives himself to God totally, as the extreme testimony of his love, together with his life of prayer and his apostolic activity. St. Gellert was a man of God, because he consecrated all his life to God with the intention of obedience. How did he obey? In accordance with the dictates of the rule and in the twofold harmony of prayer and work.

With his life, St. Gellert gave testimony of assiduous service to evangelization. He did not seek to announce his own ideas but the good news of Christ. He also understood how an ordered ecclesiastical community can arise only in this way, by seeking communion with Christ and offering one's own life to service of the brethren.

Martyrdom crowned that life dedicated to God in prayer and apostolic activity. That martyrdom was St. Gellert's final testimony of love for his new homeland, Hungary, for his new people.

The monument to St. Gellert, Monk, Apostle, Martyr, rises . . . above the Danube. With the raised crucifix in his hand, he exhorts you still today: Be testifiers of faith in Christ and of the fraternal love which is the sign of Christianity in the midst of your people! May the Spirit of Christ give you strength, through the potent intercession of the Most Blessed Virgin, *"Magna Domina Hungarorum* — Sovereign Lady of the Hungarians."

September 25

Popular Culture as Basic Morality

So-called "popular culture" means the generality of principles and values which constitute a people's ethos, the power uniting the people at a deep level and brought to maturity by historical experience, sometimes at a harsh cost, that of great collective sorrows. It constitutes a common foundation, coming before and going beyond the various ideological and political currents.

No people is formed without this foundation. No political experiment, no form of democracy may survive, if there be no appeal to a common, basic morality. No written law is enough to guarantee human society unless it draws its inward strength from a moral foundation. . . . Such "popular culture" is largely that of the Christian faith and that of education given by the Church over the centuries.

Today it is under threat, for various reasons: sometimes it seems to be in grave danger of being overturned. Watch with great care over this point: the future of the Church and of society itself depend on it.

"Popular culture" is nowadays much influenced by the mass communications media. There can be no doubt about the importance of such media for the formation of customs and public opinion. . . .

We need to multiply our efforts so that these media will not threaten that basic morality which was always the secret strength of a people.

September 26

Art and Nature

The first major exhibition of American paintings in the Vatican . . . was titled "A Mirror of Creation: 150 Years of American Nature Painting." . . . to admire these paintings . . . to reflect on nature as an example of God's handiwork, a manifestation of his power and beauty, an expression of the generosity with which he endows the world and adorns it for the good of human beings.

From these reflections on nature there emerges a deep realization of the glory of creation, the dignity of man, and above all the majesty of the Creator.

The Psalmist was moved to proclaim: "O Lord, My Lord, how glorious is your name over all the earth! You have exalted your majesty above the heavens." Artists have indeed a noble contribution to make in building the civilization of man and in promoting the Kingdom of God on earth.

September 27

Saint Vincent de Paul

The vocation of this genial initiator of charitable and social action yet lights the path of his sons and his daughters today, of laity living in his spirit, of young people seeking the key to an existence usefully and radically expended in gift of self.

To serve the poor better, Vincent willed "to gather around him churchmen free of all benefices so as to be able to apply themselves entirely under the good pleasure of the bishops, to the salvation of the poor people of the fields, through preaching, catechism and general confession, without taking any reward of any sort or manner at all." That group of priests, called "Lazarists," developed rapidly into the Congregation of the Mission. Vincent never ceased from inculcating "the spirit of our Lord" into his companions. He summed up that spirit in five fundamental virtues: simplicity, gentleness toward one's neighbor, humility as regards oneself, and then, as a condition of those three virtues, mortification and zeal, which are in some way their dynamic aspects. His exhortations to those whom he sent to preach the Gospel are full of spiritual wisdom and pastoral realism: it is not a question of being loved for one's own sake but of making Jesus Christ loved.

September 28

Saint Marie-Louise de Marillac

Another aspect of the dynamism and realism of Vincent de Paul was seen in his giving a unified and effective structure to the "Charities" which had multiplied. Under the guidance of Monsieur Vincent himself, Louise de Marillac was assigned to inspecting and supporting the "Charities." She did wonders and her radiance did much to decide a number of "good country girls," already helping in the "Charities," to follow her example of total oblation to God and the poor.

The Company of the Daughters of Charity saw the light on 29 November 1633. Vincent de Paul gave it an original and highly demanding rule: "For your monastery you shall have the chambers of the sick; for cells, rented rooms; for a chapel, the parish church; for cloisters, the city streets; for enclosure, obedience; for a grill, fear of God; for a veil, holy modesty." The Company's spirit was summed up by him as follows: "You must do what the Son of God did on earth. You must give life to these poor sick, the life of the body and the life of the soul."

Without having known the feminist movements of our time, Monsieur Vincent knew how to find intelligent and generous, loyal and constant auxiliaries in the women of his time. The history of the Company singularly lights up what is undoubtedly the most profound aspect of femininity: that of the vocation to tenderness and pity, of which mankind will always have need. For there are always poor in its midst. And modern societies even give rise to new forms of poverty.

September 29

School Education

It would seem to be the case that in modern times success of a particular educational program or system has been measured, to a large extent, by the recognized qualification it provides, with a view to some career prospect. This would appear to be felt most in the secondary sector of education, where direction for future prospects is crucial.

Hence the emphasis, until now, on a diploma-oriented curriculum, with the diploma seen as virtual guarantee of career expectations. . . .

But nowadays, as we have been made only too aware, the possession of a diploma does not bring automatic employment. Indeed, this harsh reality has brought about not only deep frustration among young people, many of whom have worked so hard, but also a sense of malaise in the educational system itself.

Hence the question: what has gone wrong? What has specialization achieved in our day in real terms, in terms of life? Wherein lies the remedy?

Perhaps we could reflect on the philosophy behind education: *education as the completing of the person.* To be educated is to be more fitted for life; to have a greater capacity for appreciating what life is, what it has to offer, and what the person has to offer in return to the wider society of man. Thus, if we would apply our modern education skills and resources to this philosophy, we might succeed in offering something of lasting value to our pupils and students, an antidote to often immediate prospects of frustration and boredom, not to mention the uncertainty of the long-term future ... giving due emphasis to education as development of the whole person; not only intellectual ability but also emotional, physical and social development.

September 30

The Ethos of the Catholic School

The development of the whole person, the spiritual dimension of education and the involvement of parents have always been central to the ethos of the Catholic school. This has been particulary true of the primary school, with the close bond among the family, school, parish and local community. Nor has this been absent in the more complex situation of the secondary sector, where the diocese often provides chaplains, above all for the school as a community of faith centered on the Eucharist and also, where possible, to serve as a pastoral link with the local parish.

However, always mindful of the constant need for improvement, the Catholic school ought to make full use of suitable new opportunities available, for no other reason than to fulfil its own identity and role. And we do well at this point to recollect what precisely is the *identity and purpose* of the Catholic school.

Such a reminder is conveniently provided in the document of that title, "The Catholic School," published by the Holy See's Sacred Congregation for the Christian Education in March 1977: "The Catholic School," it declares, "is committed ... to the development of the whole man, since in *Christ, the Perfect Man,* all human values find their fulfilment and unity. Herein lies the specifically Catholic character of the school. Its duty to cultivate human values in their own legitimate right in accordance with its particular mission to serve all men has its origin in the figure of Christ. . . . Its task is fundamentally a synthesis of culture and faith, and a synthesis of faith and life."

October

October 1

St. Theresa of the Child Jesus

A spirit . . . makes us cry out "Abba! Father!" It would perhaps be difficult to find words more incisive, and at the same time more gripping, to describe the particular charisma of Thérèse Martin, that which constituted the quite special gift of her heart and became a particlar gift to the Church through her heart. A gift marvellous in its simplicity, a universal and at the same time unique gift.

It may be said with conviction of Theresa of Lisieux that the Holy Spirit permitted her heart to reveal the fundamental mystery, the reality of the Gospel, directly to the people of our time. The "little way" is the way of the "holy childhood." There is something unique in this way — the genius of St. Theresa of Lisieux.

This most fundamental and most universal truth was in a certain sense rediscovered through the interior experience of her heart and the form which her whole life took, a life of only twenty-four years. She left behind her the memory of a child "trusting" even to heroism and consequently "free" even to heroism.

In her Carmel, Theresa felt especially united to all the Church's missions and missionaries throughout the world. She felt herself to be "missionary." She has been proclaimed patroness of the missions by the Church. Abba! Father! Thanks to her, the whole Church has found again all the simplicity and all the freshness of that cry, which has its origin and source in the heart of Christ himself.

October 2

The Central Point of Catholic Education

Implicit throughout ... terms of reference for the Catholic School is the imperative of *Christian commitment* on the part of its teachers. The Catholic school "must be a community whose aim is the transmission of values for living. Its work is seen as promoting a faith relationship with Christ in whom all values find fulfillment. But faith is principally assimilated through contact with people whose daily life bears witness to it."

In reflecting on the value of Catholic schools and the importance of Catholic teachers and educators, it is necessary to stress the central point of Catholic education itself. *Catholic education is above all a question of communicating Christ, of helping to form Christ* in the lives of others. Those who have been baptized must be trained to live the newness of Christian life in justice and in the holiness of truth. The cause of Catholic education is the cause of Jesus Christ and of His Gospel at the service of man.

Nor must we ignore the *integrity of the catechetical message* as taught: "The person who becomes a disciple of Christ has the right to receive 'the word of faith' *(Rom* 10:8) not in mutilated, falsified or diminished form but whole and entire. . . . Thus no true catechist can lawfully, on his own initiative, make a selection of what he considers unimportant, so as to teach the one and reject the other. . . . The method and language used must truly be means for communicating the whole and not just part of "the paths of life" *(Acts* 2:28, quoting *Ps* 16:11).

October 3

The University, High Point of Education

From its very origins and by reason of its institution, *the purpose of the university* is the acquiring of a scientific knowledge of the truth, of the whole truth. Thus it constitutes one of the fundamental means which man has devised to meet his need for knowledge.

But, as the Second Vatican Council observed: "Today it is more difficult than it once was to synthesize the various disciplines of knowledge and the arts. While, indeed, the volume and the diversity of the elements which make up culture increase, at the same time the capacity of individual men to perceive them and to blend them organically decreases, so that the image of universal man becomes even more faint." Any interpretation of knowledge and culture, therefore, which ignores or even belittles the spiritual essence of man, his apsirations to the fullness of being, his thirst for truth and the absolute, the questions that he asks himself before the enigmas of sorrow and death, cannot be said to satisfy his deepest and most authentic needs. And since it is in the university that young people experience the high point of their formative education, they should be able to find answers not only about the legitimacy and finality of science but also about higher moral and spiritual values — answers that will restore their confidence in the potential of knowledge gained and the exercise of reason, for their own good and for that of society. . . .

It becomes necessary, therefore, on the part of all, to recover an awareness of the primacy of moral values, which are the *values of the human person* as such. The great task that has to be faced today for the renewal of society is that of recapturing the ultimate meaning of life and its fundamental values.

And, as Christians, we believe that the ultimate meaning of life and its fundamental values are indeed revealed in Jesus Christ. It is he — Jesus Christ, true God and true man — who says to you, "You address me as 'Teacher' and 'Lord', and fittingly enough, for that is what I am" (*Jn* 13:13–14).

October 4

St. Francis of Assisi

St. Francis! We all know what the birth of the great Saint of Assisi has meant for mankind!

With him, Dante said, "a sun was born to the world." There are many reasons why he exerted and goes on exerting a marked fascination in the Church, and outside her as well: his was an optimistic vision of the whole of creation as the epiphany of God and the homeland of Christ, whom he celebrated in his very well known "Canticle of Creatures"; he chose poverty as the expression of his whole life, and called it "My Lady — Madonna," the term used by knights to their ladies and by Christians to the Mother of God.

But supporting it was an integrally practiced theological virtue. He rarely calls it by name, because it became his state of mind and made him concentrate everything on God, made him expect everything from Him, made him happy not to possess anything but from Him. He expressed this state of mind in passionate tones in the "*Chartula*," the "Little Charter" which he gave to Friar Leo on Mount La Verna: "Thou art the good, very good, the supreme good, Lord, God, living and true. . . . Thou art our hope." Yes, because true hope, this gift of the

Spirit which does not disappoint (cf. Rom 5:5) derives from unique certainty that "the Son of God . . . loved me and gave himself for me" (Gal 2:20).

Recovery of this certainty is urgent for the world of today, furrowed by so many disquiets, which are like an assault upon the hope brought by Christ to all: "Take courage! I have overcome the world" (Jn 16:33).

October 5

The Catholic University

The Christian faith enables us believers to interpret the deepest needs of the human being better than anyone else and, with serene and tranquil certainty, indicates the ways and means for fully satisfying them. So this is the testimony which the Christian community and the world of culture itself expect of [university] teachers and students. . . :

——To show through the facts that intelligence is not only not handicapped but rather is stimulated and strengthened by that incomparable source of comprehension of human reality which is the Word of God; to show by the facts that it is possible to construct a community of men and women around this Word, and they can carry on their researches in the various fields and sectors without losing contact with the essential reference points of a Christian vision of life.

—— A community of men and women seeking particular answers to particular problems, but borne up by joyful awareness of jointly possessing the ultimate answers to the ultimate problems; a community of men and women, above all, trying to incarnate in their own existences and in their special environment that announcement of salvation which they received from Him who is "the true light which enlightens every man."

—— A community of men and women who — with respect for the rightful autonomy of earthly reality, created by God, dependent on Him and ordained by Him — feel committed to "writing the divine law into the life of the earthly city."

October 6

The Holy Rosary, Prayer of the Redeemed

This month of October is traditionally dedicated to the Holy Rosary. In this month, therefore, I wish to consecrate the Angelus thought to the prayer so dear to the hearts of Catholics, so beloved by me and so much recommended by the popes, my predecessors. . . .

The Rosary also takes on fresh perspectives and is charged with stronger and vaster intentions than in the past. It is not a question now of asking for great victories, as at Lepanto and Vienna, rather is it a question of asking Mary to provide us with valorous fighters against the spirit of error and evil, with the arms of the Gospel, that is, the Cross and God's Word.

The Rosary prayer is man's prayer for man. It is the prayer of human solidarity, the collegial prayer of the redeemed, reflecting the spirit and intent of the first of the redeemed, Mary, Mother and Image of the Church. It is a prayer for all the people of the world and of history, living and dead, called to be the Body of Christ with us and to become heirs together with Him of the glory of the Father.

When we consider the spiritual directions suggested by the Rosary, which is a simple, evangelical prayer, we find the same intentions which St. Cyprian noted in the Our Father: "The Lord, master of peace and unity, did not will that we should pray individually and alone. In fact, we do not say, 'My Father, who art in heaven.' Nor do we say, 'Give me my daily bread.' Our prayer is for all; so that, when we pray, we should not do so for one only but for the whole people, so that with all the people we are one thing.

October 7

The Meaning of the Holy Rosary

The evangelist Luke tells us that Mary "was troubled" at the words of the archangel Gabriel, addressed to her at the moment of the annunciation and wondered "what his greeting meant."

This meditation of Mary constitutes the prime model of the prayer of the Rosary. It is the prayer of those who hold the angel's greeting to Mary dear. Persons who recite the Rosary take up Mary's meditation in their thoughts and hearts and as they recite the prayer they wonder "what his greeting meant."

First of all, they repeat the words addressed to Mary by God himself, through his messenger. Those who hold dear the angel's greeting to Mary repeat words *coming from God.* As we recite the Rosary, we utter these words many times. This is not just simple repetition. The words addressed to Mary by God himself and announced by the divine messenger *contain an inscrutable content.*

"Hail, Mary, full of grace, the Lord is with thee. . . ." "Blessed art thou among women." This content is closely united with the mystery of the redemption. The words of the angel's greeting to Mary lead into this mystery and find their explanation in it at the same time.

October 8

The Holy Rosary:
Participation in Mary's Meditations

The words heard by Mary at the Annunciation revealed that *the time was come for accomplishing the promises* contained in the Book of Genesis. . . . The mystery of the the Redemption is about to be accomplished. The message from the eternal God greets "the woman." This woman is Mary of Nazareth. It greets her in consideration of the "stock" which she must receive from God himself: "The Holy Spirit will come upon you and the power of the Most High will overshadow you. . . . You shall conceive and bear a son and give him the name Jesus."

Really *decisive words*. The angel's greeting to Mary constitutes the beginning of God's greatest works in the story of man and the world. This greeting opens up near prospects of redemption. It is no wonder that, having heard the words of this greeting, Mary was "troubled." *The approach of the living God always arouses awe.* Nor is there any reason to wonder that Mary asked "what his greeting meant." The archangel's words put her before an inscrutable divine mystery. Moreover, they involved her in the orbit of that mystery. This needs to be meditated on again and again and ever more deeply. It has the power of filling not only life but also eternity. The angel's greeting is dear to all of us. Let us therefore try to participate in Mary's meditations. Let us try to do so above all when we recite the Rosary.

October 9

Memory and Remembrance of Pius XII

Pius XII, Eugenio Pacelli, stood forth as *a strenuous and passionate servant of peace* in his first message, delivered on the day after his election, from the Sistine Chapel. He directed an invitation and exhortation to peace to all the Church's children and to all mankind. He tirelessly wrote and labored for the terrible Second World War not to break out. Then he did everything to reduce the harmful and tragic effects of the immense conflict, which kept on spreading and claiming millions of victims. He made use of all means to hasten peace and to alleviate the sufferings of the harsh postwar period. "With peace nothing is lost; with war all can be lost!" That was his anguished exclamation, his cry almost on the eve of the disaster. Sadly, it was not heard, but it was a prophecy!

He delivered nineteen Christmas speeches, which his successor described as "a monument of his sagacity and his apostolic fervor." In them, he spoke of peace as harmony of justice and charity; peace of conscience, peace in families, social peace, international peace. Pope Paul VI could say of him, "We must remember Pius XII as a strong and loving man, one active in defense of justice and peace, concerned for every human misfortune, such as became manifold and immense especially in the war period."

We will here recall that unforgettable Pope's luminous magisterium in the biblical, theological, moral and social fields; the new translation of the Psalter; the excavations around St. Peter's tomb; the proclamation and accomplishment of the Holy Year of 1950; the solemn definition of the dogma of the Assumption of Mary Most Holy, on 1 November of the same Holy Year of 1950.

October 10

The Holy Rosary Introduces Us to the Divine Mysteries of Christ

Through the words uttered by the messenger at Nazareth, Mary glimpsed, in God, *the whole of her life* on earth and her eternity.

Why was it that when she heard that she had to become mother of the Son of God, she did not respond with spiritual transports, but first of all with the humble "*fiat* — be it done." "I am the servant of the Lord. Let it be done to me as you say?"

Was it not because she already felt the piercing pain of that promise that he shall reign on "the throne of David," which was made to Jesus?

The archangel announced at the same time that "His reign will be without end."

Through the words of the angel's greeting to Mary, all the mysteries whereby the salvation of the world will be accomplished begin to be revealed: the Joyful, Sorrowful and Glorious Mysteries. So, as in the Rosary, Mary, who asked "what his greeting meant," seems to enter into all the mysteries and introduces us to them too. She introduces us to the mysteries of Christ and to her own mysteries at the same time. Her act of meditation at the moment of the annunciation *opens the way to our meditations* during the recital of the Rosary and thanks to it.

The Rosary is the prayer through which, by repeating the angel's greeting to Mary, we try to draw considerations of our own on the mysteries of the redemption from the Most Blessed Virgin's meditation. Her reflection began at the moment of the annunciation and continues in the glory of the assumption.

In eternity, Mary is profoundly immersed in the mystery of the Father, of the Son, and of the Holy Spirit. As our Mother, she joins in the prayer of those who hold the angel's greeting dear and express it in their recital of the Rosary.

October 11

In the Holy Rosary, Mary Prays for Us and with Us

We join with her in this prayer as did the apostles gathered in the cenacle after Christ's ascension. "Together they devoted themselves to constant prayer. There were some women in their company, and Mary the mother of Jesus, and his brothers."

Through that prayer they prepared themselves to receive the Holy Spirit on the day of Pentecost. Mary, who had obtained the Holy Spirit in lofty plenitude on the day of the Annunciation, prayed with them. That particular fullness of the Holy Spirit determined a particular plenitude of prayer in her. Through that singular fullness, Mary prays for us — and prays with us.

She presides at our prayer maternally. The Church thus continually prepares herself to receive the Holy Spirit, as on the day of Pentecost.

The first centenary of Pope Leo XIII's encyclical *Supremi apostolatus* occurs this year [1983]. With that encyclical, that great pontiff decreed that the month of October should be particularly dedicated to devotion to the Virgin of the Rosary. He vigorously stressed in that document what extraordinary effectiveness this prayer has, when recited with a pure and devout mind, so as to obtain from the Heavenly Father, in Christ, and through the intercession of the Mother of God, protection against the gravest evils which may threaten Christianity and mankind itself, thence to attain to the supreme goods of justice and peace among individuals and peoples.

With that historic gesture, Leo XIII set hmself by the side of numerous pontiffs who had preceded him — among them St. Pius V — and left an assignment to those who were to follow him in promoting the practice of the Rosary. For this reason, I too would say to you all: make the Rosary "the gentle chain linking you to heaven" through Mary.

October 12

The Church in Service to the Family

In our time, the family has been involved in the broad, deep and rapid transformations of society and culture as with other institutions, and perhaps more so. Many families live with this situation in fidelity to those values which constitute the foundation of the institution of the family. Others have become unsure and bewildered, when faced with their duties, or are even doubtful and, as it were, ignorant of the ultimate meaning and of the truth of married and family life. Other families, again, are impeded by various situations of injustice from attaining their fundamental rights.

Once again, the Church feels the urgency of the need to announce the Gospel, that is, the "good news," to all without distinction, especially to all who are called to matrimony and are preparing for it and to all spouses and parents in the world. She is profoundly convinced that only through acceptance of the Gospel can every hope which man rightfully places in matrimony and the family find full realization. Matrimony and the family were willed by God together with creation itself; they are interiorly ordained to being accomplished in Christ. They need his grace for being healed of the wounds of sin and brought back to their "principle," that is, to original full consciousness and integral accomplishment of God's design.

This is an historic moment when the family is the objective of numerous forces seeking to destroy it or at any rate deform it. The Church is aware that the good of society and her own well-being are profoundly bound up with the well-being of the family. She therefore has a keener and more stringent sense of her mission to proclaim God's plan for matrimony and the family to all, to ensure them full vitality and human and Christian advancement. She thus contributes to renewing society and the People of God at the same time.

October 13

Consecration of the World to the Immaculate Heart of Mary

Be blessed above all things, Handmaid of the Lord, who obeyed the Divine Call in the fullest way! Be greeted, you who united yourself entirely with Your Son's redemptive consecration! Mother of the Church! Enlighten the People of God on the way of faith, hope, and charity!

Help us to live with all the truth of the consecration of Christ for the entire human family in the contemporary world. By entrusting, O Mother, the world, all individuals and all peoples to you, we also entrust to you the very consecration of the world, putting it in your Maternal Heart.

O, Immaculate Heart! Help us to overcome the threat of evil, which so easily takes root in the hearts of men today and, with its incommensurable effects, already weighs upon our contemporary existence and seems to close the way toward the future!

Free us from hunger and war! From nuclear war, from incalculable self-destruction, from every kind of war, free us! From the sin against the life of man at its dawning, free us! From the hatred and from debasement of the children of God, free us! From every kind of injustice, national and international, free us! From the ease treading down God's commandments, free us! From sins against the Holy Spirit, free us! Free us!

Receive, O Mother of Christ, this cry charged with the sufferings of all mankind! Charged with the sufferings of entire societies. Reveal yourself once again, in the story of the world, to be merciful! May this cry halt evil! May it transform consciences!

May the light of hope reveal itself to all in your Immaculate Heart! Amen.

October 14

The Great Divine Trial

I desire to share with you, at least briefly, what was the content of my meditations in that period of months when I partook of *a great divine trial.* I say divine trial, because, although the events of 13 May [the attempted assassination] had their purely human dimension, this can obscure an even deeper dimension: that of the trial permitted by God.

God permitted me to experience suffering over the past months; he permitted me to experience the peril of losing my life. He permitted me at the same time to understand clearly and thoroughly that this was *a special grace* for me as a man and at the same time that it was — in consideration of the service which I do as Bishop of Rome and Successor of St. Peter — a grace for the Church.

So, dear brothers and sisters, I know that I have experienced a great grace. And as I recall the event of 13 May and the whole of the subsequent period together with you, I cannot but speak of that above all.

Christ, Light of the World and Shepherd of his Fold, above all, Prince of Pastors, granted me the grace of being able *to bear witness to his Truth and his Love,* through suffering and with danger to my life and health. I consider that this was precisely the particular grace imparted to me.

It is therefore with great gratitude to the Holy Spirit that I think of that weakness, which he consented to let me experience from 13 May on, believing and humbly trusting that it was able to help strengthen the Church and my humble person as well. This is the dimension of the divine trial, not easy to reveal to man.

October 15

St. Teresa of Avila, Doctor of the Church

Theresa of Jesus is the stream which points back to the spring; she is the splendor which leads to the light. And her light is Christ, the "Master of Wisdom," the "Living Book," in whom she learned her truths. He is "the light of heaven," the Spirit of Wisdom, which she invoked that he might speak in her name and guide her pen. Teresa of Jesus, *first woman doctor of the universal Church,* made herself a living word with God, she called to friendship with Christ, she opened up new paths of fidelity and service to Holy Mother Church.

I know that she reached the hearts of bishops and priests so as to renew desires for Wisdom and Holiness in them, to be "light to the Church." She exhorted the religious "to follow the evangelical counsels with all perfection" so as "to be servants of love." She lit up the experience of Christian laypeople with her doctrine of prayer and charity, the universal way of sanctity. For, like the Christian life, prayer does not consist "in thinking much, but in loving much" and "all by their nature are capable of loving."

Her voice has resounded beyond the Catholic Church; it has aroused response at the ecumenical level and has given rise to bridges of dialogue with the treasures of spirituality of other religious cultures. I am happy above all to know that St. Teresa's word has been enthusiastically accepted by the young.

Among the holy women of the Church's history, Teresa of Jesus is undoubtedly the one who responded to Christ with greatest fervor of heart. Christ Jesus, Redeemer of Mankind, was Teresa's model.

October 16

St. Hedwig of Silesia, Spouse

We look back over more than seven centuries to St. Hedwig, in whom we see a great light, which illuminates human problems, those of the land of our neighbors and those of our native land at the same time. In her life was expressed almost all the fullness of the Christian vocation. St. Hedwig read the Gospel thoroughly she read all its enlivening truth. There was no divergence in her between the vocation of the widow — founder of the convent of Trzebnica — and the vocation of the spouse — mother of the house of the Piasts, of Henry. One thing happened after another and one thing was deeply rooted in the other at the same time. Hedwig lived for God from the beginning; she lived above all in Love of God, just as the first commandment of the Gospel says. So she lived in matrimony as wife and mother. And when she was left a widow, she easily saw how this love for God could now become exclusive, above all for the divine Spouse. She followed that vocation.

The deepest spring of man's spiritual development is found in the evangelical commandment of love. . . . I hope and pray with all my heart that your personal, family and social lives shall be based on the commandment of love according to her model. This is at once the deepest source of moral culture for people and nations. It is on moral culture that their progress essentially depends. Man is a being created in God's likeness. Hence, his essential development and true culture arise from acknowledgement of this image and likeness.

October 17

The Christian Family in the Modern World

In the Apostolic Exhortation regarding the role of the Christian Family in the modern world I underlined *the positive aspects of family life today,* which include: a more lively awareness of personal freedom and greater attention to the quality of interpersonal relationships in marriage, greater attention to promotion of the dignity of women, to responsible procreation, to the education of children. But at the same time I could not fail to draw attention to *the negative phenomena*: a corruption of the idea and experience of freedom, with consequent self-centeredness in human relations: serious misconceptions regarding the relationship between parents and children; the growing number of divorces; the scourge of abortion; the spread of contraceptive and anti-life mentality.

Besides these destructive forces, there are social and economic conditions which affect millions of human beings, undermining the strength and stability of marriage and family life. In addition there is the cultural onslaught against the family by those who attack married life as "irrelevant" and "outdated." All of this is a serious challenge to society and to the Church. As I wrote then: "History is not simply a fixed progression towards what is better, but rather an event of freedom, and even a struggle between freedoms that are in mutual conflict."

Married couples, I speak to you of *the hopes and ideals that sustain the Christian vision of marriage* and family life. You will find the strength to be faithful to your marriage vows in your love for God and your love for each other and for your children. Let this love be the rock that stands firm in the face of every storm and temptation.

October 18

St. Luke the Evangelist

At the shrine of St. Luke, on the Colle della Guardia, beneath the ancient image of Mary Most Holy, which a pious and meaningful tradition attributes to the evangelist St. Luke, I would put a query to you. . . . How have you responded to this call from Jesus, who wishes to make you collaborators, more intimate successors to his salvific mission? How do you respond today?

Be generous with Jesus! Look to her, to Mary, as St. Luke presents her in his account of the mystery of the Annunciation — we might say, as he paints her in his Gospel, with extraordinary effectiveness and intense delicacy. God chose her for the singular, unique vocation of being Mother of the Messiah, Son of the Most High. After the initial upset troubling her before the exceptional privilege, she replied: "*Ecce ancilla Domini, fiat mihi secundum verbum tuum* — I am the servant of the Lord, let it be done to me as you say." Imitate Our Lady's *absolute readiness* in the face of God's project. You too say to the call of Jesus: "Here I am, let what you have said occur in me."

October 19

Marriage, an Unbreakable Alliance

In a marriage a man and a woman pledge themselves to one another in *an unbreakable alliance of total mutual self-giving*. A total union of love. Love that is not a passing emotion temporary infatuation, but a responsible and free decision to bind oneself completely, "in good times and in bad," to one's partner. It is the gift of oneself to the other. It is a love to be proclaimed before the eyes of the whole world. It is unconditional. To be capable of such love calls for careful preparation from early childhood to wedding day. It requires the constant support of Church and society throughout its development.

The love of husband and wife in God's plan leads beyond itself, and new life is generated, a family is born. The family is a community of love and life, a home in which children are guided to maturity. *Marriage is a holy Sacrament.* Those baptized in the name of the Lord Jesus are married in His name also. Their love is a sharing in the love of God. He is its source.

The marriages of Christian couples are images on earth of the wonder of God, the loving, life-giving communion of Three Persons in one God, and of God's covenant in Christ, with the Church. Christian marriage is a sacrament of salvation. *It is the pathway to holiness* for all members of a family. With all my heart, therefore, I urge that your homes be centers of prayer; homes where families are at ease in the presence of God; homes to which others are invited to share hospitality, prayer and the praise of God.

October 20

Interpersonal Relationship in Marriage

Saint Paul, addressing husbands and wives, recommends them to defer to one another out of reverence for Christ" *(Eph* 5:21). Here it is a question of *a relationship of a double dimension or degree:* reciprocal and communitarian. One clarifies and characterizes the other. The mutual relations of husband and wife should flow from their common relationship with Christ. St. Paul speaks of the "reverence for Christ," above all a case of respect for holiness, for the *sacrum.* It is a question of *pietas,* which arising from a profound *awareness of the mystery of Christ,* should constitute the basis of the reciprocal relations between husbands and wives.

In saying "Wives should be submissive to their husbands as if to the Lord" *(Eph* 5:22), the author does not intend to say that the husband is the "lord" of the wife and that the interpersonal pact proper to marriage is a pact of domination of the husband over the wife. The husband and the wife are in fact "subject to one another" and are mutually subordinated to one another. The source of the mutual subjection is to be found in Christian *pietas* and its expression is love.

Love makes the husband simultaneously subject to the wife, and thereby subject to the Lord himself, just as the wife to the husband. The community or unity which they should establish through marriage is constituted by a reciprocal donation of self, which is also a mutual subjection. Christ is the source and also the model of that subjection, which, being reciprocal "out of reverence for Christ," confers on the conjugal union a profound and mature character, giving rise to a new and precious "fusion" of the bilateral relations and conduct.

October 21

Children, the Most Precious Gifts to Matrimony

According to God's design, matrimony is the basis of the wider community which is the family, for the very institution of matrimony and married love are ordained for procreation and education of offspring and find their crown in the offspring.

In its deepest reality, love is essentially giving and, while conjugal love leads the spouses to reciprocal "knowledge" which makes them "one flesh," it does not end within the couple; it makes them capable of the greatest possible giving whereby they become cooperators with God for the gift of life and a new human person. So, while the spouses give to each other, they give the reality of the child out beyond themselves, as a living reflection of their love, a permanent sign of married unity and a living and inseparable synthesis of their being father and mother.

In becoming parents, spouses receive the gift from God of a new responsibility. Their parental love is called to become the visible sign to the children of God's own love, that of him "from whom all fatherhood in heaven and on earth is named."

However, it must not be forgotten that, even when procreation is not possible, it does not mean that married life loses its value. Physical barrenness may be the occasion for the spouses to take on other services important for the life of the human person, for example, adoption, various kinds of educational work, aid to other families, poor children or the handicapped.

October 22

Inauguration of the Apostolic Ministry of John Paul II

It was to Christ the Redeemer that my feelings and my thoughts were directed on 16 October [1978] ... when, after the canonical election, I was asked: "Do you accept?" I then replied: "With obedience in faith to Christ, my Lord, and with trust in the Mother of Christ and of the Church, in spite of the great difficulties, I accept." Today I wish to make that reply known publicly to all without exception, thus showing that there is a link between the first fundamental truth of the Incarnation ... and the ministry that, with my acceptance of my election as Bishop of Rome and Successor of the Apostle Peter, has become my specific duty in his See.

I chose the same names that were chosen by my beloved predecessor John Paul I. Indeed, as soon as he announced to the Sacred College on 26 August 1978 that he wished to be called John Paul — such a double name being unprecedented in the history of the papacy — I saw in it a clear presage of grace for the new pontificate. Since that pontificate lasted barely 33 days, it falls to me not only to continue it but in a certain sense to take it up again at the same starting point. This is confirmed by my choice of these two names. By following the example of my venerable predecessor in choosing them, I wish like him to express my love for the unique inheritance left to the Church by Popes John XXIII and Paul VI and my personal readiness to develop that inheritance with God's help.

Through these two names and two pontificates I am linked with the whole tradition of the Apostolic See and with all my predecessors in the expanse of the twentieth century and of the preceding centuries. I am connected, through one after another of the various ages back to the most remote, with the line of the mission and ministry that confers on Peter's See an altogether special place in the Church.

October 23

Bringing Up Children

The task of education has its roots in the parents' primary vocation to share in God's creative work. By begetting in love and for love, a new person having the vocation to growth and development in him, the parents take on the task of effectively helping that new person to live a fully human life: "Since parents have conferred life on their children, they have a most solemn obligation to educate their offspring. Hence parents must be acknowledged as the first and foremost educators of their children. Their role as educators is so decisive that scarcely anything can compensate for their failure in it. For it devolves on parents to create a family atmosphere so animated with love and reverence for God and man, that personal and social development will be fostered among the children. Hence the family is the first school of those social virtures which every society needs" (Vatican II).

The parents' right and duty is described as *essential*, connected as it is with transmission of human life; it is described as *original and primary*, as regards other educational functions, because of the uniqueness of the love relationship which exists between parents and children; it is described as *irreplaceable and unalienable*, therefore as not being able to be totally delegated to others, nor usurped by others.

Away and beyond these characteristics, the most radical element — that which characterizes the parents' educational duty — is paternal and maternal love. This finds the accomplishment of the task of education making its service to life full and perfect. The parents' love turns from being *source* into *soul*, thence into *norm*, inspiring and guiding the whole of the concrete work of education, and enriching it with those values of gentleness, constance, goodness, service, disinterestedness, spirit of sacrifice, which are the most precious fruit of love.

October 24

Blessed Luigi Guanella

Luigi Guanella felt strongly the call to love the poor and the abandoned from childhood. He was consecrated a priest at Como on 26 May 1866, with his plan for work and apostolate already clearly in his mind. This man was extremely sensitive to the situations of the marginal, the handicapped, of the orphans, of the aged, of the invalids, of people without homes and love. He desired to be always the Good Samaritan of the Gospel to all and dedicated his life completely to works of mercy. You well know how much he had to suffer in order to realize this sublime torment of his.

The specific message left us by Don Guanella is that of "fatherhood" in God, that is, of God's love, of his providence, of his affectionate and merciful presence in the affairs of mankind. "It is God who does it. Everything is from God," he said, "though the Lord usually wills that everything down here follow the ordinary routes."

"How can God not think of what he has willed?" he asked. Although he used all resources and all means of divine and human providence, Luigi Guanella was convinced that being authentic "Servants of Charity" means being first of all and always "Servants of the Truth."

He prayed and acted. He caused others to pray and to act! Thus, he said, "Victims are needed in everything, and there is special need of victims conforming to the great Victim of Calvary, to raise towers of salvation for souls." He exhorted his Sisters [of Charity] with the words, "You have to rot in prayer and hiding like the wheat which gives bread to all."

An austere message, sometimes a heroic one. But how relevant today! The divine bounty wishes to be visible today as well, present though our love too: this is the assignment left us by Don Luigi Guanella.

October 25

The Christian Family and the Priestly Vocation

We can see how the reality of the family is important for holy vocations to the priesthood to arise, as for any other state in life! Here we have one of the clearest proofs of that very close link and mutual complementarity which bind up matrimony and family with celibacy "for the kingdom of heaven's sake."

In the priesthood as in the religious life, with its testimony of God's absoluteness and of universal fraternity and spiritual fatherhood and motherhood, consecrated celibacy helps married couples and family members to keep the conscience and the practice of the loftiest ideals of their union alive. On the other hand, truly Christian family affections but prepare the best of souls in the hearts of the children for the Divine Sower to sow his seed there fruitfully, if and when He will, the seed of His call to follow Him in the priesthood.

Be close in your prayers to the family member who is preparing to be a priest. The goal of priesthood is very beautiful and not disappointing but not always easy to reach. There is need for tenacity, conviction, a spirit of sacrifice, great submissiveness to the Holy Spirit and the Church, so as to become, as St. Catherine of Siena said, "ministers of the blood." Fathers of souls, saints and sanctifiers.

So, these your sons need to be sustained by much, much prayer. Your prayers especially, dear mothers. Yes, like Mary Most Holy, Mother of Priests, you have a very special mission in preparing your sons for the priesthood, You ought to help them, like true Christian mothers, to discover new and boundless horizons: those of a love "which eye has not seen, ear has not heard, nor has it so much as dawned on man."

October 26

Blessed Luigi Orione

Today you rightly exult and feel that the gentle and austere personage . . . Don Luigi Orione is nearer to you and more confiding to you today. With his far-sighted intelligence [he] . . . perfectly understood the characteristics and necessities of this century of ours. Now, after his beatification especially, he will enlighten you, encourage you, comfort you, so that you shall ever be his worthy sons and daughters, intrepid testifiers to the Christian faith, ardent consolers of mankind in its recurrent miseries, faithful and concrete apostles of the charity of Christ.

These are difficult times and sometimes the mind is perturbed and depressed. Well, exactly for this our time and for these moments in time, Luigi Orione says to you, from the happiness which he has attained: "Lift up your hearts, dear children! Be most happy to suffer: you are suffering with Jesus Crucified and with the Church. You can do nothing more dear to the Lord and the Most Blessed Virgin. Be glad to suffer and to give your lives for love of Jesus Christ!"

I hope from my heart that . . . this . . . shall remain in your minds, as perennial consolation, as radiation of your love for God and souls, in his footsteps.

It seems almost as if Don Orione himself were here . . . with his kind and trustful smile, his serene and energetic face. I would here therefore leave you one single exhortation, springing from the pastoral concern of him who presides over the whole Church: Keep his spirit! Maintain it, whole and entire, focused in yourselves . . . in all places where you are called upon to labor!

October 27

Matrimony and Virginity

Virginity and celibacy for the Kingdom of God's sake do not contradict the dignity of matrimony but presuppose and confirm it as well. When there is no esteem for matrimony, neither can consecrated virginity exist. When human sexuality is not regarded as a great value bestowed by the Creator, renouncing it for the Kingdom of Heaven's sake loses its meaning.

In virginity, man is in expectation — in mind and body — of Christ's eschatological marriage with the Church. He is in this state of expectation through his gift of himself whole and entire to the Church, in hope that Christ will give himself to the Church in the full verity of eternal life. A person who is a virgin thus anticipates the new world of the future resurrection already in his own flesh (*Mt* 22:30).

By virtue of this testimony, virginity keeps consciousness of the mystery of matrimony alive in the Church and defends it from being reduced in any way and from all impoverishment. It renders man's heart free in a special way (*1 Cor* 7:32-35) "so as to inflame it more with charity toward God and towards all mankind." Virginity testifies that God's reign and his justice are that precious pearl which is to be preferred to every other value, however great. That is why, throughout her history, the Church has always defended the superiority of this charism in comparison with matrimony, by reason of the quite singular link that it has with the Kingdom of God. Although he or she has renounced physical fecundity, the virgin is a person who becomes spiritually fecund, the father or mother of many, by cooperating in realizing the family according to God's plan.

These reflections on virginity may enlighten and help those who, for reasons independent of their will, have not been able to marry and have then accepted their position in a spirit of service.

October 28

The Family, Prime, Vital Cell of Society

"Because the Creator of all things has established matrimony as the principle and foundation of human society," the family has become the "prime and vital cell of society." The family has vital and organic links with society, because it constitutes its foundation and continuous nourishment, through its function of serving life. From the family are born citizens who find their earliest school in those social virtues which are the soul of life and of development of society itself. So, by virtue of its nature and vocation, far from shutting itself in upon itself, the family opens out to other families and to society, taking on its social task.

The very experience of communion and of participation, which ought to mark the family's daily life, represents its prime and fundamental contribution to society. Relations among members of the familial community are inspired and guided by "the law of gratuity." This means respect and favor for one and all by reason of their personal dignity as the sole title to value. It becomes cordial openness, willingness to meet and to carry on dialogue, disinterested readiness, generous service, profound solidarity.

Thus, the encouragement of authentic and mature communion of persons in the family becomes the prime and irreplaceable school of sociability, the example and stimulus for ampler community relationships under the sign of respect, justice, dialogue, love. So the family is constituted as the home, the most effective means of humanization and personalization of society. The family collaborates in an original and profound way in construction of the world, making a properly human life possible, particularly by safeguarding and transmitting virtues and values.

October 29

The Social and Political Task of the Family

The social task of the family certainly may not be limited to the work of begetting and bringing up children, even though it has its prime and irreplaceable form of expression in that task.

Families, whether alone or in association with others, can, and therefore ought, devote themselves to manifold works of social service, especially for the sake of the poor, and all persons in situations which the public authorities' aid and assistance organizations cannot reach.

It is particularly desirable to bring out the ever greater importance assumed in our society by hospitality, in all its forms. This runs from opening the door of one's home — the door of one's heart even more — to requests of the brethren, to concrete commitment to ensuring that every family has its own home, the natural ambience where it is safeguarded and can grow. The Christian family is particularly called to listen to the Apostle's recommendation, "Be generous in offering hospitality." It is then called to imitate the example and participate in the charity of Christ by providing a welcome to a needy brother, "Whoever gives a cup of fresh water to one of these lowly ones because he is a disciple will not want for his reward."

The family's social function is also expected to be expressed in *political intervention*. This means that families must be the first to busy themselves so that the state's laws and institutions not only shall not offend, but shall also positively sustain and defend the family's rights and duties. In this sense, families must grow in awareness of being the foremost actors in so-called "family policy" and take on the responsibility of transforming society. Otherwise families will be the first victims of those evils which they limited themselves to watching with indifference.

October 30

Blessed Jeremias of Wallachia

Jeremias of Wallachia was a Capuchin friar. He was a son of Romania, that noble nation which bears the imprint of Rome in its language and name. Glorification of this faithful servant of the Lord has been left to us after three centuries of mysterious hiding. It has been kept for our time of seeking after ecumenicism and solidarity among the peoples at the international level.

Blessed Jeremias of Wallachia came from Romania to Italy, he linked East and West in his own historical experience, he built an emblematic bridge between the peoples and the Christian churches.

The inexhaustible source of his interior life was prayer. It made him grow every day in love for the Father and for the brethren. He obtained inspiration by virtue of assiduous meditation of the crucifix, from intimacy with Jesus in the Eucharist and from filial devotion to the Mother of God. He gave himself generously for the sake of the poor and labored to relieve their misery by all means. He served the sick tirelessly, assisting them, keeping the humblest and most laborious services for himself, as if they were a sought-after privilege. He chose to look after the most difficult and demanding of the sick. Such extraordinary charity could not remain circumscribed within the friary walls. Churchmen, nobles, ordinary people asked for a visit from the Wallach friar when they fell ill. . . .

In . . . two thousand years of history, rich in the values of the Faith, Jeremias of Wallachia is the first Romanian to ascend officially to the honors of the altar. He achieved a harmonious synthesis in his life between his native homeland and his adopted one. Now that he has been proclaimed "Blessed," may he contribute to promoting *peace among nations* and *unity among Christians,* by pointing out the high road — charity in working for the brethren.

October 31

The Family's Own, Original Ecclesiastical Task

The Christian family is called to take a vital, responsible part in the Church's mission, in its own, original way. That is, by putting itself, its being and its acitivity, at the service of the Church and of society, and to do so because it is *an intimate community of life and love.* If the Christian family is a community, then its participation in the Church's mission ought to come about *according to a community mode*: the couple together, therefore, as a couple; parents and children together as a family. That is how they ought to live their service to the Church and the world. In the faith they ought to be "one heart and one soul," through the common apostolic spirit animating them and in the collaboration committing them to works of service in the ecclesiastical and civil communities.

Then the Christian family builds up God's Kingdom in the world through those same daily realities which concern and distinguish its life condition. It is in *conjugal and family love* that the Christian family's participation in the prophetical, priestly and kingly mission of Jesus Christ and his Church is realized. Love and life therefore constitute the kernel of the Christian family's saving mission in the Church and for the Church.

The Second Vatican Council reminds us of this: "The family will generously put its spiritual riches in common with other families. In this way the Christian family, which arises out of matrimony as the image of and participation in the pact of love between Christ and the Church, will make the living presence of the Savior of the world and the genuine nature of the Church manifest to all, through love, generous fecundity, the unity and fidelity of the spouses and loving cooperation on the part of all its members."

November

November 1

The Solemnity of All Saints

Let us all rejoice in the Lord on this Solemnity of All the Saints! Ours is a sheer, limpid joy, a strengthening one, like that found in a big family, when it is the kind having its roots there, drawing the new blood of its own life and its own spiritual identity from there.

With our spirit today we are immersed in this numberless host of saints, of the saved. They offer us courage and sing together a chorus of glory to Him whom the psalmists call 'the God of my gladness and joy' (*Ps* 43:4). At the center of this communion is God himself. He not only calls us to holiness but he gives it to us in Christ's blood as well and so overcomes our sins. We should always sing a hymn of thanksgiving to the Lord, as Mary did, so to give joyous proclamation to the bounty of the Father "for having made you worthy to share the lot of the saints in light" (*Col* 1:12). So the Feast of All Saints calls upon us never to fall back only on ourselves, but to look to the Lord so as to be radiant (*cf. Ps* 34:6). Not to presume on our own strength but to trust as sons in him who has loved us, never to grow weary of doing good.

All the saints have ever been, and are, poor in spirit, meek, afflicted, hungry and thirsty for justice, merciful, pure of heart, peacemakers, persecuted because of the Gospel. They have been these things in varying degrees. We have to be like them. "God's will" is our sanctification (*1 Thes* 4:3).

November 2

Commemoration of All Departed Souls

Dear brothers and sisters . . . meditate on our own future lot, as each of us thinks of his and her dear ones who have gone before us in the sign of faith and sleep the sleep of peace. "We are God's children now; what we shall be later has not yet come to light (*1 Jn* 3:2). So there is a gap between what we are and what we shall become. Between these two poles lies our waiting and our hoping goes well beyond death, because it considers death only as a transition towards definitive meeting with the Lord, so as to be "like him, for we shall see him as he is" (*1 Jn* 3:2).

Today we are called to live a particular communication with our deceased. In faith and prayer, we reestablish our family links with them; they watch us, follow after us and assist us. They already see the Lord just "as he is." So they encourage us to continue on the way, that pilgrimage which still remains to us on earth. The fact is that we "have no lasting city" here (*Heb* 13:14). The important thing is for us not to grow weary, above all not to lose sight of the ultimate goal. Our departed are there where we too shall be. Indeed there is common ground between us and them, which makes us neighbors. It is the ground of our mutual introduction into the trinitarian mystery of Father, Son and Holy Spirit, on the basis of the same baptism. We here touch hands, because death does not exist on this ground; there is but a single flow of unending life.

November 3

Family Prayer

The Church prays for the Christian family and educates it to live in generous understanding of the priestly gift and task, which are received from Christ the High Priest. In reality, the baptismal priesthood of the faithful, when lived in the sacrament of matrimony, constitutes the foundation of a priestly vocation and mission for the spouses and for the family. Their daily existence is thereby transformed into "spiritual sacrifices pleasing to God through Jesus Christ." This is also what happens with the life of prayer, with the Father's prayerful dialogue through Jesus Christ in the Holy Spirit.

Family prayer has its characteristics. It is prayer offered *in common,* husband and wife together, parents and children together. Communion in prayer is in time the fruit and requirement of that communion which is given by the sacraments of baptism and matrimony. "In truth I say to you: where two or three are gathered in my name, there am I in their midst." Such prayer as its original content has *the family's very life,* which is interpreted in all its various circumstances as a vocation from God, and is actuated as a filial response to his call.

Joys and sorrows, hopes and sadnesses, births and birthdays, parents' marriage anniversaries, departures, absences and returns, important and decisive choices, deaths of dear ones, etc., mark the intervention of God's love in the family's story, just as they ought to mark the favorable moments for thanksgiving, for imploring, for the family's trusting self-abandonment to the common Father who is in heaven.

Then, the dignity and the responsibility of the Christian family as a domestic Church can be lived only with incessant aid from God. This will be unfailingly granted if it be implored with humility and trust in prayer.

November 4

St. Charles Borromeo

To all those who join with me in prayer on the feast day of my patron saint, I desire to repeat the words of the letter to the Ephesians: "Pray for me that God may put his word on my lips, that I may courageously make known the mystery of the gospel . . . for which I am an ambassador" (*Eph* 6:18-20). St. Charles was indeed one of those saints to whom was given the word, "in order to make known the Gospel," of which he was "ambassador," because he had inherited the mission from the Apostles. He accomplished that mission in an heroic manner, with total dedication of his powers. When speaking to the bishops of Lombardy, he exhorted them. "Christ pointed out the sublimest motivation of our ministry to each of us bishops and taught that love above all must be the master and teacher of our apostolate, the love which he (Jesus) wills to express *through us* to the faithful entrusted to us."

Where did St. Charles find the strength for this zealous churchly service? The secret of his success lay in his spirit of prayer. "Souls," he used to say, "are conquered on one's knees." And in his discourse to his last synod: "Nothing is so necessary to all men of the church as is mental prayer, as precedes all our actions, accompanies them, and follows them . . . when you administer the Sacraments, O brother, meditate on what you are doing. If you celebrate Mass, think of what you are offering up. If you sing in the choir, think of whom and of what you are singing. If you guide souls, meditate on that blood whereby we and they are redeemed. . . . Thus shall we have the strength to generate Christ in us and in others."

November 5

Mixed Marriages

Couples living in mixed marriages have particular requirements. . . . First of all, obligations upon the Catholic partner, deriving from the faith, must be borne in mind. They concern free practice of the faith and the consequent obligation to provide, so far as lies in one's power, for the children to be baptized and brought up in the Catholic faith. There is need to bear in mind the particular difficulties inherent in relations between husband and wife as regards respect for religious liberty. This may be violated by means of undue pressures aimed at obtaining an alteration in the partner's religious convictions and by means of impediments raised against free religious practice. As regards the liturgical and canonical form of the marriage, ordinaries have wide powers to make use of their faculties in accordance with varied necessities.

The following points must be kept in mind when dealing with those special requirements: In the proper course of preparation for this type of marriage, every reasonable effort must be made to ensure that there be comprehension of Catholic doctrine on the qualities and demands of matrimony and also to ensure that pressures and obstacles such as I have indicated shall not be applied in the future. It is of supreme importance that, with support from the community, the Catholic party shall be strengthened in his or her faith and aided positively to ripen comprehension and practice of it, so as to become a really credible witness within the family, through his or her life itself, and the quality of love shown to the other spouse and the children.

November 6

Ecumenical Spirit in Mixed Marriages

Marriages between Catholics and other baptized persons present, with their particular characteristics, numerous elements which it is good to value and to develop, both by reason of their intrinsic worth and by reason of the contribution they can make to the ecumenical movement.

This is particularly true when both partners are faithful to their religious duties. The common baptism and the dynamism of grace furnish spouses in such marriages a basis and motivation for expressing their unity in the sphere of moral and spiritual values. To this end, cordial collaboration between the Catholic and the non-Catholic minister is to be sought, from the time when preparation for the marriage and the wedding begins. This is for the purpose of bringing out the ecumenical importance of such a mixed marriage, lived fully in the faith of the two Christian spouses. Not that such cordial collaboration is always found to be easy. . . .

In your country, there are many marriages between Catholics and other baptized Christians. Sometimes these couples experience special difficulties. To these families I say: You live in your marriage the hopes and difficulties of the path to Christian unity. Express that hope in prayer *together,* in the unity of love. Together invite the Holy Spirit of love into your hearts and into your homes. He will help you to grow in trust and understanding.

Brothers and sisters, "Christ's peace must reign in your hearts. . . . Let the word of Christ, rich as it is, dwell in you" (*Col* 3:15-16).

November 7

Difficult Marriages

We cannot overlook the fact that *some marriages fail*. But still it is our duty to proclaim the true plan of God for all married love and to insist on fidelity to that plan, as we go towards the fullness of life in the Kingdom of heaven. Let us not forget that God's love for his people, Christ's love for the Church, is everlasting and can never be broken. And the covenant between a man and a woman joined in Christian marriage is as indissoluble and irrevocable as this love.

This truth is a great consolation for the world and, because some marriages fail, there is an ever greater need for the Church and all her members to proclaim it faithfully. Christ himself, the living source of grace and mercy, is close to all those whose marriage has known trial, pain or anguish. Throughout the ages, countless married people have drawn from the Paschal Mystery of Christ on the Cross and Resurrection the strength to bear Christian witness, at times very difficult, to the indissolubility of Christian marriage.

As I explained in my apostolic exhortation *"Familiaris Consortio,"* the Church is vitally concerned for the pastoral care of the family in all difficult cases. We must reach out with love — the love of Christ — to those who know the pain of failure in marriage; to those who know the loneliness of bringing up a family on their own; to those whose family life is dominated by tragedy or by illness of mind or body. I praise all those who help people wounded by the breakdown of their marriage by showing them Christ's compassion and counseling them according to Christ's truth.

To the public authorities, and to all men and women of good will I say: Treasure your families. Protect their rights. Support the family by your laws and administration. Allow the voice of the family to be heard in the making of your policies. The future of your society, the future of humanity, pass by the way of the family.

November 8

For an Effective Pastorate of the Family

It must be said that the problem of the family was not only discussed, studied, faced in the 1980 Synod; it was also in a certain sense suffered. This was because there is a human reality, the family.

On the one hand, it already fascinates us with its beauty and its grandeur, when we look at the ideal, the divine design for the family which we have to preach and propound to our brothers and sisters. On the other hand, that reality, the family, makes us suffer when we look at the various human experiences, the various difficulties, the manifold conflicts.

I would not wish to dwell too much on this point, but I would only say that the document, *Familiaris consortio*, which issued from that synod, really constitutes the "*a-b-c*" of the pastorate of the family and ought to be assiduously read and studied. A reading of this document must be made. I actually think that an effective pastorate of the family, in every diocese, then in every parish, consists in ever deeper study of *Familiaris consortio*. It should be read not in the mechanical sense of the word only but read pastorally, read in terms of a certain task, the pastoral task.

This pastoral task is entrusted to the Church, it is entrusted to us. As regards the family, the task is entrusted to it itself but with our help; we ought to help the family to be the evangelizer of itself. The fundamental program of the pastorate of the family consists in this: helping the family to be itself, to carry out those tasks, to discover its human and Christian identity, to discover its vocation. All this is to be found in *Familaris consortio*.

November 9

There Is a Spirituality of Work

In its subjective dimension, work is always a personal action, *actus personae*. It follows that the whole man, body and spirit, partakes of it, independently of whether it be manual or intellectual labor.

The Word of the Living God, the evangelical message of salvation, is also directed to the whole man, for we find that many of the contents of that message are concerned with human work; they are like special lights shining upon it. Now, adequate assimilation of those contents is necessary.

There is need for interior effort of the human spirit, guided by faith, hope and charity, to give, through the aid of those contents, the labor of the concrete man the significance which it has in God's eyes. Through this significance, labor enters into the work of salvation, together with its normal operations and components, which are particularly important at the same time.

The Church considers it a duty to make pronouncements on work from the point of view of its human value and the moral order to which it pertains. The Church sees there an important task in the service which she renders to the entire Gospel message. At the same time, she sees a particular duty of her own to form a spirituality of work, such as may help all people get closer to God, the Creator and Redeemer, by its means; partake in his saving plans for man and the world and deepen friendship with Christ in their lives by gaining lively participation in his threefold mission through faith: his mission of being Priest, Prophet, and King, as the Second Vatican Council teaches us in a marvelous expression.

November 10

Human Labor Shares in the Creator's Work

This fundamental truth is written very profoundly in the Word of divine Revelation: Man, created in God's image, participates in the Creator's work through his labor and, to the degree of his possibilities, continues in a certain sense to develop and complete it by advancing more and more in discovery of the resources and values enclosed in everything created.

We find this truth at the very beginning of Holy Scripture, in the Book of Genesis, for the very work of creation is there presented in the form of a "labor" accomplished by God over "six days," with "repose" on the seventh. And the last book of Holy Scripture proclaims, "Great and marvelous are your works, Lord God Almighty."

This description of creation, which we already find in the first chapter of the Book of Genesis is, at the same time and in a certain sense, the first "Gospel of Work." It demonstrates in what the dignity of labor consists; it teaches that, when working, man ought to imitate God, his Creator, because he alone bears in himself that singular element which is resemblance to God. Man ought to imitate God both when working and when resting, because God himself presented his own creative work to man under the form of *labor and rest*. This work of God in the world goes on always. Therefore, human labor does not only require the repose "of the seventh day," but it cannot consist only in exerting human powers in exterior activity; it must leave an inner space as well, and there, as he becomes more and more what he ought to be by God's will, man prepares himself for that "repose" which the Lord reserves for his servants and friends.

November 11

St. Martin of Tours

Today the liturgy has us celebrate the feast of St. Martin. He was a Roman officer, converted from paganism and baptized when he was about twenty years old. He became a deacon, then a presbyter, finally Bishop of Tours in France.

What characterized his life in a special way? Courage in the faith and generosity to all. Through fidelity to Christ's message, he had to struggle, suffer, commit himself boldly against heathens, heretics and unbelievers. He consecrated the whole of his life to love of neighbor, beginning from that famous night when he, still a catechumen, was making the rounds one night in the depth of winter. He met a poor, half-naked man. He took his sword, cut his cloak in two, and gave half to that poor man. The following night, he saw in a dream Jesus himself wearing that half of his cloak.

You, too, be courageous in living and testifying to your Christian faith, convinced that it is truly the solution to the gravest problems of life! You, too, be generous, always, toward all, with love, with charity, in spirit of sacrifice, sure that real joy is found in loving and giving! I sincerely hope and pray that your days shall pass by in peace and you may be able to taste the joy of being truly Christians, in perfect accord with the Lord's will and in obedience to his will, as we ask in today's Holy Mass.

With this prayer and with great affection, I impart my blessing to you and gladly extend it to all your dear ones.

November 12

The Value of Ordinary Daily Activity

Consciousness that human labor is participation in God's work should, as the Second Vatican Council teaches, "permeate *ordinary daily activities* as well. When men and women work to gain a living for themselves and their families and carry out their activities in such a way as to do proper service to society as well, they may rightly maintain that they are extending the Creator's work through their work; they are making themselves useful to their brethren and are making a personal contribution to accomplishing God's providential plan in history."

So it is necessary for this Christian spirituality of labor to become the common heritage of all. There is need for the spirituality of labor to demonstrate, especially in our time, that maturity which is demanded by tensions and anxieties in minds and hearts.

The knowledge that man participates in the work of creation through his labor constitutes the deepest motivation for starting out in various sectors. "The faithful," we read in the constitution *Lumen gentium,* "should therefore recognize the intimate nature of all creation, its value, and how it is ordained to praise of God; and they should help each other to live holier lives and also undertake appropriate secular activities, so that the world may be imbued with the spirit of Christ and more effectively attain its goal in justice, in charity and in peace. Therefore, with their abilities in worldly disciplines and through their activities they make a valuable contribution to created goods inwardly elevated by the grace of Christ enjoying progress through human labor, technology and the culture of civilization, according to the Creator's dispositions and in the light of his Word."

November 13

Christ Fulfills and Teaches the Gospel of Work

In his parables on the Kingdom of God, Jesus Christ continually refers to human labor. He speaks of the work of the shepherd (*Jn* 10:1-16), of the farmer (*Mk* 12:1-12), of the physician (*Lk* 4:23), of the sower (*Mt* 4:1–9), of the householder (*Mt* 13:52), of the servant (*Mt* 24:45; *Lk* 12:42–48), of the administrator (*Lk* 16:1–8), of the fisherman (*Mt* 13:47–50), of the merchant (*Mt* 13:45), of the laborer (*Mt* 20:1–16). And he speaks of various kinds of women's work. He presents the apostolate in the likeness of the manual labor of the reaper (*Mt* 9:37; *Jn* 4:35-38), and of the fisherman. He refers to the work of scholars (*Mt* 13:52).

This truth, whereby through his labor man shares in the work of God himself, his Creator, was brought out in a special way by Jesus Christ. Jesus not only proclaimed the word of the eternal wisdom, he also fulfilled it, first of all, through the work of the Gospel entrusted to him. Therefore this is the "Gospel of Work" too, because he who proclaimed it was a workman, a man dedicated to a craft, as was Joseph of Nazareth. Was it not he who said, "My Father is the vinegrower. . . ." Did he not transfer the fundamental truth on work into his teaching in various says, the truth already expressed in the whole of the Old Testament tradition, beginning from the Book of Genesis?

November 14

Work as Sharing in Christ's Cross and Resurrection

There is yet another aspect of human labor, an essential dimension of it, where spirituality founded on the Gospel enters deeply. Every kind of work, whether manual or mental, is inevitably linked with effort and fatigue.

In a certain sense, the Gospel has its last word to say on this matter as well, in the paschal mystery of Jesus Christ. It is necessary to seek there the answers to these problems which are so important for the spirituality of human labor. *The paschal mystery contains the cross of Christ,* his obedience unto death, which the Apostle contrasts with that disobedience which weighed upon man's history on earth from the beginning. Contained in it also is *the elevation of Christ*: through the death on the cross, he returns to his disciples with the power of the Spirit in the resurrection.

The Christian finds a little bit of the cross of Christ in human work, and he accepts it in the same spirit of redemption in which Christ accepted his cross for our sake. Thanks to the light entering us from the resurrection of Christ, we always find *a gleam of new life,* of new good, in labor, by way, as it were, of announcement of "a new heaven and a new earth," which are really shared by man and by the world through the effort of work. Through effort and fatigue, never without it. On the one hand, this confirms the indispensability of the cross in the spirituality of human labor; on the other hand, it discovers a new good in this cross and in effort, a new good arising from labor itself. . . .

November 15

St. Albert the Great, Doctor of the Church

In his lifetime, Albert carried on manifold activities as a religious and a preacher, as a religious superior, as a bishop and mediator of peace in his own city of Cologne. Posterity described him as the *"doctor universalis."* The Church refers to him as one of her "doctors."

In his long life, he was also a great man of science, a spiritual son of St. Dominic and the teacher of St. Thomas Aquinas. He was one of the great intelligences of the thirteenth century. More than anyone else, he joined faith with reason, God's wisdom with the wisdom of the world.

I will pause to meditate together with you on the words with which the liturgy celebrates him: "If this is the will of the Lord, he shall be great, filled with spirit of understanding. Like rain, he will pour out words of wisdom, in prayer he will render praise to the Lord. He will direct his counsel and his science, he will meditate on the mysteries of God. He will cause the doctrine of his teaching to shine, he will exalt the law of the Lord's alliance. Many will laud his intelligence, he shall never be forgotten, memory of him shall not fade, his name shall live from generation to generation. The peoples will speak of his wisdom, the assembly shall proclaim his praises." These words perfectly describe the image of that man who was a joy to the whole Church, Albert the Great, universal doctor. Albert the Great: a true "disciple of the kingdom of God."

Christ actually says: "Every scribe who is learned in the reign of God is like the head of a household who can bring from his storeroom both the new and the old" *(Mt* 13:52). St. Albert was like that householder!

November 16

St. Gertrude, the Theologian of the Sacred Heart

I wish you abundant heavenly favors, in your commitment to preparing yourselves for the tasks awaiting you in life and accomplishment of good . . . a propitious occasion for living the Christian life intensely and opening the doors of your hearts to Christ.

I would particularly remind you of the great German mystic St. Gertrude (1256-1301). Her liturgical feast occurs today and she has rightly been described as "the theologian of the Sacred Heart." It is important indeed to know the personalities and spiritualities of our saints, so as to be able to imitate them in the life of grace and testimony and to call upon them at moments of bewilderment and of temptation.

As St. Gertrude often recommended, I exhort you also to have always total trust in Jesus, our Redeemer and Friend, so as to be good . . . and worthy of esteem, making yourselves and those who love you happy.

I impart my blessing to all from my heart.

November 17

St. Elizabeth of Hungary

Saint Elizabeth was of the dynasty of Arpad, a sweet-smelling flower blooming in the dynasty of St. Stephen, a splendid example of young woman and mother who lived scarcely twenty-four years.

She learned early from her mother to love Jesus and Mary. She won the hearts of those about her with her dynamic personality and her unprejudiced love. She desired only to follow the will of Christ. Love of Christ radiated from her person. She took off her crown as she knelt before the crucifix, saying: "How could I bear a crown of gold when the Lord bears a crown of thorns? And bears it for me!"

Her life was accomplished in the love of the Landgrave of Thüringen, Ludwig. She was only fourteen years old, he only twenty-one. They loved each other in God, and helped each other to love God more and more. They accepted the gift of a new life from God with profound thankfulness. Who could remain indifferent to the overwhelming joy of a mother of fifteen years and the immense love of Ludwig and Elizabeth! Urged by love of Christ, the young mother visited the poor, the sick, the foundlings. Elizabeth had become the mother of all.

Joy was never extinguished in her heart, she gave with evangelical joy: "We ought to give everything we can with joy and good grace," she said. The sick, the abandoned came to her in floods. She — living ceaselessly in God's presence — restored health and the peace of God to many. "You see, as I told you, it is necessary to make people happy."

She died in the night of the 16–17 November 1231. Ever united with Christ and with her dear ones, Elizabeth has ever since been a flaming torch to all who imitate Christ in service to their neighbors.

November 18

Europe Has Need of Christ

We have in fact a Europe of culture, that of the great philosophical, artistic and religious movements which distinguish her and make her the teacher of all the continents. We have the Europe of labor which, through scientific and technological research, developed through various stages of civilization, finally to arrive at the present epoch of industry and of cybernetics.

But there is also the Europe of tragedies of peoples and of nations, the Europe of blood, of tears, of night, of fractures, of cruelties of the most fearful kind. Upon Europe too, in spite of the message of the great spirits, the heavy and terrible drama of sin has made itself felt, the drama of evil, which according to the Gospel's words, sows baleful discord in the field of history.

The problem which assails us today is that of saving Europe and the world from further catastrophes! *Europe has need of Christ!* There is need to enter into contact with

Him, take over His message, His love, His life, His pardon, His eternal and exaltation certainties! It is necessary to understand that the Church, founded by Him, and willed by Him, has the sole purpose of transmitting and guaranteeing the Truth revealed by Him, to keep the means of salvation instituted by Him himself, that is, the sacraments and prayer, alive and relevant today. This was understood by elect and thoughtful spirits, such as Pascal, Newman, Rosmini, Soloviev, Norwid.

We find ourselves in a Europe where the temptation to atheism and skepticism grows stronger and stronger. In it, aligned with painful moral uncertainty, disintegration of the family, degeneration of customs, a perilous conflict of ideas and movements holds sway. The crisis of civilization (Huizinga) and the decline of the West (Spengler) but signify the extreme topicality and necessity of Christ and the Gospel.

November 19

The Unity of Europe

The cultural unity of the European continent continues, in spite of all crises and tensions. It is not comprehensible without the content of the Christian message. This unity, fused in a marvellous manner with the ancient spirit, constitutes a common inheritance to which Europe owes her wealth and her strength, the flourishing development of her arts and sciences, her cultural formation and her search for philosophy and cultivation of the spirit.

The Christian picture of man has especially determined the culture of Europe in the context of this Christian spiritual inheritance. The conviction of man's likeness to God and his Redemption through Jesus Christ, the son of man, has given an historico-religious foundation to consideration of the dignity of the person and respect for his requirement for the free development of human solidarity. So it was by a logical consequence that the formulation and proclamation of human rights in general arose from the West.

Let us put this Europe, united and formed by faith in Christ, once more under the sign of the Cross, for "in the Cross is hope." In the Cross lies hope of a Christian renewal of Europe, but only if Christians themselves take the message of the Cross seriously. The Cross means love is stronger than hatred and vengeance; giving is more joyful than receiving; devoting oneself is better than asking. The Cross means there is no shipwreck without hope; there is no dark without dawn; nor storm without haven. The Cross means God is always bigger than we men and is salvation even in the greatest failure.

Life is always stronger than death.

November 20

The United Nations

The special bond of cooperation that links the Apostolic See with the United Nations Organization . . . is shown by the presence of the Holy See's Permanent Observer to this Organization. The existence of this bond, which is held in high esteem by the Holy See, rests on the sovereignty with which the Apostolic See has been endowed for many centuries. The territorial extent of that sovereignty is limited to the small State of Vatican City, but the sovereignty itself is warranted by the need of the papacy to exercise its mission in full freedom and to be able to deal with any interlocutor, whether a government or an international organization, without dependence on other sovereignties. Of course the nature and aims of the spiritual mission of the Apostolic See and the Church make their participation in the tasks and activities of the United Nations Organization very different from that of the states, which are communities in the political and temporal sense.

Besides attaching great importance to its collaboration with the United Nations Organization, the Apostolic See has always . . . expressed its esteem and its agreement with the historic significance of this supreme forum for the international life of humanity today.

This confidence and conviction on the part of the Apostolic See are the result not of merely political reasons but of the religious and moral character of the mission of the Roman Catholic Church. As a universal community embracing faithful belonging to almost all countries and continents, nations, peoples, races, languages and cultures, the Church is deeply interested in the existence and activity of the Organization whose very name tells us that it unites and associates nations and states. It unites and associates: it does not divide and oppose.

November 21

On Contemplatives

Silent, separated life is a leaven of renewal and of the presence of the Spirit of Christ in the world. That is why the [Vatican] Council said that "contemplative women religious keep a quite eminent place in the Mystical Body of Christ, and bring forth most abundant fruits of holiness; they are an honor and example to the People of God, to which they give increase with mysterious apostolic fecundity."

The Lord who chose you [contemplatives], by identifying you with his Paschal mystery, unites you with himself in his work of sanctifying the world. This ought to be every day's prospect of faith and spiritual joy: for him, with him, and in him. So, have no doubt in this regard, one day, in the very name of Christ, the Church took possession of all your capacity for living and loving. That was the meaning of your monastic profession. Renew it frequently! In so doing, you follow the example of the saints. Consecrate yourselves, immolate yourselves more each time without even asking to know how God uses your collaboration.

Your virginal fecundity ought to be situated in the midst of the universal Church and your particular churches. Your monasteries can also be centers of Christian welcome for those persons, young persons especially, who are often in search of a simple, open life, in contrast with that which the consumer society offers them. I make an appeal to Christian communities and their pastors, reminding them of the indispensable place of the contemplative life in the Church. We all should value and esteem the dedication of contemplatives' souls to adoration, praise and sacrifice. They are prophetesses and living teachers to all; *they are the Church's vanguard on the road to the Kingdom.*

November 22

The United Nations and Religion

It is certainly a highly significant fact that among the representatives of the states, whose *raison d'être* is the sovereignty of powers linked with territory and people, there is also today the representative of the Apostolic See and the Catholic Church. This Church is the Church of Jesus Christ, who declared before the tribunal of the Roman judge Pilate that he was a king, but with a kingdom not of this world (*cf. Jn* 18:36-37). When he was then asked about the reason for the existence of this kingdom among men, he explained, "The reason I was born, the reason why I came into the world, is to testify to the truth" (*Jn* 18:37). . . .

The invitation extended to the Pope to speak . . . shows that the United Nations Organization accepts and respects the religious and moral dimension of those human problems that the Church attends to, in view of the message of truth and love that it is her duty to bring to the world. The questions that concern your functions, especially in the fields of culture, health, food, labor and the peaceful uses of nuclear energy, certainly make it essential for us to meet in the name of man in his wholeness, in all the fullness and manifold riches of his spiritual and material existence.

November 23

To the United Nations

The problems that the human family faces today may seem overwhelming. I, for my part, am convinced that there is immense potential with which to face them. History tells us that the human race is capable of reacting and of changing direction every time it perceives clearly the warning that it is on the wrong course.

You are privileged to witness . . . how the representatives of the nations endeavor to chart a common course in order that life on this planet will be lived in peace, order, justice and progress for all. But you are also aware that every individual must work towards the same end. It is individual actions put together which bring about today and tomorrow the total impact which is either beneficial or harmful for humanity.

The various programs and organizations that exist within the framework of the United Nations Organization, as well as the specialized agencies and other intergovernmental bodies, are an important part of that total effort. In the area of its own specialization — be it food, agriculture, trade, environment, development, science, culture, education, health, disaster relief, or the problems of children and refugees — each one of these organizations makes a unique contribution not only to providing for peoples' wants, but also to fostering respect for human dignity and the cause of world peace.

My cordial greeting goes to the representatives of the various Protestant, Jewish and Moslem associations, and in a particular way to the representatives of the international Catholic organizations. May you never lose sight of the ultimate aim of your efforts: to create a world where every human person can live in dignity and loving harmony as a child of God.

November 24

Diplomacy, the Art of Making Peace

In the cause of service to humanity the diplomatic corps and the Holy See stand together, each one in its own sphere, each one faithfully pursuing its own mission, but united in the great cause of understanding and solidarity among peoples and nations. . . . [Diplomacy] is a noble task. Despite unavoidable difficulties, setbacks and failures, diplomacy retains its importance as one of the roads that must be travelled in the search for peace and progress for all mankind.

"Diplomacy," in the words of my predecessor Paul VI, "is the art of making peace." The efforts of diplomats, whether in a bilateral or in a multilateral setting, do not always succeed in establishing or in maintaining peace, but they must always be encouraged, today as in the past, so that new initiatives will be born, new paths tried with the patience and tenacity that are the eminent qualities of the deserving diplomat. As one who speaks in the name of Christ, who called himself "the way, and the truth, and the life" (*Jn* 14:6), I would also like to make a plea for the fostering of other qualities that are indispensable if today's diplomacy is to justify the hopes that are placed in it: the ever deeper insertion of the supreme values of the moral and spiritual order into the aims of peoples and into the methods used in pursuit of these aims.

November 25

Truth, the Power of Peace

First among the ethical imperatives that must preside over the relations among nations and peoples is *truth*. . . . I am confident that the governments and the nations . . . will, as they have so admirably done in the past, associate themselves once again with this lofty aim: to instill truth into all relationships, be they political or economic, bilateral or multinational. Bringing truth into all relations is to work for peace, for it will make it possible to apply to the problems of the world the solutions that are in conformity with reason and with justice — in a word, with the truth about man.

And this brings me to the second point I would like to make. If it is to be true and lasting, peace must be truly human. The desire for peace is universal. It is embedded in the hearts of all human beings and it cannot be achieved unless the human person is placed at the center of every effort to bring about unity and brotherhood among nations.

November 26

To the Knights of Columbus

I greet all the Knights of Columbus, the more than one million, three hundred thousand Catholic laymen all over the world, who display a spirit of profound attachment to their Christian faith and of loyalty to the Apostolic See. Many times in the past ... you have given expression to your solidarity with the mission of the Pope. I see in your support a further proof — if further proof were ever necessary — of your awareness that the Knights of Columbus highly value their vocation to be part of the evangelization effort of the Church. I am happy to recall here what my revered predecessor, Paul VI, said about this task in his apostolic exhortation *Evangelii nuntiandi,* as he emphasized the specific role of the laity: "Their own field of evangelizing activity is the vast and complicated world of politics, society and economics, but also the world of culture, of the sciences and the arts, of international life, of the mass media. It also includes other realities which are open to evangelization, such as human love, the family, the education of children and adolescents, professional work and suffering."

These words of one who never ceased to encourage you clearly indicate the road which your association must travel. I am aware of the many efforts you make to promote the use of mass media for the spreading of the Gospel and for the wider diffusion of my own messages. May the Lord reward you and through your efforts bring forth abundant fruits of evangelization in the Church.

November 27

To Representatives of the Mass Media

The world of today is often an immense audience, one sole public, gathered about the same cultural, political and religious events. Yours is a service of incalculable import.

I just then uttered a well-weighed word: *Service*. Because you really serve through your work, and you have to serve the cause of man as a whole — his body, his spirit, his need for honest diversion, cultural and religious nourishment and a correct moral criterion for his individual and social life. This is a noble mission. It elevates whoever lives it worthily, because it offers a most valid contribution to the good of society, its equilibrium and its development.

The Church attributes very great importance to the field of social communications and that of transmission of culture, where such lofty values are at stake. There are many things in common between your mission and mine. You and I are servants of communication among men. It is for me, in a singular fashion, to transmit *the Good News* of the Gospel to mankind, and with it, the message of love, of justice and of peace, the message of Christ. These are values which you can favor a great deal through your effort to construct a world more united, more pacific, more humane, where truth and morals may shine. So, you will be able to offer a service of communication responding to the profound truth of man.

Respect the truth, defend rightful professional secrecy, avoid sensationalism, give high value to the importance of moral education for childhood and youth, promote coexistence in legitimate pluralism among individuals, groups, and peoples. . . . God bless your work.

November 28

The Physical and Moral Values of Sport

Sport finds support from the Church, by reason of everything good and healthy which it bears in itself. The Church cannot but encourage everything serving harmonious development of the human body, which is rightly regarded as the masterpiece of all creation, not only through its proportions, vigor, and beauty, but also and above all because God has made it the dwelling and instrument of an immortal soul, by infusing into it that "breath of life" (*Gen* 2:7) whereby man is made in his image and likeness. Then, if we consider the supernatural aspect, St. Paul's words are an enlightening admonition: "Do you not see that your bodies are members of Christ? . . . You must know that your body is a temple of the Holy Spirit, who is within — the Spirit you have received from God. . . . So glorify God in your body" (*1 Cor* 6:15, 19–20). . . .

There we have glimpses of what revelation teaches us on the greatness and dignity of the human body, created by God and redeemed by Christ. This is why the Church never ceases recommending proper appreciation and employment of this marvelous instrument through suitable physical education such as shall, on the one hand, avoid turning into a cult of the body and, on the other hand, will train body and spirit in effort, courage, balance, sacrifice, nobility, fraternity, courtesy and, in a word, fair play. If you use sport in this way, it will help you to become above all citizens who love social order and peace.

November 29

The Many Sides of Tourism

Tourism is an important component of the use of leisure time. In its many-sided aspects it entails free choices, both on the part of those who enjoy tourism and on the part of those who organize it. Such free choices will be morally positive if they conform to the right use of liberty.

Tourism worthy of man can never be evasion from moral duties; the Christian is expected to realize the gospel ideal "in" and "through" all moments of existence. When we reflect upon it well, free time is eschatological, like all time established by Christ, It is eschatological inasmuch as it is ultimate and definitive time. It, too, must therefore be ordered toward eternal salvation, through constant commitment, because "the way of earthly life is one." It is therefore up to you consciously to favor the use of free time in terms of appreciating and employing natural and spiritual resources for the benefit of the entire community.

Tourism is furthermore recognized as a factor for meetings and of peace among peoples. It is actually due to tourism that this earth of ours, soaked with Christ's blood for universal salvation, appears more and more as "everyone's home."

So the ultimate end of the development of tourism does not lie in economic advantage, even though this may be on a national scale. Rather it lies in service offered to the individual, considered as a whole, that is, with consideration for his material and spiritual needs as well.

I express the most lively and heartfelt wish that tourism shall contribute more and more to glorification of God, Creator of the Universe, to increasing appreciation of human dignity, reciprocal knowledge, spiritual fraternity, and recreation for body and spirit, and that it may accomplish this through the work of those responsible for it and organizing it.

November 30

St. Andrew, Apostle and Brother of St. Peter

On this feast of Saint Andrew, Apostle of Jesus Christ, brother of Simon Peter, we look to Saint Andrew himself for a fresh inspiration. To Jesus Christ, Andrew bears witness with that wonderful announcement made to his brother, "We have found the Messiah!" (*Jn* 1:41). Andrew finds Jesus, he leads Peter to Jesus, and then Jesus leads Peter, and with him all of us, to the Father. Andrew thus proclaims to the world the One who was awaited for centuries: "We have found the Messiah!" We are called to proclaim him to so many people who still await his coming to their hearts and into their lives.

Like Andrew, we have, by God's grace, discovered the Messiah and the meaning of his message of hope to be transmitted to our people. The Lord himself is constantly inviting us to newness of life, in expectation of the final moment when he will definitively proclaim, "See, I make all things new" (*Rev* 21:5). The message, therefore that I proclaim today is one of fresh hope in the infinite power of Christ's Paschal Mystery, in which he sends his Holy Spirit into our hearts. To all the faithful of every generation I offer *the great treasure of the Church:* Jesus Christ and his word, Jesus Christ and his promises, Jesus Christ and communion with His Father in the unity of the Holy Spirit. "So that through the power of the Holy Spirit you may have hope in abundance (*Rom* 15:13).

The Moveable Feasts and Special Occasions

First Sunday of Advent

Message of Hope and Summons

First Sunday of Advent.

What is the truth which penetrates and enlivens us today?

What message does the Church our Mother announce?. . .

The message of hope and summons. . . .

Here is what the Apostle Paul said to the Romans of those days but which we ought to take to heart today. . . as well:

"You know the times in which we are living. It is now the hour for you to wake from sleep. . . . The night is far spent, the day draws near" *(Rom* 13:11–12). . . .

They seemed to have been induced to believe that human signs give the lie to the message . . . of the liturgy. But in fact . . . it foretells the divine design which never fails, which does not change, even though men can change, and programs, human progress, as well can change. . . .

It is the design of the salvation of mankind in Christ. But man can be deaf and blind to all that.

He can multiply the works of darkness, even though day draws near.

He can multiply the works of darkness even though Christ offers him "the weapon of light."

411

Hence the Apostle's pressing invitation: "Put on the Lord Jesus Christ" (*Rom* 13:14).

This expression is in a certain sense the definition of the Christian.

Being Christian means "putting on Christ."

Advent is the new summons to put on Jesus Christ.

Second Sunday of Advent

Man's Spiritual Progress

The Messiah is very near!

The Liturgy . . . is full of the historic content of Advent.

Through this content, a *liturgical summons* is revealed, linked not only with the distant past, but also with our contemporary Advent too. . . .

This Advent is alive not only with preparations for what *shall be accomplished* but also with full awareness of what *has been accomplished*. . . .

This liturgical Advent is expectation of what has been accomplished — which expectation must nonetheless be continually renewed in memory and heart, so that it shall not occur only in the past but also continually constitute our present and our future.

On that night of the nativity of the Lord at Bethlehem . . . the Lord was to change the destiny of Zion. . . . With the coming of the Messiah, the sadness of human souls, wearied by sowing of life . . . was to be turned into joy. . . .

Advent is therefore preparation for a *great and glorious change*. This alteration will radically mutate man's situation in the world. . . .

Advent is nothing other than annual meditation . . . on the work of salvation and sanctification, the work of grace and love, which the Lord "began" and continually "begins" in every man and in every generation *down to the last coming* of Jesus Christ, when this work shall be brought to completion.

Third Sunday of Advent

The Path to God

This is the Third Sunday of Advent. . . .
Advent not only reveals God's coming to us but also indicates the path leading us to God. . . .
This is above all the path *of conduct in conformity with conscience.* . . .
Conduct yourselves rightly.
Do your duty conscientiously.
Know how to give of yourselves to others.
Share what you have with the needy.
The way to God is above all *the way of conscience and morality.*
The commandments lead man along this way. . . .
The path to God does not consist in observing the commandments only but also in profound purification of the soul from attachment to sin, concupiscence and passions. . . .
But such purification sometimes is costly to man: it is linked with grief and suffering, but it is *indispensable,* since the soul has to preserve what is noble, honest and pure in itself. . . .
Man is afraid of the purifying power of God and of His grace. . . .

The desire for salvation, that is, of the life of God's grace, ought to overcome the fear with which man defends himself from God's purifying power.

As the evil rooted in the soul yields little by little, and sinful attachments are weakened, God comes closer, and joy and peace come to the soul together with Him. . . .

Fourth Sunday of Advent

The Time of Invitation

The whole of Advent is a period of waiting and preparation for the coming of the Lord. The last week of Advent might be called *the time of invitation*, for over the days immediately preceding Christmas the Church issues invitations.

Her invitations are given by means of the whole of her Liturgy, in which an important place is taken by the so-called Great Antiphons, joined with the singing of the *Magnificat* during Vespers. They are very beautiful antiphons and, at the same time, their content is simple as well as profound. Today's antiphon . . . it addresses Him Who Is to Come with the following words:

"O Emmanuel, God-with-us, our King and legislator, the awaited of the peoples and their liberator, come to save us with Your presence, Lord our God."

Emmanuel! This is the ultimate invocation, the last word of these bidding antiphons. It seems to testify that the invitation has been accepted, because "Emmanuel" means "God who is with us." So, therefore, the last of the grand Advent antiphons expresses certainty of the coming of the Lord. It already speaks of His presence among us.

When we take account of the circumstances of God's birth, when we remember that "there was no room for them in the place where travelers lodged" (*Lk* 2:7), we shall get an even better understanding of the Advent liturgy's invitation and will express it with deeper inner peace. With *greater love for Him who is about to come.*

O Emmanuel, God-with-us! What else can we wish for if not that God may be with us? So I wish the same for you with all my heart.

Sunday within the Octave of the Nativity

Solemnity of the Holy Family of Nazareth

This Sunday, within the octave of the Nativity, is also the solemnity of the Holy Family of Nazareth.

The Son of God came to the world through the Virgin whose name was Mary. He was born at Bethlehem and grew up at Nazareth, under the protection of a just man called Joseph.

Jesus was the center of their great love from the beginning, a love full of concern and affection. He was their great vocation. He was their inspiration. He was the great mystery of their lives. He "progressed steadily in wisdom and age and grace before God and men" (*Lk* 2:52). He was obedient and submissive, as a son should be toward his parents. This Nazarene obedience of Jesus to Mary and Joseph fills almost all the years lived by Him on earth and therefore constitutes the longest period of the whole and uninterrupted obedience which He paid to the heavenly Father. Jesus did not dedicate as many years to the service of the Good News and finally to the Sacrifice of the Cross.

On the solemnity of the Holy Family of Nazareth, the Church extends her best and most fervent wishes to all families in the world, through the liturgy of the day. From the letter of St. Paul to the Colossians, I will take just these two very meaningful phrases: "Christ's peace must reign in your hearts" (*Col* 3:15).

Peace is actually the sign of love and confirmation of it a family's life. Peace is the joy of hearts. It is comfort in daily efforts. Peace is the support which husband and wife offer each other and which the children find in the parents, the parents in the children.

May all families in the world receive the wish of such peace.

Sunday between January 2 and 8

Epiphany, God's Challenge

They came from the East . . . strange pilgrims: Wizard Kings, the Magi. They passed through Jerusalem.

They were led by a mysterious star, by outer light itself. . . . But they were led even more by faith, by inner light. They arrived . . . and prostrated and adored him. . . .

Through that pilgrimage to Bethlehem, the Magi . . . became the beginning and symbol of all those who come to Jesus through faith. . . .

They became the beginning and prefiguration of those who come from beyond the frontiers of the Chosen People of the Old Alliance, and reached, and keep on reaching Christ through faith. . .

Epiphany is *the feast of the vitality of the Church.* . . . The Church is herself when men — like the Shepherds and the Kings from the East — reach Jesus Christ through faith. When they find God in Christ-Man and through Christ.

So Epiphany is *the great feast of faith.*

Taking part in this feast are those who have already reached the faith and those who are still on the way to it. They take part with thanksgiving for the gift of faith, as did the Magi, who were full of gratitude and kneeled before the Child. The Church takes part in this feast and every year becomes more conscious of the vastness of her mission. To how many people must she still bring the faith!. . . . But the Church can never call a halt, because she is aware of that great gift, the gift of the incarnation of God. She must go on always seeking the way to Bethlehem for every person and every time.

Epiphany is *the feast of God's challenge!*

Sunday after Epiphany

The Baptism of the Lord

In the Liturgy the Church celebrates the Solemnity of the Baptism of the Lord. . . .

This ceremony of Baptism is intended to mean . . . that the Church lives and acts solely in view of the eternal salvation of mankind and with the prospect of giving mankind "grace," that is, eternal life, that which Jesus, the Incarnate Word, came to bring to earth. . . .

Jesus . . . told the apostles: "Make disciples of all the nations. Baptize them in the name of the Father and of the Son and of the Holy Spirit" *(Mt* 28:19). . . .

That is the new and definitive Baptism which eliminates "original sin" from the soul, that sin which is inher-

417

ent in fallen human nature because of the first two rational creatures' refusal of love. He returns to the soul "sanctifying grace," that is, participation in the very life of the Most Blessed Trinity. . . .

Here is a clamorous, marvelous thing; the rite is simple, but its meaning is sublime!

The fire of God's Creative and Redemptive Love *burns away sin* . . . and takes possession of the soul, which becomes the dwelling of the Most High!. . . .

Baptism is a
supernatural gift,
a radical transformation of human nature,
grafting of the soul into God's very life, concrete and personal realization of the Redemption.

Ash Wednesday

A New Spiritual Season

Ash Wednesday!

This is a day which opens up a particularly demanding spiritual season for every Christian who wishes to prepare himself or herself worthily for celebrating the Paschal Mystery, that is, the remembrance of the suffering, death and resurrection of the Lord.

This major time of the liturgical year is marked by the Biblical message which may be summed up in a single word, "*metanoeite* — be converted." This imperative is recalled to the minds of the faithful by the austere rite of the laying on of the Holy Ashes. Through the words, "Be converted and believe in the Gospel," and the expression, "Remember, man, you are but dust, and to dust you must return," this rite invites all to reflect upon the duty of conversion by remembering the inexorable decline and ephemeral frailty of human life, which is subject to death.

The moving ceremony of the distribution of the ashes raises our minds to the eternal reality which never passes away, to God who is the beginning and the end, the *alpha* and *omega* of our existence. Conversion is actually nothing less than a return to God, through evaluating earthly realities in the unfailing light of His truth. This evaluation leads us to ever clearer consciousness of the fact that we are but in transit through the wearisome affairs of this earth. It urges and stimulates us to make every effort for the kingdom of God to be established within us and for His justice to triumph.

Synonomous with conversion is also the word *penitence.* . . . Penitence as medicine, reparation, as change of mentality. . . . Penitence as the expression of a free and joyous commitment to follow Christ.

First Sunday of Lent

The Church Has Need of Faith

Today is the first Sunday of Lent!

Christ — Redeemer of Man — is present in the Church which He washed with His own blood on the cross. And in Christ's name, the Church every year announces the message of Lent to man: the gospel of conversion and of pardon. In Christ the Church finds hope for her own renewal and at the same time certainty of her mission.

Christ lets us know that He willed to be subjected to trials and sufferings for love of us. "*Christum Dominum pro nobis tentatum er passum, venite adoremus!* — Come let us adore Christ the Lord, who was tried and suffered for us!"

Various are the trials and sufferings of mankind, of the nations, of the peoples, of families and of every human being. Various are the trials to which the Lord subjects His Church, trials from inside and outside.

The Church lives in the midst of individuals and peoples. The Church is the witness of the generations and the centuries. She cannot be exempt from trials and sufferings.

There is need for the Church of our time to be fully conscious of the trials she is going through. She must also be aware of the temptations which these times are preparing for her.

The Church cannot be free from temptations because the Lord Himself took temptations on Himself. Consciousness of being subjected to temptations is in a certain sense the prime condition of penitence, that is, of conversion.

Second Sunday of Lent

"This is My Son. . . Hear Him"

What does hearing Christ mean?

This is a question which a Christian cannot evade. Neither his consciousness nor his conscience can get around it.

What does listening to Christ mean?

The whole Church always must respond to this question in the dimension of the generations, of the epochs, of changing social, economic and political conditions.

The answer given has to be authentic, it has to be sincere — as Christ's teaching is authentic and sincere, His Gospel, and then His Gethsemane, the Cross and the Resurrection. And each of us must always give a response to this question if our Christianity and lives are in conformity with our faith, if they are authentic and sincere.

The Christian must give this response unless he wants to risk having his own belly as his god *(cf. Phil* 3:19) and behave as an enemy "of the cross of Christ" *(Phil* 3:18).

The response will be a little different every time. The response given by the father and mother of a family will be different, that of an engaged couple will be different, that of children will be different again, a boy's and a girl's will be different, so will an aged person's response be different, that of the sick one nailed to a bed of pain, that of the man of science, of the politician, of the intellectual, of an economist, all will be different, that of a man doing very heavy work will be different, as will that of a sister or a brother in religion, a priest's response will be different, so will that of a pastor of souls, a bishop and the Pope.

Third Sunday of Lent

My Father's House

"My Father's house."

Today Christ pronounces these words on the threshold of the Temple at Jerusalem.

He appears on that threshold to "vindicate," to claim back His Father's House in the face of men, to claim his rights to that House. Men had made it into a marketplace. Christ rebuked them severely. He put Himself decidedly against that error.

He was eaten up by zeal for the House of God (*cf. Jn* 2:17). He therefore did not hesitate to expose himself to the malevolence of the elders of the Jewish people and all those responsible for what had been done against the House of His Father, the Temple.

That was a memorable event. It was a memorable scene. Through the words of His holy wrath, Christ wrote the law of the holiness of God's House deep into the Church's tradition. By uttering those mysterious words regarding the temple of His Body, "Destroy this temple . . . and in three days I will raise it up" (*Jn* 2:19), Jesus consecrated all the temples of the People of God once for all.

These words take on a quite special richness of meaning in the period of Lent, when we meditate on Christ's Passion and death — the destruction of the temple of His Body — so as to prepare ourselves for the solemnity of Easter, for the moment, that is, when Jesus will reveal Himself to us again *in the same temple of His Body,* newly raised up by the power of God, who wills to build the spiritual edifice of the new faith, hope and charity in it from generation to generation.

Fourth Sunday of Lent

The Parable of the Prodigal Son

How many people over the course of the centuries, how many in our time find in this parable the basic outlines of their own personal stories?

There are three key stages in the story of that young man, with which each of us identifies, in a certain sense, when he or she commits a sin.

The first stage: the departure. We depart from God, as that son departed from his father, when we begin to behave towards all the good that is in us as he behaved in regard to the part of his father's good he had received as inheritance. We forget that good is given to us by God as a task, as an evangelical talent. Unfortunately, we behave at times as if that good in us — that of the soul and the body, the abilities, the faculties, the strength — were our own exclusive property, which we can use and abuse in any way we like, wasting and squandering it.

The second stage in our parable is that of the return to right reason and of the process of conversion. Man has to face up sadly to what he has lost, what he has deprived himself of by committing sin, living in sin, so that that decisive step may ripen in him; "I will break away and return to my father" (*Lk* 15:18). He must once more see the face of that Father upon whom he had turned his back.

Finally, *the third stage*: the return. The return will occur as Christ speaks of it in the parable. The Father awaits the son, forgetting all evil done by him, no longer considering all the waste of which the son is guilty. One thing alone is important to the Father now: his son has been found; he has not thoroughly lost his humanity; in spite of everything, he now has a determined resolve to live as a son again. . . .

Fifth Sunday in Lent

Rend Your Hearts

"Tear your hearts. . . ."

This is the invitation of the day in the season of Lent, above all in these two last weeks preceding Easter. The invitation is addressed to every person, to his and her inward part, the conscience.

The conscience is the measure of man. It testifies to his greatness, his profundity. For this depth to open, for man not to let himself be deprived of such greatness, God speaks to him with the word of the cross.

Verbum Crucis — the word of the cross: this is the last, definite word. God chose to use this word to confront man and always uses it to touch the conscience, which has the power to lacerate the human heart.

The inner man must ask himself why God chose to speak with this word. What meaning has this decision of God's in the history of man? This is the fundamental question put by Lent and the liturgical season of the Suffering of the Lord. Contemporary man experiences the threat of spiritual unfeelingness and even death of the conscience. This death is something deeper than sin: it is a slaying of the sense of sin. Many factors work together today to kill the consciences of people of our time. This corresponds to what Christ called "the sin against the Holy Spirit." Such sin begins when the Word of the Cross no longer speaks to man as the last cry of love, with power to tear hearts.

Scindite corda vestra — rend your hearts.

Palm Sunday

The Beginning of Holy Week

The liturgy of Palm Sunday is marvellous, just as the events of that day to which they refer were marvellous.

A deep shadow lay across the enthusiasm of the *hosannas* in greeting the Messiah — *the shadow of the approaching Passion.* How significant are the words of the prophet which are fulfilled on this day: "Fear not, daughter of Zion! Your king approaches you on a donkey's colt" (*Jn* 12:15; *cf. Zec* 9:9). On the day of the general enthusiasm of the people at the coming of the Messiah, can the Daughter of Zion have reason to fear? Yes, indeed. The time is now near when the words of the psalmist will be accomplished on the lips of Jesus of Nazareth, "My God, my God, why have you forsaken me?" (*Ps* 22:2). He himself was to utter those words from the height of the cross. So, instead of the enthusiasm of the people singing *hosanna,* we shall be witnesses of the scorn and sneers in Pilate's courtyard and on Golgotha, as the psalmist proclaimed: "All who see me, scoff at me, they mock me with parted lips, they wag their heads: He relied on the Lord; let him deliver him, let him rescue him, if he loves him" (*Ps* 22:8–9)

Today's liturgy — that of Palm Sunday — permits us to linger by Christ's triumphal entry into Jerusalem and so conducts us at the same time to the end of the passion.

"They have pierced my hands and my feet; I can count all my bones. . . ." And later, "They divide my garments among them, and for my vesture they cast lots (*Ps* 22:18–19). As if the psalmist already saw the events of Good Friday with his own eyes. On that day indeed — it is imminent — Christ will make himself obedient unto death, and that death will be that of the cross. *(cf. Phil* 2:8). But exactly this term means *the beginning of exaltation.* The exaltation of Christ is included in his denudation. *Glory has its beginning and source in the Cross.*

Monday in Holy Week

The Cross and the Resurrection

The messianic message of Christ and His activity among people end with the cross and resurrection. We have to penetrate deeply into this final event — which especially in the language of the Vatican Council is defined as the *Mysterium Paschale* — if we wish to express in depth the truth about mercy, as it has been revealed in depth in the history of our salvation. At this point of our considerations, we shall have to draw closer still to the content of the encyclical *Redemptor hominis.* If, in fact, the reality of the Redemption, in its human dimension, reveals the unheard-of greatness of man, *qui talem ac tantum meruit habere Redemptorem,* at the same time *the divine dimension of the redemption* enables us, I would say, in the most empirical and "historical" way, to uncover the depth of that love which does not recoil before the extraordinary sacrifice of the Son, in order to satisfy the fidelity of the Creator and Father towards human beings, created in His image and chosen from "the beginning," in this Son, for grace and glory.

The events of Good Friday and, even before that, in prayer in Gethsemane, introduce a fundamental change into the whole course of the revelation of love and mercy in the messianic mission of Christ. The one who "went about doing good and healing" and "curing every sickness and disease" now Himself seems to merit the greatest mercy and to *appeal for mercy,* when He is arrested, abused, condemned, scourged, crowned with thorns, when He is nailed to the cross and dies amidst agonizing torments. It is then that He particularly deserves mercy from the people to whom He has done good, and He does not receive it. Even those who are closest to Him cannot protect Him and snatch Him from the hands of His oppressors. At this final stage of His messianic activity the words which the prophets, especially Isaiah, uttered concerning the Servant of Yahweh are fulfilled in Christ: "Through his stripes we are healed."

Christ, as the man who suffers really and in a terrible way in the Garden of Olives and on Calvary, addresses Himself to the Father — that Father whose love He has preached to people, to whose mercy He has borne witness through all of His activity. But He is not spared — not even He — the terrible suffering of death on the cross: *"For our sake God made him to be sin who knew no sin,"* St. Paul will write, summing up in a few words the whole depth of the cross and at the same time the divine dimension of reality of the Redemption.

Tuesday in Holy Week

Let All Mankind Believe in Mercy

The cross of Christ on Calvary stands *beside the path of* that *admirabile commercium,* of that *wonderful self-communication of God to man,* which also includes *the call* to man to share in the divine life by giving himself, and with himself the whole visible world, to God, and like an adopted son to become a sharer in the truth and love which is in God and proceeds from God. It is precisely beside the path of man's eternal election to the dignity of being an adopted child of God that there stands in history the cross of Christ, the only-begotten Son, who, as "light from light, true God from true God," came to give the final witness to the wonderful *covenant of God with humanity, of God with man* — every human being. This covenant, as old as man — it goes back to the very mystery of creation — and afterwards many times renewed with one single chosen people, is equally the new and definitive covenant, which was established there on Calvary, and is not limited to a single people, to Israel, but is open to each and every individual. . . .

Believing in the crucified Son means "seeing the Father," means believing that love is present in the world and that this love is more powerful than any kind of evil in which individuals, humanity, or the world is involved. Believing in this love means *believing in mercy.* For mercy is an indispensable dimension of love; it is as it were love's second name and, at the same time, the specific manner in which love is revealed and effected vis-à-vis the reality of the evil that is in the world, affecting and besieging man, insinuating itself even into his heart and capable of causing him to "perish in Gehenna."

Wednesday in Holy Week

The Cross Overcomes Evil and Death

The cross of Christ on Calvary is also a witness to the strength of evil against the very Son of God, against the one who, alone among all the sons of men, was by His nature absolutely innocent and free from sin, and whose coming into the world was untainted by the disobedience of Adam and the inheritance of original sin. And here, precisely in Him, in Christ, justice is done to sin at the price of His sacrifice, of His obedience "even to death." He who was without sin, "God made him sin for our sake." Justice is also brought to bear upon death, which from the beginning of man's history had been allied to sin. Death has justice done to it at the price of the death of the one who was without sin and who alone was able — by means of his own death — to inflict death upon death. In this way *the cross of Christ,* on which the Son, consubstantial with the Father, *renders full justice to God,* is also *a radical revelation of mercy,* or rather of the love that goes against what constitutes the very root of evil in the history of man: against sin and death.

The cross is the most profound condescension of God to man and to what man — especially in difficult and painful moments — looks on as his unhappy destiny. The cross is like a touch of eternal love upon the most painful wounds of man's earthly existence.

Holy Thursday

O Sacrum Convivium!

"The Father who had handed everything over to him. . .
(Jn 13:3).

Before the paschal supper, Christ had the clear consciousness that the Father had given everything into his
hands. He is free, with all the fullness of liberty which
the Son of Man, the Incarnate Word, enjoys. He is *free*
with a freedom not belonging to any other man. Everything that was done during the Last Supper had its
source in *the Son's perfect liberty as regards the Father.* He
was soon to take that human liberty of his to Gethsemane,
and say: "Father, if it is your will, take this cup from me;
yet not my will but yours be done" *(Lk* 22:42). He was
then to accept the suffering coming upon him, suffering
which was at the same time *the object of a choice* — suffering of a dimension inconceivable to us.

But the choice was already made during the Last
Supper. Christ acted with full consciousness of the
choice made.

Only such understanding explains that fact that he
took a loaf and "giving thanks, he broke it and gave it to
them, saying, 'This is my body to be given for you'"
(Lk 22:19). And after having supped, he took the chalice,
saying, "This cup is the new covenant in my blood," as St.
Paul recalls *(1 Cor* 11:25), while the Gospels add, "in my
blood, which will be shed for you" *(Lk* 22:20) or "the
blood of the covenant, to be poured in behalf of many"
(Mt 26:28; *Mk* 14:24).

When pronouncing those words in the cenacle, Christ
had already made his choice. He had made it for some time.
Now he made it again. And he was to make the choice
once more at Gethsemane accepting in sorrow all the
immensity of the suffering linked with such a choice.

"The Father . . . had handed everything over to him."
Everything, the Father had given the whole plan of salvation over to his perfect liberty.

And *to his perfect love*.

Good Friday

The Agony of Calvary and the Cross

Crucem tuam adoremus — let us adore your cross.

Yes, this is the day when we honor the cross in a special way. The Cross of Christ. This sign, the instrument of shameful death, has risen ever since dawn before us, and penetrates the hours of Good Friday, during which we hasten with concerned thoughts and hearts to follow the sufferings of the Lord: along the way from Pilate's Praetorium to Calvary; the agony on Calvary. The death. The Way of the Cross: *crucifixion – death – entombment*.

Through how many parts of the earth has this cross passed? Through how many generations? For how many disciples of Christ has it become the principal reference point on the earthly pilgrimage?

How many has it prepared for suffering and death? How many for martyrdom for Christ? For bloody or bloodless testimony? And how many is it continually preparing for all that? The Church's history, on the various continents and in the various countries, can record only part of that general martyrology. The Church's altars have not been able to find room in their glory for all those who have given testimony for Christ through the Cross. We have only to think of those who have lived in our own century. The Cross is the gate through which God entered definitely into man's history. And remains in it. The cross is the gate through which God ceaselessly enters our lives.

The Cross opens us to God. The Cross opens the world to God. And blessing is given in the sign of the cross.

Dearest brothers and sisters, may this day of Good Friday, dedicated to the mystery of the Cross, which we have meditated upon, bring us ever nearer the Living God, Father, Son and Holy Spirit. May the sign of Christ's death enliven his presence and his power in us. Amen.

Holy Saturday

The Silence of the Tomb

The word "death" is pronounced with a lump in the throat. Mankind has become accustomed to some degree, after so many generations, to the reality of death and to its inevitability. Yet, death is always a deeply troubling event. Christ's death entered deeply into the hearts of those near him and into the consciousness of all Jerusalem. The silence which then fell filled the evening of Good Friday and the whole of the Sabbath which followed.

The three women of whom today's Gospel speaks well remembered the heavy stone with which the entrance to the sepulcher was sealed. They remembered that stone; they may have said something about it among themselves as they went to the sepulcher the day after the Sabbath. It also symbolizes *the weight which crushed their hearts.* It was the stone which separated the Dead One from the living, the boundary stone between life and death, the weight of death.

The women who went to the sepulcher the morning after the Sabbath day did not speak of death but of the stone. When they got there, they found that it was no longer blocking the entrance to the tomb. It had been rolled away. They did not find Jesus in the sepulcher. They looked for him, in vain! "He is not here. He has been raised, exactly as he promised" (*Mt* 28:6). They had to go back to the city and report to the disciples that He had been brought back to life and they should see him in Galilee. The women were not capable, however, of uttering a word. The news of the death had been given in hushed tones, the news of the resurrection was quite hard for them to put into words. It was difficult to repeat the words they heard, so much had the reality of the death affected a person's thought and heart.

And exactly because of this, the Paschal Vigil, the day following Good Friday . . . is *the day of the great awaiting*. It is the paschal wake: day and night spent in waiting for the Day that the Lord had made.

Easter Day

Christ Has Risen!

On the third day he rose again. . . . Today, together with the whole Church, we repeat these words with particular emotion. We repeat them with the same faith with which they were pronounced the first time. We utter them with the same certainty that was put into the sentence by the eyewitnesses of the event. On the third day he rose again. . . .

This is the truth, upon which, as upon a cornerstone, is based the whole construction of our faith; today we wish to share it among ourselves as fullness of the Gospel, we confessors of Christ, we Christians, we the Church.

How can we not rejoice at the victory of this Christ, who went about the world doing good to all and preaching the Gospel of the Kingdom, in which the fullness of God's redemptive goodness is expressed? In it, man has been called to the greatest of dignity. How can we not rejoice at the *victory* of Him, who was so unjustly condemned to the most terrible suffering and death on the Cross. At the victory of Him who was first scourged, buffeted, covered with spittle, with so much human cruelty.

Behold the day of universal hope, The day on which all human sufferings, disappointments, humiliations, crosses, violated human dignity, disrespected human life, all are gathered up and associated with the Risen One, and loudly cry out, "To the Paschal Victim, let sacrifice of praise be raised today!" The Risen one does not depart from us. The Risen One returns to us. . . . "Peace to you." How necessary his presence is for the world . . . the order coming from His Commandment of Love, that individuals, families, nations, continents, may enjoy peace.

Monday in the Octave of Easter

Alleluia!

Alleluia! Our cry expresses the joy of Easter!

It is the exclamation which still resounds in the middle of the night of expectation and brings the joy of the morning with it. It brings the certainty of resurrection. What the lips of the women before the sepulcher and the mouths of the apostles did not have the courage to utter is now uttered by the Church. Thanks to their testimony, she utters their *alleluia*.

This song of joy, sung near midnight, announces the great day to us. (In some Slav tongues, Easter is called "Great Night," and after the Great Night arrives the Great Day, "The Day Which the Lord Has Made.")

That great moment does not permit us to remain outside ourselves. It constrains us to enter into our own humanity. Christ not only revealed the victory of life over death to us but, with his Resurrection, he also brought us the New Life. He gave us such new life.

This is how St. Paul puts it: "Are you not aware that we who are baptized into Christ Jesus were baptized into his death? Through baptism into his death we were buried with him, so that, just as Christ was raised from the dead by the glory of the Father, we too might live a new life" *(Rom* 6:3-4).

The words, "we were baptized into his death," tell us much. Death is the water wherein Life recommences: the water which leaps "up to provide eternal life" *(Jn* 4:14). We must be immersed in this water; in this Death, so as to come out of it as the New Man, the New Creature, to become new, that is, enlivened by the Power of the Resurrection of Christ!

Tuesday in the Octave of Easter

The Stone Removed

"She saw that the stone had been moved away" (*Jn* 20:1). . . .

That stone placed over the entrance to the tomb had become primarily a mute witness to the death of the Son of Man. With such a rock was the course of the lives of many people of those days ended, in the cemetery of Jerusalem. Indeed, so were concluded the lives of all men, in graveyards.

Under the weight of the tombstone, behind its massive barrier, the work of death is accomplished in the silence of the tomb. That is, man drawn out of dirt, returns slowly to dirt (*Gen* 3:19).

The stone was set over Jesus' tomb on the evening of Good Friday. Like all tombstones, it became the silent witness of the death of the Man, of the Son of Man.

What testimony did this stone give on the day after the Sabbath, in the dawn hours? What does it tell us? What does the stone rolled away from the sepulcher declare?

"I shall not die, but live, and declare the works of the Lord. . . . The stone which the builders rejected has become the cornerstone. By the Lord has this been done; it is wonderful in our eyes" (*Ps* 117:17, 22–23).

Those who worked the death of the Son of Man "kept it under surveillance of the guard after fixing a seal to the stone" (*Mt* 27:66). Often builders of the world, to die for which Christ came, have tried to set a final stone upon his tomb. But the stone has always been removed from the tomb; the stone, the witness to death, has become witness to the resurrection: "The right hand of the Lord has struck with power" (*Ps* 117:16).

The Church is continually announcing Christ's Resurrection anew. The Church joyfully repeats to men the words of the angels and of the women, uttered on that radiant morning when death was defeated. The Church announces that he who has become our Pasch is alive. He who died on the cross reveals the fullness of life.

Wednesday in the Octave of Easter

The Death of God

This world today, unfortunately, seems in various ways to will "the death of God." But let it listen to the message of the Resurrection.

All you who announce "the death of God," who try to expel God from the human world, halt and think for "the death of God" can also carry with it "the death of man."

Christ rose again so that man may retrieve the authentic meaning of existence, *so that man may live his life fully:* that man, who comes *from God,* may live *in God.*

Christ rose again. He is the cornerstone. Already an attempt had been made then to reject and overcome him by means of the stone before the sephulcher, sealed and guarded. But that stone was rolled away, Christ rose again.

Do not reject Christ, you who construct the human world.

Do not reject Christ, you who construct the world of today and of tomorrow, in whatever way and in whatever sector: the world of culture and of civilization, the world of the economy and of politics, the world of science and of information.

You who construct the world of peace . . . or of war? You who construct the world of order . . . or of terror? Do not refuse Christ: He is the cornerstone!

Let no one refuse him, for all are responsible for their destiny, constructor or destroyer of their own existence.

Christ rose even before his angel had rolled back the tombstone. Then he revealed himself as the cornerstone, upon which is built the history of all mankind and of each of us.

Christ, "our Pasch," does not cease from being a pilgrim with us upon the road of history and each of us may meet him, for he does not cease from being a brother to mankind in every epoch and at every moment.

Thursday in the Octave of Easter

"Our Pasch"

We once again find ourselves in the atmosphere of the Solemnity of the Pasch. There an indescribable spiritual experience lets us taste the profound truth of our faith in the Risen Christ, "our Pasch, our Passover" (*1 Cor* 5:7). He immolated himself for us but did not exhaust his mystery and his mission when, hanging upon the cross, he uttered the words, "Now it is finished" (*Jn* 19:30).

At that very moment, the accomplishment of God's saving design actually opened a fresh stage in human history, which Christ himself consecrated with his resurreaction from death. It is the new *kairós* (time) or certainty of life, founded on that demonstration of divine omnipotence.

Christ rose again, as he had promised, because his profound Ego identifies with the eternal principle of life, God, so much that he was able to say of himself, "I am . . . the life" (*Jn* 14:6), as he had also proclaimed on another occasion, "I am the resurrection and the life" (*Jn* 11:25).

With him, then, the omnipotent life force entered into the world; after the sacrifice of justice and love offered up on the Cross, it exploded in his humanity and, through his humanity, in the human race and in some way in the entire universe. From that moment on, creation encloses the secret of an ever new youthfulness and we are no longer slaves of the "fear of death" (*cf. Heb* 2:15). Christ has liberated us forever!

Rightly then, with the Church's liturgy, we may greet the Cross as "the only hope" and source of grace and pardon, not only in *hoc Passionis tempore,* this time of the Passion, as we have celebrated Good Friday, but also in *in hac triumphi gloria,* this glory of the triumph, as we shall sing on the feast of its Exaltation (14 September), echoing the Paschal *alleluia.*

Friday in the Octave of Easter

The Pasch, Guaranty of Life

St. Peter tells us in his first letter to the Christian communities of Asia Minor of this mystery of the glory pouring out from the cross (*fulget Crucis mysterium* — the mystery of the cross shines forth). That letter is a fundamental document it contains simple and clearly outlined reflections, thick with meaning for Christology; it reflects to us the Apostles and the early Christian communities as well. "Praised be the God and Father of our Lord Jesus Christ, he who in his great mercy gave us new birth; a birth unto hope which draws its life from the resurrection of Jesus Christ from the dead; a birth to an imperishable inheritance, incapable of fading or defilement" *(1 Pt* 1:3–5).

So the risen Christ dominates the scene of history, and gives a generating force of eternal hope to Christian life, in this *kairós,* in this eschatological age, already begun with the victory won over death by Him who was "chosen before the world's foundation and revealed for your sake in these last days" *(1 Pt* 1:20).

This is the certainty of which the world had need, the world in which the apostles preached the Gospel of Christ; this is the hope of him of whom humanity in our time has need, those to whom we would communicate the message and the gift of the Holy Year: Christ is risen and by rising again he has broken what seemed and still seems to many an implacable vortex of decadence, degradation and corruption in history.

The risen Christ *gives us the guaranty of a life which does not fade away,* of an "imperishable inheritance," of "a safeguard" exercised by God in favor of the just, who, liberated and renewed by the Redeemer, now belong in faith and hope to the kingdom of eternal life.

Saturday in the Octave of Easter

The Power Which Regenerates the World

Earthly history and the workings of the cosmos undoubtedly continue their course and are not identified with the rate at which the Kingdom of Christ develops. In fact, pain, evil, sin, death, yet claim their victims, in spite of the resurrection of Christ.

The cycle of one thing succeeding another, the cycle of becoming, is not at a standstill. If it were, history would be at an end! And so facts and events are continually being repeated and give rise to thoughts of an irremediable conflict here on earth between the two kingdoms, or, as St. Augustine said, between the two cities. Think, for example, of the contrast which is to be found in this Holy Year between celebration of the Redemption on the one hand and on the other hand the offenses against God, the misdeeds committed against man and, at bottom, the challenges to Christ which are continually being launched.

This is the most impressive aspect, the most mysterious dimension of the historic dialectic between the forces of good and the forces of evil: the fact that obstacles are raised or indifference is shown to the forces of Redemption let into the world by Christ through his Resurrection as the principle which resolves the conflict between death and life.

The world is in need, today as yesterday, for the "new people" to remain in its midst, among the vicissitudes, the conflicts, the variations which not seldom lead to situations which are so difficult, sometimes even dramatic. The world has need of this people which will dedicate itself with humility, courage and perseverance to service of the Redemption and give concrete form, in good Christian conduct, to the regenerating power of Christ's resurrection.

This is the function which Christians have as evangelizers and witnesses to the Resurrection in history. . . .

Low Sunday (Sunday "in Albis")

The Glorious Victory

Are unbelievers more numerous among us today than believers? Perhaps faith is dead and has been covered with a layer of secular daily habit, or even denial and contempt. . . . In today's evangelical and liturgical event there is also an unbelieving apostle, one obstinate in his unbelief. "I will never believe it" (*Jn* 20:25).

Christ then said: "Examine my hands. Put your hand into my side. Do not persist in your unbelief, but believe!" (*Jn* 20:27). Can it be that beneath unbelief *there is downright sin,* the inveterate sin which evolved people will not call by its name, so that mankind shall not call it by that name, and not seek remission?

Christ said: "Receive the Holy Spirit. If you forgive men's sins, they are forgiven them; if you hold them bound, they are held bound" (*Jn* 20:22-23). Let man name sin by its name; he is not called upon to falsify it in himself, because the Church has received the power from Christ to exert over sin, for the good of the human conscience. These, too, are essential details of today's paschal message.

The whole Church announces the paschal joy to all mankind. In that joy resounds *victory over man's fear.* Over the fear which is in human consciences and arises from sin. That was the joy of the Apostles gathered in the cenacle at Jerusalem. It is the Church's paschal joy, which has its beginning from that cenacle. It has its beginning from the empty tomb below Golgotha and the hearts of those simple men who "the evening of that first day of the week" saw the Risen One and heard the greeting from his mouth, "Peace be with you!"

The Ascension

The Two Aspects of the Ascension

"The Lord Jesus was taken up into heaven and took his seat at God's right hand" (*Mk* 16:19). Today's solemnity calls us above all to meditate on the meaning of the mystery which we are celebrating.

What does it mean that Jesus was taken up into heaven? "He took his seat at God's right hand": *this is the prime meaning of the Ascension.* And even though the expression is an imaginative one, for God has neither a right nor a left hand, it contains an important Christological message. The Risen Jesus entered fully — with his humanity as well — to share in the divine glory, to take part, indeed, in the saving activity of God himself. Christ is not only our head; he is also the "Pantocrator," he who holds sway over all things.

These statements have a very concrete meaning for our lives. But there is still another essential aspect, which is proper to the Solemnity of the Ascension and is expressed both in the first reading and in the Gospel. "Be my witnesses . . . even to the ends of the earth" (*Acts* 1:8).

"Go into the whole world and proclaim the good news to all creation" (*Mk* 16:15). There is a duty to give testimony and it derives directly from our faith. We may not celebrate the exaltation of Jesus Christ and lead an uncommitted life, taking no notice of his last, supreme command. The Ascension reminds us that the taking away of Jesus from his disciples' responsive experience of him also had the purpose of leaving the field to them. They now go on in history with his mission and pursue it with the pastoral zeal and missionary effort which he showed, even though their work is marked with many weaknesses.

It was not for nothing that, according to the account in the Acts of the Apostles, Pentecost came shortly after, with the gift of the Holy Spirit, who gave the start to the Church's missionary history.

Pentecost

Thank the Holy Spirit

Brought together like the Apostles in the cenacle, *"cum Maria Matre eius* — Mary the mother of Jesus *(Acts* 1:14) — to proclaim the *magnalia Dei"* ["the marvels God has accomplished" *(Acts* 2:11)]. I desire to thank the Holy Spirit together with you, and reconfirm with you our common faith in him, *Dominum et vivificanem,* Lord and lifegiver, at sixteen centuries from the First Council of Constantinople. I wish to pray to him together with you in order that the universal Church, which he enlivens, and of which you are splendid image today, may ever be an instrument of salvation and sanctity, a sign of unity and of truth, a worker of justice and peace.

May Christ's love unite us. May the Spirit, God's Personal Love, ever unite us likewise and, having united us, lead us along the roads of the world to carry forward, bravely, that work of evangelization which was entrusted to us. . . May he sustain us in preaching of the Gospel *in omni patientia et doctrina,* in all patience and doctrine, like Peter at Pentecost, like Paul, like the other apostles, witnesses to Christ "to the ends of the earth" (*Acts* 1:8). That we may have ever fresh strength for announcing to our brothers and sisters that Jesus alone is "the way, and the truth, and the life" (*Jn* 14:6) and that "there is no other name in the whole world given to men by which we are to be saved" (*cf. Acts* 4:12).

To you, to all the dearly beloved faithful . . . to all the Churches of the world, whose hearts beat today in accord with the Church of Rome and that of Constantinople, I impart with great affection my Apostolic Benediction.

Trinity Sunday

The Mystery of the Trinity

"O Lord our Lord, how glorious is your name over all the earth" (*Ps* 8:2). These words from the psalm bring us trembling and adoring before the great mystery of the Most Blessed Trinity, the feast of which we solemnly celebrate today. Yet, the extent of the world and the universe, though boundless, does not equal the immeasurable reality of the life of God. Before him, we must more than ever humbly accept the call of the wise man in the Bible when he says: "Let not your heart be quick to make a promise in God's presence. God is in heaven and you are on earth" (*Eccl* 5:2).

God is actually the only reality beyond our powers of measuring, observing, controlling, of gaining exhaustive knowledge. That is why he is God: because he measures us, rules us, watches us, understands us, even when we might be unaware of it. But if this be true for the Godhead in general, it is all the truer for the mystery of the Trinity, the typically Christian mystery, of God himself. He is at the same time Father, Son and Holy Spirit. But it is not a matter of three separate Gods — that would be blasphemy — nor of simply diverse and impersonal modes of presenting himself on the part of one Divine person. This would mean radically impoverishing the richness of his interpersonal communion.

We are in a position to know more about what the One and Triune God is not than about what he is. If we could explain him adequately with our reason, that would mean that we should have captured and reduced him to the measure of our minds.

However, this is the Christian novelty: *the Father* loved us so much as to give us his Only Begotten Son; through love, *the Son* poured out his blood for our sake; and *the Holy Spirit* was actually "given to us" in such a way as to bring into us that same love with which God loves us (*Rom* 5:5).

Corpus Christi

The Body and Blood of Christ

For many centuries now, the Church has chosen the Thursday following the feast of the Most Holy Trinity as the day dedicated to particular public veneration of the Eucharist. This is the day of "Corpus Christi," the day of this *holiest of Sacraments:* the Sacrament of the Body and the Blood of the Lord. The Sacrament of the Divine Pasch. The Sacrament of Death and Resurrection. The Sacrament of the sacrifice and the banquet of the redemption. The Sacrament of communion of souls with Christ in the Holy Spirit. The Sacrament of the faith of the pilgrim Church and of hope in eternal union. The Food of souls. The Sacrament of Bread and Wine, of the poorest of species, which become our greatest treasure and wealth. "Behold the bread of angels, the bread of pilgrims."

Why was Thursday chosen for the solemnity of Corpus Christi? It is easy to answer that. This solemnity refers to the mystery which is historically linked with that day, Holy Thursday.

We celebrate the solemnity of the Body and Blood of Christ on the Thursday after Trinity Sunday, to draw attention to that *Life* which the Eucharist gives us. It is a fuller echo of the Most Holy Trinity, in such a way that the Divine Life is shared *by our souls* through this Sacrament. This is a deepest, innermost mystery and we accept it with all our hearts, with all our interior "ego." We live it in secret, in the most profound recollection.

However, there is but one day, and one time, when we desire to give particular external and public expression to this reality. That day is today. It is an expression of love and veneration.

Holy Church, praise your Lord! Amen.

Feast of the Sacred Heart

That Unique Heart

Heart of Jesus, formed by the Holy Spirit in the womb of the Virgin Mary, have mercy on us! So do we pray in the litany of the Most Sacred Heart of Jesus.

This invocation refers directly to the mystery on which we meditate when we recite the "Angelus": through the operation of the Holy Spirit the Humanity of Christ, Son of the Eternal Father, was formed in the womb of the Virgin of Nazareth.

Through operation of the Holy Spirit, the Heart was formed in this Humanity! The heart is the central organ of the human organism of Christ, it is at the same time the true symbol of his inner life, of his thought, his will, his sentiments. Through this Humanity, Christ's Humanity is "God's Temple" in a particular way and, at the same time, also through this Heart, it remains incessantly open to man and everything which is human: "Heart of Jesus, from whose fullness we have all received." The month of June is dedicated in a special manner to veneration of the Divine Heart. Not only one day of the month, that, when the liturgical feast occurs usually in June, but every day of the month. With this is linked the devout practice of reciting or singing the litany of the Sacred Heart every day.

It is a marvellous prayer, wholly concentrated on the interior mystery of Christ: God-Man. The litany of the Heart of Jesus draws abundantly on Biblical sources; at the same time it reflects the deepest experiences of human hearts. It is a prayer of veneration and authentic dialogue at the same time. In it we speak *of the heart,* and enable hearts to speak to *that unique Heart.*

When recited and meditated, this prayer becomes *a real school for the interior man:* the school of the Christian.

Feast of the Immaculate Heart of Mary

The Message of Fatima

When Jesus said on the Cross, "Woman, there is your son," he opened his mother's heart in a new way, he showed her the Immaculate Heart and revealed the new dimension of love and the new significance of love, to which she was called in the Holy Spirit with the power of the sacrifice of the Cross. We seem to find this dimension of maternal love again in the words of Fatima, a love which lights up with its rays the path of all men to God.

The path is that which leads across the earth, it is that which goes beyond the earth, through purgatory.

The solicitude of the Mother of the Savior is solicitude for the work of salvation, the work of her Son. It is concern for salvation, for the eternal salvation of all mankind... Since that 13 May 1917, it is difficult not to see how this saving love of the Mother embraces our century with its rays in a special manner. We understand the whole message of the Lady of Fatima in the light of motherly love.

What directly sets itself up against man's movement toward God is sin, perseverance in sin and, finally, negation of God. The programmed cancellation of God from the world of human thought. Detachment of all man's earthly activity from him. Refusal of God on man's part. If it becomes definite, it leads to damnation.

Can the Mother ... remain silent? No, she cannot. Hence, the message of Fatima, so maternal, is strong and decisive at the same time. It seems severe. It calls for penance. It warns. It calls for prayer. It recommends the Rosary. *All the individuals of our time are the object of its concern,* and with them societies, nations and peoples.

Devotion to the Most Sacred Heart of Jesus

The Heart of the Redeemer enlivens the whole Church and draws men who have opened their hearts "to the inscrutable wealth" of this unique Heart....

I desire in a special way to join spiritually with all those *who inspire their human hearts from this Divine Heart.*

It is a numerous family. Not a few congregations, associations and communities live and develop in the Church, taking their vital energy in a programmed way from the Heart of Christ. This spiritual bond always leads to a great reawakening of apostolic zeal. Adorers of the Divine Heart become people with sensitive consciences. And when it is given to them to have a relationship with the Heart of our Lord and Master, then need also reawakens in them to do reparation for the sins of the world, for the indifference of so many hearts, for their negligence.

How necessary these ranks of vigilant hearts are in the Church, so that the Love of the Divine Heart shall not remain isolated and without response! In these ranks, special mention deserves to be made of all those who offer up their sufferings as living victims in union with the Heart of Christ pierced on the cross. Transformed in that way by love, human suffering becomes a particular leaven of Christ's saving work in the Church. . . .

The Most Sacred Heart of Jesus reminds us, above all, of those moments when this Heart was "pierced by the lance," and, thereby, opened in a visible manner to man and the world. By reciting the litany and venerating the Divine Heart in general, we learn the mystery of the Redemption in all its divine and human profundity.

Consecrate the World to the
Immaculate Heart of Mary

The Immaculate Heart of Mary was open to the word, "Woman, there is your son." It went to meet spiritually the heart of the Son opened by the soldier's lance. The Heart of Mary was opened by the same love for man and for the world with which Christ loved man and the world, offering up himself even on the cross, even to that lance stroke from the soldier.

Consecrating the world to the Immaculate Heart of Mary means approaching the same Source of Life, through the Mother's Intercession, that life which flowed forth from Golgotha, the source which gushes out ceaselessly with redemption and grace. Reparation for the sins of the world is continually being accomplished in it. It is ceaselessly the fount of new life and holiness.

Consecrating the world to the Immaculate Heart of the Mother means returning under the *Cross of the Son*. More: it means consecration of this world to the pierced Heart of the Savior, by bringing the world back to the very source of its Redemption. Redemption is always greater than man's sin and "the sin of the world." The power of the Redemption infinitely surpasses the whole range of evil in man and in the world.

The Heart of the Mother is aware of it, more than anyone in the whole cosmos, visible and invisible. This is why she calls. She does not call only to conversion; she also calls upon us to let ourselves be helped by her, the Mother, to return to the source of the Redemption.

Second Sunday in May

Mother's Day

We cannot but observe that a broad and widespread social and cultural tradition in the more specific field of the family chose to reserve the task of being wife and mother solely to the woman without giving her adequate open-

ing to assume public tasks which were generally reserved for males. There is no doubt that the equal dignity and responsibility of man and woman fully justify
woman's access to public tasks. On the other hand, true
advancement of the woman also requires that the value
of her maternal and family task be acknowledged, compared with all other public tasks and all other callings.

The Church therefore can and ought to help contemporary society by tirelessly calling upon all to acknowledge and honor the irreplaceable value of woman's work in the home. This is of particular importance
in bringing up children. The right must also be recognized for women, as for men, to have access to the various public offices. Society ought also to structure itself in
such a way that wives and mothers should not be obliged
to work outside the home, and their families should be
able to live decently and prosperously, even though wives
devote themselves entirely to their families. It is also
necessary to overcome that mentality according to which
the honor of a woman derives more from her outside
work than from her family activities.

However, it is clear that all this means for the woman
is not that she should give up her femininity, nor that she
should imitate the masculine character, but the fullness
of her true female humanity. This should find expression in her activity both in the family and outside of it. At
the same time, the variety of customs and cultures
should not be forgotten.

Father's Day

Venerate Joseph, the just man, Joseph, who loved Mary, of the house of David, all the more deeply for having accepted her mystery. We venerate Joseph in whom the Fatherhood of God Himself is reflected more fully than in all earthly fathers. We venerate Joseph who built a family home on earth for the Eternal Word, just as Mary gave Him a human body. "The Word became flesh and made His dwelling among us" *(Jn* 1:14).

Let us turn our eyes from that great mystery of the faith and direct our thoughts to our homes, to so many couples and families. Joseph of Nazareth is a special revelation of the dignity of human fatherhood. Joseph of Nazareth, the carpenter, the man of labor. . . . The family rests upon the dignity of human paternity — on the responsibility of man, husband and father, as it does also on his work. Joseph of Nazareth testifies to that.

God addressed the following words to him: "Joseph, son of David, have no fear about taking Mary as your wife" *(Mt* 1:20). Are not these words perhaps addressed to each of you? Dear brothers, husbands and fathers of families! "Do not be afraid to take. . . ." Do not desert! It was said at the beginning, "A man leaves his father and his mother and clings to his wife, and the two of them become one body" *(Gen* 2:24). And Christ added, "Therefore let no man separate what God has joined" *(Mk* 10:9).

The *compactness* of the family, its *stability*, is one of the fundamental goods of man and society. At the basis of the compactness of the family lies the *indissolubility* of matrimony. If man, if society, seek ways depriving marriage of its indissolubility and the family of its compactness, then they cut away almost the very root of its moral strength and its health; they deprive themselves of one of the fundamental goods on which human life is built.

Labor Day

God created man "in His own image and likeness." His fundamental and original intention in regard to him was not cancelled out even when man heard the words, "By the sweat of your face shall you get bread to eat."

These words refer to the effort and fatigue, sometimes heavy effort, which has accompanied human labor ever since. But they do not alter the fact that it is the way by which man realizes the dominion which is proper to him, dominion won over the visible world by "subjugating" the earth. This effort is a universally acknowledged fact because it is a universal experience.

Men who do manual labor know it, their labor sometimes carried out under exceptionally burdensome conditions. Farmers and peasants know it, spending long days in cultivating the soil, which sometimes only "produces thorns and thistles." It is known by miners underground and stonecutters in quarries, steelworkers in front of their furnaces, men working in housebuilding and other construction tasks, frequently risking their lives and in danger of losing their health. Intellectuals tied to their benches and desks know it, scientists know it, those men and women know it who bear the weight of grave responsibility for decisions destined to have vast social effects. Doctors and nurses know it as they stand watch night and day by the sick. Those women know it who, sometimes without adequate acknowledgement on the part of society and even their own families, bear the daily burden of responsibility for the home and the upbringing of children. All working people know it, and because it is true that work is a universal vocation, all mankind knows it.

Yet, with all that effort and fatigue, and maybe because of it, in a certain sense, labor is a good thing for man.

World Mission Day

I desire that all the faithful would allow themselves to become involved and to bring their personal contribution to the great movement of "missionary cooperation."

Animation on the part of the leaders of the People of God is indispensable because a concrete awareness by the faithful of the problem of evangelization and therefore their commitment in the area of cooperation depend on this. A commitment so much more necessary and urgent when one considers that missionary activity, which also includes the indispensable construction of churches, schools, seminaries, universities, social assistance centres, etc., for the religious and human advancement of many of our brothers, is greatly conditioned by many difficulties of an economic character.

And for actualizing this program and for organizing the network of universal charity, to what better structure can one resort than the Pontifical Missionary Societies?

On World Mission Day, therefore, the Church, Mother and Teacher, solicitous for the good of all, extends her hand through the Pontifical Societies mentioned above to gather aid from men of good will. The new code of canon law, too, explicitly sanctions the obligation of all the faithful to collaborate, each according to his own responsibility, which stems from the intrinsically missionary nature of the Church.

Thus missionary cooperation is to be promoted in all the dioceses according to these four basic directives: the promotion of missionary vocations; the necessary assistance of priests for missionary initiatives, above all for the development of the Pontifical Missionary Societies; the celebration of World Mission Day; the annual collection of material assistance for the missions, to be sent to the Holy See.

Thanksgiving Day

Should we not think in terms of every grace which we have received from the fullness of Jesus Christ, God and Man? . . . to give thanks for every one of those graces, and for all at the same time?. . .

Grace is an interior reality. It is a mysterious pulsation of the divine life in human souls. It is an interior rhythm, that of God's intimacy with us, hence also of our intimacy with him. It is the source of every true good in our life. And it is the foundation of the good which does not pass away. Through grace, we already live in God, in the unity of the Father, of the Son and of the Holy Spirit, although our lives continue to go on in this world. Grace gives supernatural value to every life, even though, humanly speaking and according to the criteria of time, this life may be very poor, insignificant and hard.

So today we ought to give thanks for every grace of God which has been conveyed to anyone, not only to each of us . . . but also to every brother and sister of ours in every part of the world.

In this way, our hymn of thanksgiving will become a great synthesis, as it were. The whole Church will be present in this synthesis, because, as the [Vatican] Council teaches us, she is a sacrament of human salvation.

Prayer to Mary Most Holy

Hail Mary, Mother of Christ and of the Church! Hail, our life, our sweetness, and our hope!

To your care I entrust all the necessities of all families, the joys of children, the desires of the young, the worries of adults, the pains of the sick, the serene old age of senior citizens! I entrust to you the fidelity and the abnegation of Your Son's ministers, the hope of all those preparing themselves for this ministry, the joyous dedication of virgins in cloisters, the prayer and concern of men and women religious, the lives and the commitment of all those who work for Christ's reign on this earth.

In your hands, I set the fatigue and the sweat of those who work with their hands; the noble dedication of those who transmit knowledge, and the efforts of those who learn it; the beautiful vocation of those who alleviate the pains of others through their science and their service; the commitment of those who seek truth through their understanding and intelligence.

In your heart I leave the aspirations of those who uprightly seek the prosperity of their brethren through economic activities; of those who, in service to truth, inform and correctly form public opinion; of those who, in politics, in armies, in labor and trades unions, or in service to civic order, lend their honest collaboration in favor of just, peaceful and secure social life.

Come to the aid of those suffering misfortunes, those suffering because of loneliness, of hunger, of lack of work. Strengthen the weak in faith.

Blessed Virgin, increase our faith, strengthen our hope, reawaken our charity.

Feast of Christ the King

"The Lord reigns."

On the last Sunday of the annual cycle of the liturgy, the Church desires to pronounce this truth in a solemn manner: Christ reigns over the universe, which he created. *He is King because he is Creator.* The Church proclaims the work of creation and "through the work of creation," she proclaims "the reign of God" in the world: the Reign of God *is*.

At the same time, the Church prays as Christ taught, "May your reign come." God's kingdom already belongs to our contemporary reality but even more to the future. In Jesus Christ, God is he who is, who was, but at the same time "he who comes." Through the work of redemption, God's reign over humanity has its past, present and future. "It has its history," which develops together with the history of mankind. Jesus Christ is found at the center of it.

Jesus Christ is a "King who loves." Because he loved us humans to the shedding of his blood. Because he loves, he has liberated us from sin, because only love is capable of freeing us from sin. By liberating us from sin, he made from us the kingdom of God. His reign "never fades." "The Kingdom" of truth, of love, of grace and of pardon knows no sunset. His reign does not pass away. And the reign of man does not decline in him. Only in him, though living in the world, where truth and love are threatened in various ways, where sin more and more acquires the right of citizenship, where man may become victim of the horrible energies he has liberated.

Let us look now with "the eyes of faith" to Christ's kingdom, and repeat, "May your reign come."

SOURCES

ABBREVIATIONS

AAS   Acta Apostolicae Sedis
Enc.   Enciclica "Dives in Misericordia," n. 8
IGP   Insegnamenti di Giovanni Paolo II
OR   L'Osservatore Romano

DECEMBER

1. IGP, 29 November 1981, Vol. IV, 2, pp. 781–2. — 2. IGP, 3 December 1978, Vol. I, pp. 271–2. — 3. IGP, 28 November 1982, Vol. V, 3, pp. 1465–72. — 4. IGP, 16 December 1982, Vol. V, 3, pp. 1618–20. — 5. IGP, 16 December 1982, Vol. V, 3, pp. 1620–3. — 6. IGP, 16 December 1982, Vol. V, 3, p. 1623. — 7. IGP, 30 November 1980, Vol. III, 2, pp. 1466–8. — 8. IGP, 8 December 1982, Vol. V, 3, pp. 1557–8. — 9. IGP, 8 December 1979, Vol. II, 2, pp. 1351–2. — 10. IGP, 6 October 1979, Vol. II, 2, pp. 653–4. — 11. IGP, 19 March 1982, Vol. V, 1, pp. 933–4. — 12. January, 1979, Mexico. — 13. IGP, 16 December 1982, Vol. V, 3, pp. 1621–2. — 14. IGP, 4 November 1982, Vol. V, 3, pp. 1138–40. — 15. IGP, 2 December 1979, Vol. II, 2, p. 1317. — 16. IGP, 19 December 1980, Vol. III, 2, pp. 1731–2. — 17. IGP, 19 December 1980, Vol. III, 2, p. 1732. — 18. IGP, 19 December 1980, Vol. III, 2, pp. 1733–4. — 19. IGP, 22 December 1982, Vol. V, 3, pp. 1664–5. — 20. IGP, 22 December 1982, Vol. V, 3, pp. 1665–6. — 21. IGP, 12 December 1982, Vol. V, 3, pp. 1599–1601. — 22. IGP, 22 December 1982, Vol. V, 3, pp. 1666–7. — 23. IGP, 23 December 1980, Vol. III, 2, p. 1787. — 24. IGP, 23 December 1982, Vol. V, 3, pp. 1671–2. — 25. IGP, 25 December 1980, Vol. III, 2, pp. 1799–1801. — 26. IGP, 26 December 1980, Vol. III, 2, pp. 1806–7. — 27. IGP, 2 July 1979, Vol. II, 2, p. 12. — 28. IGP, 25 December 1982, Vol. V, 3, pp. 1688–91. — 29. IGP, 25 December 1978, Vol. I, pp. 419–22. — 30. IGP, 30 December 1981, Vol. IV, 2, pp. 1265–6. — 31. IGP, 31 December 1980, Vol. III, 2, pp. 1843–5.

JANUARY

1. IGP, 1 January 1979, Vol. II, p. 6. — 2. IGP, 8 May 1982, Vol. V, 2, pp. 1457–8. — 3. IGP, 8 May 1982, Vol. V, 2, p. 1457. — 4. AAS, 1 January 1981, Vol. 73, pp. 152–3. — 5. IGP, 1 January 1979, Vol. II, pp. 4–5. — 6. IGP, 4 October 1979, Vol. II, 2, p. 590. — 7. IGP, 24 January 1979, Vol. II, pp. 111–2. — 8. IGP, 6 January 1982, Vol. V, 1, pp. 47–8. — 9. IGP, 6 January 1982, Vol. V, 1, pp. 48–9. — 10. IGP, 11 January 1981, Vol. IV, 1, pp.

41–2. — 11. IGP, 10 January 1982, Vol. V, 1, pp. 67–9. — 12. IGP, 20 February 1981, Vol. IV, 1, pp. 476–7. — 13. IGP, 3 January 1979, Vol. II, pp. 9–10. — 14. IGP, 20 January 1980, Vol. III, 1, pp. 161–2. — 15. IGP, 20 January 1980, Vol. III, 1, pp. 164–5. — 16. IGP, 20 January 1980, Vol. III, 1, pp. 162–3. — 17. IGP, 28 December 1980, Vol. III, 2, p. 1812. — 18. IGP, 21 January 1981, Vol. IV, 1, pp. 121–2, 125–6. — 19. IGP, 20 January 1980, Vol. III, 1, pp. 157–8. — 20. IGP, 3 November 1982, Vol. V, 3, pp. 1090–2. — 21. IGP, 21 January 1980, Vol. III, 1, pp. 167–8. — 22. IGP, 29 September 1979, Vol. II, 2, pp. 443–5. — 23. IGP, 7 October 1979, Vol. II, 2, pp. 693–4. — 24. IGP, 29 November 1979, Vol. II, 2, pp. 1263–7. — 25. IGP, 25 January 1982, Vol. V, 1, pp. 212–3. — 26. IGP, 25 January 1983, Vol. III, 1, pp. 184–5. — 27. IGP, 7 June 1981, Vol. IV, 1, pp. 1232–3. — 28. IGP, 13 September 1980, Vol. III, 2, pp. 609–10. — 29. IPG, 29 May 1982, Vol. V, 2, pp. 1947–8, 1942. — 30. IGP, 17 November 1980, Vol. III, 2, pp. 1254–7. — 31. IGP, 1982, Vol. V, 1, pp. 267–72.

FEBRUARY

1. IGP, 1 February 1981, Vol. IV, 1, pp. 207–8. — 2. IGP, 2 February 1982, Vol. V, 1, pp. 284–5. — 3. IGP, 2 February 1982, Vol. V, 1, pp. 285–6. — 4. IGP, 17 November 1980, Vol. III, 2, pp. 1272–5. — 5. IGP, 20 February 1981, Vol. IV, 1, pp. 423–5. — 6. IGP, 26 February 1981, Vol. IV, 1, pp. 565–6. — 7. IGP, 20 February 1980, Vol. III, 1, pp. 438–9. — 8. IGP, 25 December 1981, Vol. IV, 2, pp. 1247–8. — 9. IGP, 25 January 1981, Vol. IV, 1, pp. 168–9. — 10. IGP, 10 February 1980, Vol. III, 1, pp. 364, 695–6. — 11. IGP, 11 February 1980, Vol. III, 1, pp. 372–4. — 12. IGP, 13 February 1982, Vol. V, 1, p. 396. — 13. IGP, 11 February 1982, Vol. V, 1, pp. 348–59. — 14. AAS, 14 February 1981, Vol. 73, pp. 263–4. 15. AAS, 14 February 1981, Vol. 73, pp. 264–5. — 16. AAS, 14 February 1981, Vol. 73, pp. 265–6. — 17. IGP, 2 January 1980, Vol. III, 1, pp. 13–4. — 18. IGP, 30 January 1980, Vol. III, 1, p. 218. — 19. IGP, 26 March 1981, Vol. IV, 1, pp. 785–6. — 20. IGP, 13 April 1980, Vol. III, 1, pp. 882–4. — 21. IGP, 13 April 1980, Vol. III, 1, pp. 884–5. — 22. IGP, 22 February 1980, Vol. III, 1, pp. 466–8. — 23. IGP, 13 April 1980, Vol. III, 1, pp. 885–6. — 24. IGP, 13 April 1980, Vol. III, 1, pp. 886–7. — 25. IGP, 30 March 1979, Vol. II, p. 739. — 26. IGP, 30 March 1979, Vol. II, pp. 739–40. — 27. IGP, 30 March 1979, Vol. II, pp. 740–1. — 28. IGP, 2 January 1981, Vol. IV, 1, pp. 16–7.

MARCH

1. IGP, 24 February 1982, Vol. V, 1, pp. 689–90. — 2. IGP, 1 March 1982, Vol. V, 1, pp. 732–5. — 3. IGP, 1 March 1983, Vol.

V, 1, pp. 737–8. 4. IGP, 4 March 1981, Vol. IV, 1, pp. 596–7. —
5. IGP, 26 March 1981, Vol. IV, 1, pp. 786–7. — 6. IGP, 15
March 1981, Vol. IV, 1, pp. 668–9. — 7. IGP, 22 February 1980,
Vol. III, 1, pp. 459–60. — 8. IGP, 15 March 1981, Vol. IV, 1,
pp. 670–1. — 9. 20 February 1983; OR, 21–2 February 1983, p.
1. — 10. IGP, 8 March 1981, Vol. IV, 1, pp. 642–3. — 11. IGP,
26 March 1981, Vol. IV, 1, p. 790. — 12. IGP, 26 March 1981,
Vol. IV, 1, p. 791. — 13. IGP, 26 March 1981, Vol. IV, 1, pp.
792–3. — 14. IGP, 19 February 1980, Vol. III, 1, p. 426. — 15.
IGP, 18 March 1979, Vol. II, pp. 672–3. — 16. IGP, 16 March
1980, Vol. III, 1, pp. 558–9. — 17. IGP, 29 September 1979,
Vol. II, 2, pp. 423–4. — 18. IGP, 18 March 1979, Vol. II, pp.
673–4. — 19. IGP, 19 March 1982, Vol. V, 1, pp. 935–7. — 20.
IGP, 19 March 1981, Vol. IV, 1, pp. 717–8. — 21. IGP, 8 March
1981, Vol. IV, 1, pp. 641–2. — 22. IGP, 15 March 1981, Vol. IV,
1, pp. 664–5. — 23. IGP, 9 March 1980, Vol. III, 1, pp. 534–5.
— 24. IGP, 9 March 1980, Vol. III, 1, p. 535. — 25. IGP, 25
March 1982, Vol. V, 1, p. 1000. — 26. IGP, 25 March 1982, Vol.
V, 1, pp. 1001–2. — 27. IGP, 16 March 1980, Vol. III, 1, pp.
570–1. — 28. IGP, 16 March 1980, Vol. III, 1, pp. 573–4. — 29.
IGP, 20 February 1980, Vol. III, 1, pp. 443–5. — 30. IGP, 26
March 1981, Vol. IV, 1, pp. 788–9. — 31. 16 February 1983;
OR, 18 February 1983, pp. 1–2.

APRIL

1. IGP, 28 February 1979, Vol. II, pp. 488–9. — 2. IGP, 28
February 1979, Vol. II, pp. 489–90. — 3. IGP, 14 March 1979,
Vol. II, p. 540. — 4. IGP, 24 February 1982, Vol. V, 1, p. 673. —
5. IGP, 24 February 1982, Vol. V, 1, pp. 673–4. — 6. 17 February 1983; OR, 17 February 1983, p. 2. — 7. IGP, 21 November
1981, Vol. IV, 2, pp. 696–700. — 8. IGP, 4 April 1979, Vol. II,
pp. 777–8. — 9. IGP, 4 April 1979, Vol. II, pp. 778–9. — 10.
IGP, 20 February 1980, Vol. III, 1, pp. 436–7. — 11. IGP, 5
June 1979, Vol. II, pp. 1443–4. — 12. IGP, 30 March 1982, Vol.
V, 1, pp. 1040–2. — 13. IGP, 30 March 1982, Vol. V, 1, pp.
1042–3. — 14. IGP, 1 April 1979, Vol. II, pp. 770–1. — 15. IGP,
5 April 1980, Vol. III, 1, pp. 817–8. — 16. IGP, 11 April 1982,
Vol. V, 1, pp. 1168–70. — 17. IGP, 19 April 1981, Vol. IV, 1,
pp. 974–5. — 18. 3 April 1983; OR, 5–6 April 1983, p. 1. — 19.
IGP, 26 April 1981, Vol. IV, 1, pp. 1028–9. — 20. 3 April 1983;
OR, 5–6 April 1983, p. 1. — 21. 3 April 1983; OR, 5–6 April
1983, pp. 1–2. — 22. IGP, 14 April 1982, Vol. V, 1, p. 1189. —
23. IGP, 18 April 1982, Vol. V, 1, pp. 1234–5. — 24. IGP, 18
April 1982, Vol. V, 1, p. 1237. — 25. IGP, 18 April 1982, Vol.
V, 1, pp. 1238–9. — 26. IGP, 7 May 1982, Vol. V, 2, p. 1441. —
27. Enc., 30 November 1980, n. 8. — 28. IGP, 5 April 1980, Vol.
III, 1, pp. 818–9. — 29. IGP, 29 April 1980, Vol. III, 1, pp.
1020–1. — 30. IGP, 9 April 1980, Vol. III, 1, pp. 840–1.

MAY

1. IGP, 19 March 1982, Vol. V, 1, pp. 921–2; 931–2. — 2. IGP, 11 February 1982, Vol. V, 1, p. 350. — 3. IGP, 3 May 1982, Vol. V, 2, p. 1400. — 4. IGP, 3 May 1982, Vol. V, 2, pp. 1399–1400. — 5. IGP, 24 March 1982, Vol. V, 1, p. 979. — 6. IGP, 24 March 1982, Vol. V, 1, p. 980. — 7. IGP, 24 March 1982, Vol. V, 1, pp. 980–1. — 8. IGP, 11 February 1982, Vol. V, 1, pp. 348–9. — 9. IGP, 14 February 1982, Vol. V, 1, p. 351. — 10. IGP, 9 May 1982, Vol. V, 2, pp. 1460–1. — 11. IGP, 9 May 1982, Vol. V, 2, p. 1461. — 12. IGP, 12 May 1982, Vol. V, 2, pp. 1484–5. — 13. IGP, 17 May 1981, Vol. IV, 1, pp. 1210–1. — 14. IGP, 12 May 1982, Vol. V, 2, pp. 1495–6. — 15. IGP, 12 May 1982, Vol. V, 2, p. 1543. — 16. IGP, 12 May 1982, Vol. V, 2, p. 1544. — 17. IGP, 12 May 1982, Vol. V, 2, pp. 1544–6. — 18. IGP, 12 May 1982, Vol. V, 2, p. 1546. — 19. IGP, 13 May 1982, Vol. V, 2, pp. 1580–1. — 20. IGP, 30 August 1980, Vol. III, 2, pp. 507–8. — 21. IGP, 13 May 1982, Vol. V, 2, p. 1583. — 22. IGP, 10 February 1982, Vol. V, 1, pp. 872–3. — 23. IGP, 19 March 1982, Vol. V, 1, pp. 924–5. — 24. Enc., 30 November 1980, g. — 25. IGP, 18 April 1982, Vol. V, 1, pp. 1217–8. — 26. IGP, 26 May 1979, Vol. II, pp. 1320–1. — 27. IGP, 13 May 1982, Vol. V, 2, p. 1580. — 28. IGP, 13 May 1982, Vol. V, 2, p. 1578. — 29. IGP, 19 March 1982, Vol. V, 1, pp. 923–4. — 30. IGP, 30 April 1982, Vol. V, 1, pp. 1370–1. — 31. IGP, 31 May 1979, Vol. II.

JUNE

1. IGP, 30 May 1979, Vol. II, pp. 1345–6. — 2. IGP, 30 May 1979, Vol. II, p. 1346. — 3. Private source. — 4. 8 October 1983, OR, 9 October, pp. 1 & 5. — 5. IGP, 3 June 1979, Vol. II, pp. 1393–4. — 6. IGP, 31 May 1982, Vol. V, 2, pp. 2019–20. — 7. IGP, 31 May 1982, Vol. V, 2, pp. 2021–2. — 8. IGP, 25 May 1980, Vol. III, 1, pp. 1464–5. — 9. IGP, 25 May 1980, Vol. III, 1, pp. 1465–6. — 10. IGP, 29 May 1983, Vol. VI, 1, p. 1397. — 11. IGP, 29 May 1983, Vol. VI, 1, p. 1398. — 12. IGP, 30 May 1982, Vol. V, 2, pp. 1978–9. — 13. IGP, 12 September 1982, Vol. V, 3, pp. 418–9. — 14. IGP, 12 September 1982, Vol. V, 3, pp. 421–2. — 15. IGP, 25 May 1980, Vol. III, 1, pp. 1467–8. — 16. IGP, 25 May 1980, Vol. III, 1, p. 1468. — 17. IGP, 30 May 1982, Vol. V, 2, p. 1993. — 18. IGP, 30 May 1982, Vol. V, 2, pp. 1993–4. — 19. IGP, 22 May 1983, Vol. VI, 1, pp. 1346–8. — 20. IGP, 22 May 1983, Vol. VI, 1, pp. 1348–9. — 21. IGP, 22 May 1983, Vol. VI, 1, pp. 1348–9. — 22. IGP, 28 May 1982, Vol. V, 2, p. 1899. — 23. IGP, 1 June 1983, Vol. VI, 1, pp. 1411–2. — 24. IGP, 24 June 1979, Vol. II, pp. 1619–20. — 25. IGP, 1 June 1983, Vol. VI, 1, pp. 1412–3. — 26. IGP, 1 June 1983, Vol. VI, 1, p. 1413. — 27. IGP, 2 June 1983, Vol. VI, 1, pp. 1421–2. — 28. IGP, 2 June 1983, Vol. VI, 1, pp. 1423–4. — 29. IGP, 29 June 1979, Vol. II, pp. 1648–9. — 30. IGP, 29 June 1979, Vol. II, p. 1650.

JULY

1. IGP, 8 June 1980, Vol. III, 1, pp. 1709–10. — 2. IGP, 28 May 1982, Vol. V, 2, pp. 1907–8. — 3. IGP, 9 April 1983, Vol. VI, 1, pp. 919–20. — 4. IGP, 3 October 1979, Vol. II, 2, pp. 569–70. — 5. IGP, 4 March 1979, Vol. II, pp. 634–5. — 6. IGP, 18 October 1980, Vol. III, 2, pp. 899–902. — 7. IGP, 4 March 1979, Vol. II, pp. 618–20. — 8. IGP, 4 March 1979, Vol. II, pp. 619–20. — 9. IGP, 4 March 1979, Vol. II, pp. 629–30. — 10. IGP, 1 June 1982, Vol. V, 2, pp. 2065–6. — 11. IGP, 17 May 1979, Vol. II, pp. 1158–9. — 12. IGP, 17 May 1979, Vol. II, pp. 1159–60. — 13. IGP, 13 July 1980, Vol. III, 2, p. 266. — 14. IGP, 24 June 1980, Vol. III, 1, pp. 1829–30. — 15. IGP, 20 July 1980, Vol. III, 2, pp. 280–1. — 16. IGP, 1 June 1982, Vol. V, 2, pp. 2066–7. — 17. IGP, 18 March 1981, Vol. IV, 1, p. 681. 18. IGP, 2 June 1982, Vol. V, 2, pp. 2098–9. — 19. IGP, 2 June 1982, Vol. V, 2, pp. 2099–100. — 20. IGP, 2 June 1982, Vol. V, 2, pp. 2100–1. — 21. IGP, 18 March 1981, Vol. IV, 1, pp. 682–4. — 22. IGP, 25 January 1983, Vol. VI, 1, pp. 239–40. — 23. IGP, 12 March 1980, Vol. III, 1, pp. 537–9. — 24. 6 July 1983, OR, 7 July 1983, pp. 1–2. — 25. IGP, 1982, Vol. V, 3, p. 1250. — 26. IGP, 10 December 1978, Vol. I, pp. 327–8. — 27. 26 July 1983, OR, 27 July 1983, pp.. 1–2. — 28. IGP, 2 October 1979, Vol. II, 2, pp. 552–3. — 29. IGP, 20 July 1980, Vol. III, 2, pp. 277–9. — 30. 16 October 1983, OR, 17–8 October 1983, p. 4. — 31. IGP, 6 November 1982, Vol. V, 3, pp. 1160–2.

AUGUST

1. IGP, 6 December 1979, Vol. II, 2, p. 1327. — 2. Private source. 3. IGP, 28 January 1979, Vol. II, pp. 226–7. — 4. IGP, 28 January 1979, Vol. II, pp. 214–6. — 5. IGP, 10 August 1980, Vol. III, 2, pp. 352–3. — 6. IGP, 15 March 1981, Vol. IV, 1, pp. 669–70. — 7. IGP, 6 April 1980, Vol. III, 1, pp. 830–2. — 8. 5 September 1983, OR, 5–6 September 1983, p. 4. — 9. IGP, 27 May 1980, Vol. III, 1, pp. 1481–2. — 10. IGP, 18 October 1978, Vol. I, pp. 21–3. — 11. IGP, 5 October 1979, Vol. II, 2, pp. 634–5. — 12. IGP, 1 June 1982, Vol. V, 2, pp. 2081–2. — 13. IGP, 28 May 1982, Vol. V, 2, pp. 1914–6. — 14. IGP, 26 February 1981, Vol. IV, 1, pp. 567–8. — 15. IGP, 15 August 1979, Vol. II, 2, pp. 134–5. — 16. 15 August 1983, OR, 16–7 August 1983, p. 5. — 17. 15 August 1983, OR, 16–7 August 1983, p. 5. — 18. IGP, 31 May 1982, Vol. V, 2, pp. 1999–2000. — 19. IGP, 31 May 1982, Vol. V, 2, p. 2028. — 20. IGP, 31 May 1982, Vol. V, 2, pp. 2028–30. — 21. IGP, 1 November 1982, Vol. V, 3, pp. 1051–2. — 22. IGP, 13 January 1980, Vol. III, 1, pp. 110–2. — 23. IGP, 3 October 1979, Vol. II, 2 pp. 586–7. — 24. IGP, 24 August 1980, Vol. III, 2, pp. 431–2. — 25. IGP, 3 October 1979, Vol. II, 2, pp. 585–6. — 26. IGP, 26 August 1982, Vol. V, 3, pp. 303–6. — 27. IGP, 3 October 1979, Vol. II, 2, pp. 587–8. — 28. 25 August 1983, OR, 26 August 1983, pp. 1–2. — 29. IGP, 31 May 1982, Vol. V, 2, pp. 2036–7. — 30. IGP, 1 November 1983,

Vol. V, 3, pp. 1027–8. — 31. IGP, 28 August 1980, Vol. III, 2, pp. 471–4.

SEPTEMBER

1. IGP, 4 November 1982, Vol. V, 3, pp. 1128–31. — 2. IGP, 4 November 1982, Vol. V, 3, pp. 1131–2. — 3. IGP, 4 November 1982, Vol. V, 3, pp. 1132–3. — 4. IGP, 4 November 1982, Vol. V, 3, pp. 1135–6. — 5. IGP, 22 November 1981, Vol. IV, 2, pp. 1054–5. — 6. IGP, 22 November 1981, Vol. IV, 2, pp. 1060–1. — 7. IGP, 7 September 1980, Vol. III, 2, pp. 565–6. — 8. IGP, 9 September 1981, Vol. IV, 2, pp. 141–2. — 9. IGP, 22 November 1981, Vol. IV, 2, p. 1057. — 10. IGP, 21 November 1982, Vol. V, 3, pp. 1393–4. 11. IGP, 30 November 1980, Vol. III, 2, p. 1558. — 12. IGP, 30 November 1980, Vol. III, 2, p. 1559. — 13. IGP, 30 November 1980, Vol. III, 2, pp. 1561–2. — 14. IGP, 17 April 1981, Vol. IV, 1, pp. 960–3. — 15. IGP, 13 April 1980, Vol. III, 1, pp. 868–9. — 16. IGP, 30 November 1980, Vol. III, 2, pp. 1562–3. — 17. IGP, 30 November 1980, Vol. III, 2, pp. 1572–3. — 18. IGP, 15 June 1982, Vol. V, 2, pp. 2315–7. — 19. IGP, 20 May 1982, Vol. V, 2, pp. 1776–7. — 20. IGP, 20 May 1982, Vol. V, 2, pp. 1778–9. — 21. IGP, 23 September 1981, Vol. IV, 2, pp. 298–9. — 22. IGP, 20 May 1982, Vol. V, 2, pp. 1779–80. — 23. IGP, 20 May 1982, Vol. V, 2, pp. 1780–1. — 24. IGP, 29 September 1980, Vol. III, 2, p. 743[35]–[40]. — 25. IGP, 15 January 1982, Vol. V, 1, pp. 103–4. — 26. IGP, 23 September 1980, Vol. III, 2, pp. 711–2. — 27. IGP, 24 July 1981, Vol. IV, 2, pp. 49–51. — 28. IGP, 24 July 1981, Vol. IV, 2, pp. 51–2. — 29. IGP, 1 June 1982, Vol. V, 2, pp. 2052–3. — 30. IGP, 1 June 1983, Vol. V, 2, pp. 2054–5.

OCTOBER

1. IGP, 2 June 1980, Vol. III, 1, pp. 1659–64. — 2. IGP, 1 June 1982, Vol. V, 2, pp. 2055–6. — 3. IGP, 1 June 1982, Vol. V, 2, pp. 2056–7. — 4. IGP, 16 January 1982, Vol. V, 1, pp. 138–9. — 5. IGP, 8 December 1978, Vol. I, pp. 302–3. — 6. 2 October 1983, OR, 3–4 October 1983, p. 1, 5. — 7. 2 October 1983, OR, 3–4 October 1983, p. 5. — 8. 2 October 1983, OR, 3–4 October 1983, p. 5. — 9. 8 October 1983, OR, 9 October 1983, p. 1. — 10. 2 October 1983, OR, 3–4 October 1983, p. 5. — 11. 2 October 1983, OR, 3–4 October 1983, p. 5. — 12. IGP, 22 November 1981, Vol. IV, 2, pp. 1045–8. — 13. 16 October 1983, OR, 17–18 October 1983, pp. 1, 4. — 14. IGP, 14 October 1981, Vol. IV, 2, pp. 409–12. — 15. IGP, 1 November 1982, Vol. V, 3, pp. 1032–8. — 16. IGP, 21 June 1983, Vol. VI, 1, p. 1621. — 17. IGP, 31 May 1982, Vol. V, 2, pp. 2009–10. — 18. IGP, 18 April 1982, Vol. V, 1, pp. 1214–5. — 19. IGP, 31 May 1982, Vol. V, 2, p. 2008. — 20. IGP, 11 August 1982, Vol. V, 3, pp. 204–6. — 21.

IGP, 22 November 1981, Vol. IV, 2, p. 1058. — 22. IGP, 4 March 1979, Vol. II, pp. 611–2. — 23. IGP, 22 November 1981, Vol. IV, 2, pp. 1080–1. — 24. IGP, 28 March 1982, Vol. V, 1, pp. 1036–9. — 25. IGP, 20 March 1983, Vol. VI, 1, pp. 771–3. — 26. IGP, 27 October 1980, Vol. III, 2, pp. 1002–3. — 27. IGP, 22 November 1981, Vol. IV, 2, pp. 1059–60. — 28. IGP, 22 November 1981, Vol. IV, 2, pp. 1086–7. — 29. IGP, 22 November 1981, Vol. IV, 2, pp. 1087–8. — 30. 30 October 1983, OR, 31 October–1 November 1983, p. 2 — 31. IGP, 22 November 1981, Vol. IV, 2, pp. 1902–3.

NOVEMBER

1. IGP, 1 November 1980, Vol. III, 2, pp. 1029–30. — 2. IGP, 1 November 1980, Vol. III, 2, pp. 1031–2. — 3. IGP, 22 November 1981, Vol. IV, 2, pp. 1100–1. — 4. IGP, 4 November 1980, Vol. III, 2, pp. 1054–5. — 5. IGP, 15 December 1981, Vol. IV, 2, p. 1121. — 6. [1] IGP, 15 December 1981, Vol. IV, 2, pp. 1121–2. [2] IGP, 31 May 1982, Vol. V, 2, p. 2009. — 7. IGP, 31 May 1982, Vol. V, 2, pp. 2010–1. — 8. IGP, 17 February 1983, Vol. VI, 1, pp. 447–8. — 9. IGP, 14 September 1981, Vol. IV, 2, p. 258. — 10. IGP, 14 September 1981, Vol. IV, 2, pp. 259–60. — 11. IGP, 11 November 1981, Vol. IV, 2, pp. 598–9. — 12. IGP, 14 September 1981, Vol. IV, 2, pp. 260–1. — 13. IGP, 14 September 1981, Vol. IV, 2, pp. 261–2. — 14. IGP, 14 September 1981, Vol. IV, 2, pp. 264–5. — 15. IGP, 15 November 1980, Vol. III, 2, pp. 1194–5. — 16. 16 November 1983, OR, 17 November 1983, p. 5. — 17. IGP, 12 November 1981, Vol. IV, 2, pp. 673–4. — 18. IGP, 6 November 1981, Vol. IV, 2, pp. 569–70. — 19. 10 September 1983, OR, 12–3 September 1983, p. 2. — 20. IGP, 2 October 1979, Vol. II, 2, pp. 522–3. — 21. IGP, 1 November 1982, Vol. V, 3, pp. 1028–30. — 22. IGP, 2 October 1979, Vol. II, 2, p. 524. — 23. IGP, 2 October 1979, Vol. II, 2, pp. 541–2. — 24. IGP, 6 October 1979, Vol. II, 2, pp. 670–1. — 25. IGP, 6 October 1979, Vol. II, 2, pp. 671–2. — 26. IGP, 7 October 1979, Vol. II, 2, pp. 697–8. — 27. IGP, 2 November 1982, Vol. V, 3, pp. 1068–70. — 28. IGP, 11 October 1981, Vol. IV, 2, p. 399. — 29. IGP, 27 September 1982, Vol. V, 3, pp. 609–11. — 30. IGP, 30 November 1982, Vol. V, 3, pp. 1481–2.

MOVEABLE FEASTS

1. IGP, 30 November 1980, Vol. III, 2, pp. 1465–6. — 2. IGP, 5 December 1982, Vol. V, 3, pp. 1523–5. — 3. IGP, 12 December 1982, Vol. V, 3, pp. 1597–8. — 4. IGP, 23 December 1979, Vol. II, 2, p. 1504. — 5. IGP, 30 December 1979, Vol. II, 2, pp. 1534–5. — 6. IGP, 6 January 1979, Vol. II, pp. 17–8. — 7. 9

January 1983, OR, 10 January 1983, p. 1. — 8. 16 February 1983, OR, 17 February 1983, p. 1. — 9. IGP, 24 February 1980, Vol. III, 1, pp. 482–3. — 10. IGP, 2 March 1980, Vol. III, 1, pp. 505–6. — 11. IGP, 18 March 1979, Vol. II, pp. 677–8. — 12. IGP, 16 March 1980, Vol. III, 1, pp. 571–3. — 13. IGP, 1 April 1979, Vol. II, pp. 764–5. — 14. IGP, 4 April 1982, Vol. V, 1, pp. 1105–6. — 15. Enc. 30 November 1980, n. 7. — 16. ibid. n. 7. — 17. ibid. n. 8. — 18. IGP, 8 April 1982, Vol. V, 1, pp. 1148–9. — 19. IGP, 9 April 1982, Vol. V, 1, pp. 1152–5. — 20. IGP, 14 April 1979, Vol. II, pp. 907–8. — 21. IGP, 15 April 1979, Vol. II, pp. 911–13. — 22. IGP, 14 April 1979, Vol. II, pp. 908–9. — 23. IGP, 6 April 1980, Vol. III, 1, pp. 821–3. — 24. IGP, 6 April 1980, Vol. III, 1, pp. 823–5. — 25. IGP, 6 April 1983, Vol. VI, 1, pp. 898–9. — 26. IGP, 6 April 1983, Vol. VI, 1, p. 899. — 27. IGP, 6 April 1983, Vol. VI, 1, pp. 900–1. — 28. IGP, 13 April 1980, Vol. III, 1, pp. 889–90. — 29. IGP, 20 May 1982, Vol. V, 2, pp. 1772–4. — 30. IGP, 7 June 1981, Vol. IV, 1, pp. 1254–5. — 31. [1] IGP, 12 March 1980, Vol. III, 1, pp. 542, 544–5; [2] Enciclica "Familiaris Consortio," 22 November 1981, 34. — 32. IGP, 19 March 1981, Vol. IV, 1, pp. 718–9. — 33. IGP, 6 November 1982, Vol. V, 3, pp. 1182–3. — 34. IGP, 29 May 1983, Vol. VI, 1, pp. 1395–6. — 35. IGP, 8 June 1980, Vol. III, 1, pp. 1712–4. — 36. IGP, 27 June 1982, Vol. V, 2, pp. 2412–3. — 37. IGP, 13 May 1982, Vol. V, 2, pp. 1581–2. — 38. [1] IGP, 24 June 1979, Vol. II, p. 1617; [2] IGP, 27 June 1982, Vol. V, 2, p. 2413. — 39. IGP, 13 May 1982, Vol. V, 2, p. 1582. — 40. IGP, 14 September 1981, Vol. IV, 2, p. 231. — 41. IGP, 10 June 1983, Vol. VI, 1, pp. 1483–5. — 42. IGP, 31 December 1979, Vol. II, 2, pp. 1538–9. — 43. IGP, 21 November 1982, Vol. V, 3, pp. 1379–83.